Windows® XP Digital Music For Dummies®

Cheat Sheet

KT-444-602

My Personal Radio Dial

- **KCRW** (http://kcrw.org): Adventurous programming (like the outstanding show "Morning Becomes Eclectic") and NPR news and shows make this a great stop for Internet radio if you're not in Los Angeles.

- **WOXY** (http://woxy.com): This station recently went Internet-only after closing its Ohio broadcast studio. The station leads the way in cutting-edge music that you'll hear on MTV a few months or years later. It gets bonus points for publishing its playlists and streaming song information live right to your browser.

- **Live365** (http://live365.com): This is the Wal-Mart of online radio, except the music coming out of the speakers is better. Search for any genre or artist on this site.

- **Radio XY** (http://radioxy.com): This station also gives you a sampling of the cutting edge of music. This is coupled with the fact that it airs no commercials, which is always a bonus. You don't even have to deal with a DJ.

- **WGRE-FM** (http://www.depauw.edu/univ/WGRE/index.asp): I mention this because it was my college radio station, and I get a serious nostalgia fix whenever I tune in to WGRE.

Keep This in Mind while You Rip Files

- **What is the song's information?** At the very least, make sure that the artist's name and song title go along with your new file. You could also include an album title, the year it was recorded, and other information that could be useful in organizing your media library. If your computer is connected to the Internet, this will likely be provided for you.

- **What is the file format being used?** Make sure that you're ripping your CD to a file format that can be played by your media player or portable audio device.

- **What is the file's resolution?** You have to balance the amount of space you have available with the quality of the music. The smaller the file size, the lower the audio quality (and vice versa). Ripping songs at 128 Kbps seems to be the most popular resolution for online stores, and you can adjust your ripping preferences from there based on your personal tastes.

- **Where is the file going?** Make sure that you know where the files are saved on your hard drive. It's easier to organize your media library if you know where all the files are going.

Windows® XP Digital Music For Dummies®

Online Music Services

Different online music services use different file formats. The following table describes the most popular services and the file formats they support.

Service	Format
iTunes	AAC
Napster	WMA
Rhapsody	Real Media
eMusic	MP3
Wal-Mart	WMA
MusicMatch	WMA
BuyMusic	WMA
MusicNow	WMA
Music Rebellion	WMA or MP3

Common Media Players

These players can handle many more files than those listed here. This is just a sample of the major types of file formats you're likely to run across.

Player Name	Format
Windows Media Player	MP3, WAV, WMA
Winamp	MP3, WAV, WMA
Real	MP3, WAV, Real
iTunes	MP3, WAV, AAC
MusicMatch	MP3, WAV, WMA

Wiley, the Wiley Publishing logo, For Dummies, the Dummies Man logo, the For Dummies Bestselling Book Series logo and all related trade dress are trademarks or registered trademarks of John Wiley & Sons, Inc. and/or its affiliates. All other trademarks are property of their respective owners.

For Dummies: Bestselling Book Series for Beginners

Windows® XP Digital Music

FOR DUMMIES®

by Ryan Williams

WILEY

Wiley Publishing, Inc.

Windows® XP Digital Music For Dummies®

Published by
Wiley Publishing, Inc.
111 River Street
Hoboken, NJ 07030-5774

WILEY

About the Author

Ryan Williams is the Digital Multimedia Development Specialist for the Indiana University School of Dentistry. He graduated from the Indiana University School of Music with a master's degree in music technology, along with a bachelor's degree in communications from DePauw University. In addition, he writes for indianapolismusic.net, a Web site focused on the musical happenings in and around the greater Indianapolis metropolitan area.

As a bassist, Ryan has played in most known genres of music and some additional ones that seemed invented on the spot. While he was named "Best Bassist In Indianapolis" by shotgunreviews.com in 2002, he will happily provide you with the names of several local musicians who both inspire and embarrass him on a regular basis. He currently shares stages and studios with the members of Mother Grove, a Celtic rock band featured in shows and festivals from Ohio to Colorado.

Author's Acknowledgments

This book would not have been possible without the tireless dedication of Steve Hayes, Colleen Totz, John Edwards, and Erik Scull. Their efforts, advice, and encouragement were essential to this project.

My sincere thanks go to Matt Fecher and everyone at `indianapolismusic.net`, Doug Babb and the Indiana University School of Music, and John Gosney, Nadine Florek, Brian Lich, and the Indiana University School of Dentistry.

During my time in Indianapolis, I've been lucky to receive the patience and support of people like Candice Jackson, Matt Chandler, and all the musicians I've had the pleasure of sharing the stage with in the last few years. You all have introduced me to new possibilities and views, and I'm a better person for it.

And finally, I've been blessed with the support and love of my wonderful Jennifer. Here's to future adventures.

Publisher's Acknowledgments

We're proud of this book; please send us your comments through our online registration form located at www.dummies.com/register/.

Some of the people who helped bring this book to market include the following:

Acquisitions, Editorial, and Media Development

Project Editor: Colleen Totz

Senior Acquisitions Editor: Steve Hayes

Copy Editor: John Edwards

Technical Editor: Erik Scull

Editorial Manager: Carol Sheehan

Media Development Manager: Laura VanWinkle

Media Development Supervisor: Richard Graves

Editorial Assistant: Amanda Foxworth

Cartoons: Rich Tennant, www.the5thwave.com

Production

Project Coordinator: Maridee Ennis

Layout and Graphics: Andrea Dahl, Lauren Goddard, Joyce Haughey, Stephanie D. Jumper, Barry Offringa, Lynsey Osborn, Heather Ryan

Proofreaders: John Greenough, Joe Niesen, Brian H. Walls, TECHBOOKS Production Services

Indexer: TECHBOOKS Production Services

Publishing and Editorial for Technology Dummies

Richard Swadley, Vice President and Executive Group Publisher

Andy Cummings, Vice President and Publisher

Mary Bednarek, Executive Acquisitions Director

Mary C. Corder, Editorial Director

Publishing for Consumer Dummies

Diane Graves Steele, Vice President and Publisher

Joyce Pepple, Acquisitions Director

Composition Services

Gerry Fahey, Vice President of Production Services

Debbie Stailey, Director of Composition Services

Contents at a Glance

Table of Contents

Introduction

· ·

Right now, your home computer is probably set up to run as a standard home office machine. That means it's ready to handle things like e-mail and word processing, and maybe provide a little background music while you do all this mundane work. But it's capable of doing so much more — your Windows XP PC could have an organized collection of your music ready to go at any moment. You could be using your common home computer to download the latest music and undiscovered classics, put them on a portable audio player, and take them with you on a long road trip to avoid hearing your friends sing campfire songs (and they will sing them, unfortunately). You could even use it to unleash your inner record producer and conquer the world with your undiscovered musical genius.

Well, sure, you must have some musical genius there to begin with. But the point is that your Windows XP machine is capable of being a mighty tool in downloading, listening, and even recording the soundtrack to your life. Just as CDs replaced 8-track tapes, cassettes, and vinyl for most people, digital music files could eventually revitalize your music collection and make you listen to your old music in new ways.

The problem is that most computers arrive at their homes set up to do the mundane word and number processing I described earlier. That's useful stuff, but it's also boring. *Windows XP Digital Music For Dummies* is here to free your computer from those tasks and to make it work to bring you the best in music.

About This Book

Windows XP Digital Music For Dummies is a ground-up guide to using the audio tools that come on Windows XP computers as well as a resource for some useful tools and programs you can get after you've already bought the computer. I cover both the hardware (the actual parts of the computer) and the software (the programs run by your computer) that you need to make your computer sing.

A lot of hardware, software, and virtual record stores are out there, and you'll want to know what you need before you go in and actually lay down your money. This book is your reference point for the world of music in a Windows XP digital music environment. You can read it from front to back and gain a better overall understanding of digital music, or you can skip directly to the chapter that covers the topic you want. I've organized the information to cover the following points of interest:

- ✔ Getting your computer set up to handle music in the best way possible
- ✔ Choosing the right software and audio files to play the songs you want
- ✔ Hooking up and using a portable audio player
- ✔ Shopping for and downloading music from the Internet legally
- ✔ Venturing into the world of recording digital music

By the time you're done consulting this book, you'll be able to handle these tasks with the confidence and skill of a 14-year-old teenager raised on this kind of technology.

Conventions Used in This Book

Most of the programs I talk about in this book are menu driven, that is, you usually choose what you want to do from a list of commands or options presented to you by the program. To help you navigate these menus, I lead you through a series of commands to make the program do what you want. The instructions will be a choice followed by an arrow and the next step in the menu, as many times as necessary to get what you want. For example, if you see File⇨Import/Export⇨Audio, this means that you should choose File on the program's menu bar, select the Import/Export option, and then choose Audio from that menu.

Sometimes I also show you keyboard shortcuts for commands that could make dealing with your computer a little easier. Windows XP combines the Ctrl or Alt key with another key to make a shortcut, so I show these combinations as Ctrl+Z or Alt+B, for example.

What You Don't Have to Read

I love talking about music, and I'm fascinated by gadgets and technology. This means that I have a lot of stories to share in various places during this book. These "sidebars" are not necessary to the essence of this book. However, they can give you some background or additional understanding of the topic at hand. You can excitedly study them for new nuggets of knowledge, or you can skip them without a second thought. It's up to you.

Foolish Assumptions

It may seem obvious, but I'm going to assume that you have (or will be receiving as a birthday or lovely parting gift) a personal computer (or PC) that's powered by the Windows XP operating system. If you're using a Mac, you're in the wrong line — please step aside and head toward the Apple desk. While Windows XP comes in two flavors (Home and Professional), the differences — as far as audio and digital music programs are concerned — are nothing to worry about. Therefore, I don't differentiate between XP Home and XP Professional throughout the book.

Because you have Windows XP, you have a version of Windows Media Player installed on your computer. It's like getting a radio with the car you just bought. The player is there, and it's the first one you're going to use when you're starting to explore the world of digital music. Therefore, I talk about it the most throughout this book. As you go on, you may choose to switch out your player with another one that makes more sense to you or works better with your system. I take a look at these other players in the book, but I mainly focus on Windows Media Player as the convenient and useful default.

How This Book Is Organized

I've organized this book into five main sections. If you're looking for a general understanding of digital music in the Windows XP environment, go ahead and start reading at page 1. However, if you're pressed for time or only need the answer to a specific problem, go ahead and read the section that addresses that problem — you can still figure out what you need.

Part 1: Playing Music on Windows XP

This part explains what digital audio is and how you can recognize it when you see (and hear) it. Chapter 1 gives you a general overview of musical files, the hardware and software your computer uses, and the legal side of digital music (and isn't that where you first heard about MP3s anyway?). Chapter 2 leads you through installing and connecting the parts you need to make your computer musical (maybe a little more complicated than programming your VCR, but certainly less hassle than doing your taxes). Chapter 3 guides you through basic audio operations in Windows XP (how do I turn this down again?). Finally, Chapter 4 takes a look at a special type of Windows XP that is designed to do nothing but play your media. Windows XP Media Center

Edition only comes on special types of computers, so read this chapter only if you've purchased one of these (and trust me, by the price tag, you'll know if you bought one instead of a regular PC).

Part II: Making Windows XP Your Digital Jukebox

Here's where I show you how to take this new machine of yours and make it the centerpiece of your musical collection. Chapter 5 examines what you should look for in a media player and gives you an overview of some of the most popular entries on the market today. Chapter 6 shows you how to transfer your CDs (or even the antiquities known as vinyl records) to the realm of your computer. Chapter 7 combines two of the things that make my life happy (sorry, dear) — shopping for music and the Internet. And Chapter 8 shows you how to dial in an Internet radio station and let someone else share his or her collection with you.

Part III: Goin' Mobile: Taking Your Songs on the Road

I spend a lot of time on the computer, but I don't want to leave my music behind when it's time to step away and experience the world. This part takes a look at portable audio players and how to make them sing and dance. Chapter 9 goes over common features of the portable audio player and rates some well-known products. Chapter 10 shows you how to move your songs over to your device and organize songs for some easy listening (not necessarily elevator-music easy listening, but it's still a possibility).

Part IV: Quiet in the Studio

Part of the reason I spend a lot of time in front of the computer is because it's such a powerful, creative tool. You don't have to be a genius composer to make music on a PC — in fact, the software available today makes it easier than ever to make your own music. Chapter 11 shows you how to soup up your computer and make it a virtual studio. Chapter 12 starts you down the road to recording by looking at what to expect from digital music recording software. Chapter 13 actually takes you into the booth and shows you how to lay down basic tracks. Chapter 14 helps you mix everything together into a good song, and Chapter 15 looks at taking the finished product to disc, the Internet, and elsewhere.

Part V: The Part of Tens

This long-standing *For Dummies* tradition is a great way to gather up any loose ends and toss in some extra helpful hints. You find lists of interesting Web sites and intriguing gadgets, and even what to avoid when you're getting the most out of your music.

Icons Used in This Book

Occasionally, you'll see some pictures off to the side of the pages — these are designed to attract your attention to some important details. Here's what they look like:

Like a string around your finger, this icon emphasizes some important piece of information that you should keep in mind.

I'm a helpful guy — this information gives you some useful details that can make listening to your digital music collection easier.

You're going to be spending some money and time on this, and I don't want anything to discourage you along the way. This icon alerts you to some possible pitfalls or problems that you can avoid by following my advice. Trust me, it's better for all involved.

Windows XP is a large and intricate operating system, and there's always some minute and technical details to add to discussing the program. While it's useful, the information isn't always necessary to the basic process of working with music. This icon tells you that there's good information here, but you can move on if you don't want to get too involved with the subject. On the other hand, if you want to get really geeky, stop and stay awhile.

Where to Go from Here

All right, I've laid out the basics of what to expect from *Windows XP Digital Music For Dummies,* but I want you to keep one more thing in mind: HAVE FUN! Music, at its essence, is meant to be enjoyed. Everything else I tell you in this book is meant to enhance your enjoyment of the music you already love. The computer, the portable audio player, and all the hardware and software in between are tools to help you experience that joy you get from the first few notes of your favorite song.

Here's where the tour group splits up. I recommend starting at the beginning to make sure you have all your bases covered, but that's not necessary if you want to skip to a good part. Feel free to join me at the beginning for the scenic route, or you can catch up at the chapter that you want to learn more about.

Part I
Playing Music on Windows XP

The 5th Wave

By Rich Tennant

"It's bad enough he fell asleep waiting for a huge music file to download into his music folder, but wait until he finds out he hit the 'SEND' button instead of selecting 'DOWNLOAD'."

In this part . . .

These first few chapters introduce you to digital music. You'll learn about both the hardware and software that you'll need to find, download, and play music on your home PC. You'll also learn how to hook all of your computer components up and perform basic audio operations.

Even if you've never opened an MP3 file in your life, this part will give you the background you need to get your music system up and running.

Chapter 1

Are You XPerienced?

*W*hether you've spent years assembling a music collection or are just now buying your first albums, music must mean something to you. And now you have this Windows XP machine to open up new possibilities for storing and listening to your tunes. The potential for using your computer for music is virtually limitless — how do you want to make your music better?

In short, the answer depends on several things. Windows XP is a great environment in which to organize your music collection. First, though, you have to understand what you're dealing with. Two files may sound the same coming out of your speakers, but their inner workings could make all the difference in whether your Barry Manilow recordings make the leap successfully to your playlists or fall behind, a casualty of incorrect formats.

The Whats and Whys of Digital Sound

Some of us are old enough to remember when musical recordings were stored on cassettes or vinyl records (I had saddlebags made for my dinosaur to transport my collection around). These recordings stored sound in an *analog* format — the sound was recorded to the disc or tape as physical grooves or magnetic impulses. The medium got the song from the artist to the listener, but it still had some drawbacks.

The main drawback of these recordings is that they tend to degrade each time they are played. When you pressed the Play button, physical contact was made between the recording and the player. Like rubbing sandpaper against wood, some of the detail on the recording would be worn away. Before long, you would start to hear the cracks and pops associated with old recordings (ironically enough, these sounds have now been digitally sampled and layered onto new recordings to make them sound "vintage"). The music would get lost behind the noise, and fairly soon, you would need to go out and buy a new copy to get that wonderfully clear sound back.

Second, vinyl records were a little hard to carry around and listen to wherever you want. Unless you have a full stereo system available, it wasn't easy to hear your records in their intended glory. Cassettes made the music a little more mobile with the advent of the portable stereo and the Walkman, but the sound wasn't quite as good as that from the vinyl records. This was a symptom of the format itself — the tape on which musicians usually recorded their music was several inches wide to allow as much detail as possible to be recorded. After the sound had been mixed down to the small stereo tracks of a cassette (along with the requisite hiss that accompanies sound recorded on that cassette), it had lost a little something.

Ah, but then came the compact disc. Instead of being carved into the grooves of the record or recorded on magnetic tape, the music was encoded on the disc as numerical information. A laser reads the information and translates that into your favorite song. Music fans have their preferences — some people still insist on the superiority of analog sound. But digital music is here to stay, for many reasons. I take a look at those reasons in the following section, "The benefits of digital sound." First, it's time to acquaint yourself with digitally recorded music. It's a vastly different process, and some different terminology is associated with digital recordings.

The benefits of digital sound

When you compare digital and analog sound, the first thing you need to examine is the *sample rate*. In analog recordings, the machine is always recording any sound or noise that is coming through the microphones. In digital recording, however, you don't have a constant recording of what's going on. Instead, you have a series of samples taken from the sound being recorded.

Think of it like a movie — a motion picture strings together a series of pictures to make it look like moving action. In this case, digital recording takes a series of "pictures" of what the sound is like and turns it into a digital recording. A standard compact disc contains sound that has been sampled at 44.1 kHz, or just over 44,000 times a second (that's a lot of pictures!). However, you may run into digital sound on the Internet that's been recorded at 48 kHz, 96 kHz, or even higher. Just think of it as getting more detail from more pictures.

But how do those pictures look? The more detailed those pictures are, the better the sound is. That's where *bits* come in. By increasing the number of bits (units of information, without getting too detailed) contained in the file, the amount of detail contained in each sample is increased. It's the difference between saying "The cat has white fur" and "The purebred Siamese feline has ivory fur with charcoal roots." See the difference? Now imagine the detail that you can get from higher bit rates in your music. Again, a standard CD has 16-bit sound, although you might occasionally run into higher bit sizes on the Internet.

Now consider the *bit rate* of the file. Digital music files are measured in the amount of information they play per second. In most cases, it's measured in Kbps, or kilobits per second. This is the amount of sound information presented to the listener every second. The standard for near-CD quality is 128 Kbps, and some files go up to 320 Kbps. On the other hand, files played over Internet radio are 56 or 64 Kbps to allow faster transport over networks, like your dialup or broadband Internet connection.

In short, the benefits to using digital sound are the following:

- ✔ **Portability:** You can take digital sound anywhere on a variety of devices, and you can transfer it from network to computer very easily.
- ✔ **Durability:** Digital audio doesn't degrade like analog audio sources.
- ✔ **Options:** You can buy or record your audio in differing levels of quality and size, depending on your needs.
- ✔ **Sound Quality:** Unless you've invested thousands of dollars in audio-phile-quality analog audio gear, you'll probably note a better sound coming from digital audio systems.

The tradeoff of better sound (and what you can do to counteract it)

Like everything else in life, though, there is a tradeoff in getting this improved sound. For the increased detail and better sound, you give up space on your hard drive or memory card. The extra information and detail mean that more memory is taken up. The size of these files is usually measured in megabytes, or MB. For comparison, the size of current hard drives is measured in gigabytes, or GB. There are approximately 1,000MB in each GB. If your songs are recorded at a lower bit rate, you can fit more songs on your drive — but they won't sound as good. It all depends on what you want — more songs or better quality.

This is where *compression* comes in. To use less memory space, you can compress the data and reduce the file size while keeping the detail of the music as close as possible to the original. When the file is compressed according to the appropriate file format (see the next section), the media player needs a *codec,* or compression/decompression instructions, to read it.

Fascinating File Formats

Without the right program, digital audio is just a file in your computer. It's the media player that makes the music happen. A *media player* is a program that translates audio files into the song you wanted to hear. Windows XP comes bundled with Windows Media Player, the program you'll most likely use to listen to your songs. There are other options, but I'll talk about those later. It's important to note here that all of your digital audio files only become songs with the help of the media player.

I've talked about the basic attributes of digital sound files: size and detail. However, all of that information has to be organized and structured so that the media player can read it. It's just like being able to read and understand a different language. If the player "speaks" the language that these files are recorded in, it can reproduce the song and make beautiful music. If it can't speak the language, the numbers of the music just don't add up, and you get an error message — and no music. Because error messages are frustrating and I'm the kind author who wants to spare you grief, I take a look at the major audio file formats and give you a basic understanding of what's going on and what it means to you.

WAV

This method of presenting sound is the most detailed and rich of the available formats in Windows XP. All the detail is recorded at the chosen bit rate and sampling speed, and it's all done without compression schemes. It's digital sound presented in all its glory, and it takes up huge amounts of memory in the process. Four or five minutes of WAV sound can consume 40–50MB of memory, making it difficult to store a decent number of files. For that reason, you seldom see these files being sold over the Internet — they're just too big and bulky.

MP3

If you've listened to the news in the past decade, you've heard this term. This is the file format that basically powered the popularity of digital music. It also became associated with the controversy surrounding the "sharing" of music over services like Napster and Kazaa, but I tackle that subject in the section "Law and Order: MP3," later in this chapter. Still, at its heart, MP3 is only a way of encoding music for listening on a computer or a portable player.

MP3 is an audio layer of the larger MPEG file format. The important thing to remember here is that this is a specific way to make the music file smaller while retaining much of the quality of the original CD or WAV file. Compared to a WAV file of 50MB, a typical MP3 file is 5–6MB. Obviously, that's a huge size difference. However, you can hear the sound difference between an MP3 and a compact disc or a WAV file. The compression scheme is *lossy,* which means that some data is lost when the file is encoded. By increasing the bit rate of the file, you lose less data, but the file size increases accordingly.

Aside from size, the other advantage of MP3 is that it's almost universally recognized. It's the American Express of audio. Just about any media player or portable audio player can recognize and play an MP3 song. That makes it popular among users. It is not popular among most folks that sell music, however, because it's easily copied and distributed over the Internet due to its small size.

WMA

To go along with its Windows Media Player, Microsoft developed a compressed file format. The format is supposed to provide better sound at lower compression rates than MP3, although outside sources have taken issue with Microsoft's claims. WMA files are also not as universal as MP3s — as with anything Microsoft owns, this is well-guarded proprietary technology. You can find this technology on portable audio players or media players, and it functions well with the Windows Media Player that's bundled with Windows XP. It also allows music producers to better regulate how their music is used. WMA can be paired with licenses that restrict where and how the files may be used. This can make it difficult to transfer WMA songs to other media players and devices.

AAC

This file format is a derivative of another, more advanced MPEG encoding scheme called MPEG-4. It is currently being used primarily by Apple's iTunes service to sell music over the Internet. Apple claims this format allows better sound reproduction (sound familiar?), and Apple has made it the centerpiece of iTunes and its portable music player, iPod. Because AAC is a newer format, not all media players and portable devices are compatible with it. However,

Finding the free stuff

You can find plenty of alternatives to the main file formats, most of them provided by the open source software movement. Windows XP is proprietary software, where the inner workings are guarded and the rights to use it are restricted by the selling of the software and the license to use it. (Don't worry, you got the license when you purchased the Windows XP software or purchased the computer that it came on.) In *open source software,* the people who created it let others see how the software works, and they charge little or nothing for people to use it.

If you delve deep into the Internet, you may see file formats like Ogg Vorbis (OGG), Shorten (SHN), or FLAC (Free Lossless Audio Compression). These formats have been developed by people outside of Microsoft or Apple for use in creating and distributing digital audio.

The price is attractive — little or nothing can usually find space in your budget. Some of these formats even work with the more common media players, like Windows Media Player and Winamp. However, this is not always the case. Sometimes, the files have been written to work with only one compression scheme or player. It all depends on what the software writers had in mind when they created their particular flavor of audio.

You may want to investigate these file formats as you run across them. They could help you listen to music that you've never heard before or allow you to store your music in a way that's more convenient for you because of smaller file size. However, because this book focuses on Windows XP and the file formats that are most commonly used with it, I spend most of my time discussing the files I highlighted in the main text.

it's gaining acceptance, and it could become more prevalent. It can also handle some digital rights management, so music producers can control how and where AAC songs are distributed.

Real

This format was primarily developed as a *streaming format,* that is, a file that's listened to over a network without being saved on your computer (I talk more about this in Chapter 8). Because streaming requires a smaller size to be sent over dialup or broadband Internet connections, Real audio (designated with the file extension .ra) is usually among the smallest file size available. However, it's hampered by a comparable reduction in sound quality and the fact that nothing but the proprietary Real Player can handle these files. The Real Player is a free download, although many critics and users alike have complained that finding the free download among the many advertisements for its premium player and services is like finding dust bunnies in Martha Stewart's house — very difficult. Unless you prefer to use the Real Player, you probably won't run across the file very often.

MIDI

MIDI, or Musical Instrument Digital Interface, gets its own section because it's so different than the formats I talked about earlier. Technically, MIDI is not audio; it's a set of instructions on how something (like your computer's sound card) should create music. It's like a cookbook. The MIDI cookbook tells something that already has all the ingredients (the notes of the music) how to arrange them and play them to make music. Because it's just a set of instructions, the MIDI file size is quite small (often measured in kilobytes as opposed to the larger megabytes). How those instructions sound can vary depending on the device that is used to play those instructions. The sheet music for a Beethoven symphony makes no sound, but the music will likely sound better when played on a concert piano as opposed to a thrift-store keyboard. MIDI files are not often sold to the public as music, but MIDI does play a part in home recording. Because of this, I talk more about it in Chapter 12. You can also get a more exhaustive look at MIDI by checking out *Home Recording For Musicians For Dummies,* by Jeff Strong (published by Wiley).

Just the Facts

Along with the actual sound, the formats of your sound files can carry text information about the song. This can include the name of the artist, the title of the song, the genre in which the song belongs, the date it was produced, and any additional tidbits and morsels. This is an invaluable tool, because it allows you to organize your songs and see what you're listening to. MP3 files carry an *ID3 tag* that stores this information; the other file formats also carry similar information. Without it, looking for information about your songs could be as hard as finding something you need right after you've moved. It's all there in boxes, but without the labels, you have no idea what's in the boxes. Even if all your kitchen items end up in boxes in the kitchen, you would still have to look through each box to find what you wanted. With these labels, your media player can search and bring you the song you wanted much quicker. Your player can also use these tags to organize playlists of your songs and transfer them to other devices, like a portable media player. Look for more information on this subject in Chapter 5.

Storing and Moving the Goods

You have so many places in which you can put audio files these days. Before, sound was only available on vinyl records, cassettes, or the much-maligned 8-track cartridge. Now, you can find songs on CDs, DVDs, and portable audio players; online; on your cell phone; and just about anywhere else a little bit of circuitry and a speaker can be crammed in. This is one of the biggest advantages of digital sound — portability. Digital songs can be copied and moved quite easily, in most cases without losing any of the original sound quality.

The following are examples of where you can store your sound files on your computer:

- **Hard drive:** Storage of sound files requires some type of drive. You've probably heard the term *hard drive* associated with computers. This is the internal device that stores the majority of files and data on your computer. The hard drive can store the most amount of data in a small amount of physical space, which is why most of the popular portable audio devices use this component to store large amounts of songs. It's also the most expensive storage device in overall cost, but the cost per gigabyte is quite small. You pay a hundred or more dollars for a hard drive, but you get more memory than a flash drive at a comparable cost.

- **Optical discs:** Optical discs, like CDs and DVDs, can handle large amounts of data (up to 700MB and 4.7GB, respectively), and they're much cheaper forms of storage compared to a hard drive. You can also burn optical discs as data CDs (which hold files to be read by a computer or another device) or music CDs (which play in a standard CD player). The two are not always compatible, however. Older CD players can't read computer files.

- **Flash memory:** Flash memory is relatively small compared to the previous two storage devices (most portable media players that use flash memory top out between 512MB and 1GB), and it's impossible to accidentally skip ahead or move back the player while moving. For that reason, it's a popular choice among portable players that are meant to be used while exercising — the extra movement might disrupt other players, but not this one.

Moving data to and from all of these devices is relatively simple. You connect a wire from the computer to the device, or perhaps you use your Internet connection to download a file. The devices simply exchange a series of numbers that can later be read by a player or portable device. Or, in the case of streaming media, the data is read as soon as it is received. The moving or copying does not reduce the quality of the sound, because digital copies don't degrade. Furthermore, no physical parts can degrade.

Of course, like most technologies, the process of transferring music is more difficult in practice than in theory. Each device is built around one or two types of connections, and many are available. Most players are built around standard connections called *USB* (or Universal Serial Bus) or *FireWire,* which allows high rates of data to be transmitted quickly from device to device. For more on USB and FireWire, see Chapter 2.

Look for computers and devices that can handle both types of connections. This will make your life much easier when you're trying to find the right connector cable.

The Nuts and Bolts of Hardware

It doesn't take any special equipment to play these files. You probably already have the tools in your computer right now. But it's important to understand what makes the music happen, so I look briefly at each part of the puzzle.

Processors and memory

The processor and memory in your computer make the whole thing run. They keep the programs running and working. They are the brain and the nervous system of your computer, and the old adage "bigger is better" is true here. In this case, you're looking for faster processor speeds and more memory (or RAM) to accurately reproduce music. It takes much more power to play an audio file than it does to create a spreadsheet (or to write a book on music). The good news is that this isn't as big a concern as it was just a few years ago. Just about any computer you purchase today has more than enough speed and power to play back music. I talk more about the demands placed on processors and memory in Chapter 2.

This doesn't mean that you should try to play music, download a bunch of files, and burn a CD all at the same time. Computers with less memory or slower processors might balk at handling all of these tasks at the same time. Try reducing the amount of applications that are open on your computer to allow for better audio playback.

Sound cards

The *sound card* is the piece of hardware that makes the sound happen. Again, this piece of equipment has made huge leaps in the last few years. It is no longer a concern whether sound cards can accurately reproduce music. Now, it's a question of whether the sound is heard in stereo or perhaps more advanced formats, like 5.1 or 7.1 surround sound.

Sound cards are often not even "cards" anymore. The components that computers use to reproduce music or other sounds are often included right on the main circuitry of the computer itself (the motherboard). This can be both a blessing and a curse — if you like the sound of the computer, everything's wonderful. However, because the sound is built in, you're stuck with it unless you disable it and install something new. It's not as complicated as it may sound, but it's still extra effort. Again, I talk more about sound cards in Chapter 2.

Speakers

Speakers make the air move and create the sounds you hear. Most computers come bundled with a set of speakers that connect to the sound card (or internal sound). That's not always good enough, because these speakers are rather small and can't always faithfully reproduce the music. (Bass speakers are so big for a good reason — they need to be!) Depending on how your computer's sound is set up, you may want to consider getting surround-sound speakers (which include a main speaker, smaller satellite speakers, and a subwoofer for bass).

This assumes, of course, that the music you're playing has been designed for multiple speakers. Most standard recordings today are mixed to stereo, or two channels. Running a stereo recording through a surround-sound setup still only gives you a stereo sound output. You start hearing the differences when the audio has been specifically encoded for surround sound, like in many video games and movies. For now, because popular music is still focused on stereo, it is the main format of my discussions.

Portable audio players

This gets a much closer look in Chapter 5, but these devices are one of the most popular ways to listen to music. Portable sound started with the Walkman, which allowed people to take cassette recordings with them. Now, you can take CDs, DVDs, or your audio files with you wherever you go. Your length of enjoyment depends only on the amount of songs in the player and the juice left in your battery. These players can use any of the three types of storage media I discussed in the section "Storing and Moving the Goods," earlier in this chapter, depending on where they are used.

The Softer Side of Audio

I've looked briefly at the hardware components you need to make your computer a music machine. You also need programs to make the music happen. These programs interpret the numbers and instructions that are present in the digital file formats and do one of three things: play the music, download the music, or edit the music.

Media players

Because you have Windows XP, you already have a media player on your system (specifically, Windows Media Player). Many other commercial or free players are also available. They all handle basically the same thing: They play music or videos. Most can also handle some sort of organizational function (they can keep track of your files) and even play some sort of light show to go along with it. These players can also change how they look and interact with your computer, depending on what you want them to do. I take a closer look at media players in Chapter 5.

Download programs

A Web browser can usually handle all your download needs. Using Internet Explorer, you can bring all manner of files (digital or otherwise) into your home. However, some stores require the use of specialized download programs to bring their files onto your computer. This isn't because Internet Explorer (or your preferred Web browser) can't handle the process of downloading. It's because these stores (such as iTunes or Rhapsody) want to control how their music leaves their *servers* (a central computer that sends out the information requested by computers like yours) and where it goes. If you want to use a particular store, you use its download software. Many companies also combine a media player or organizational function with these download programs.

Editing programs

You probably won't have to use this type of program very often unless you're creating music. Music-editing programs are just like word processors for text. They allow you to record, edit, or delete sections of a recording and make it closer to what you want. This topic is covered in more detail in Chapter 13, but it may also be useful for you if you want to create transitions between songs on CDs that you burn. Some of these functions are also built into a media player. For example, Winamp can eliminate silence between songs and create automatic cross-fades with the push of a button, just like on the radio.

Law and Order: MP3

You have a basic overview of what can be done with digital music from what you've read so far. What should stick with you now is that digital music is easy to move around via networks and is easy to store on CDs and other media. And with all this moving, the sound doesn't lose quality like analog recordings do. This is great for music fans, because it's easy to get music in this format. Although the MP3 format may not be as high quality as a CD, its continuing popularity shows that most people are willing to give up the additional quality in exchange for the convenience and availability.

This convenience and availability moved the recording and distribution of music into an entirely unexplored area. Never before had there been such a widespread network available to distribute music to literally millions of listeners worldwide. Also, never before had this network been available for free. And never before have we had such legal and ethical conflicts about how this network was built.

Peer-to-peer file sharing

You probably first heard about peer-to-peer file sharing as part of a single brand name: Napster. In the late '90s, this service put the exchange of MP3 files at the attention of the nation. This service allowed computer users to *rip,* or copy, songs from a CD and convert them to MP3 files. These files could then be exchanged over the Internet by other uses of the Napster software. Napster used central servers to allow the file transfers to continue, while other services transferred files directly from a user's computer to another computer. Hence, the term *peer-to-peer (or P2P) file sharing* — where each file is transferred from one user to another — was born.

Legal setbacks

The problem is that the legality of this exchange is highly suspect. According to copyright law, a user who purchases a media product like a CD or movie can make a backup copy in case the original gets damaged. However, any more copies that are made are illegal. You've probably seen this warning message at the beginning of movies. The question was whether these digital copies were legal. And it was answered when the courts decided to shut down the original Napster network; the transmission of these files was deemed to be illegal.

While they share the same name, the current Napster service should not be confused with its previous version. The Napster brand name and logo were purchased and are being used by another company to sell music downloads via a subscription service that's endorsed by those companies who own the music.

Pandora's Box was already open, however, as many other services sprung up to take Napster's place. Names like Kazaa, Morpheus, and Limewire became more commonplace as alternatives to the now-defunct Napster. The problem is that these networks are still illegal. They are distributing copyrighted music without the permission of the owners of that music, and the owners are not being compensated for the distribution.

Two persuasive arguments are used by proponents of file sharing to justify their activities. One is the increasing cost of popular music. Indeed, the courts have determined that the major record labels did overcharge customers, and in 2003, participants in a class action suit received small payments in a judgment against the major recording labels. An additional component to this argument is that the record companies make money at the expense of the artists. (Trust me; as a musician, I'm sympathetic to this argument.) However, the files being shared are still illegal copies. That does not affect the legality of file sharing. It's still considered piracy.

File-sharing proponents have also claimed that previewing music is an important part of the music-buying process and that people are buying more music because they can listen to it before they buy it. While this may be true, legal ways exist to obtain previews of songs before purchase. Web sites like iTunes and Amazon have sections where buyers can listen to songs before they purchase them; it's just like having a listening station in a traditional record store. Again, that does not eliminate the fact that file sharing uses illegal copies of copyrighted material.

This section applies only to files that are distributed without permission of the owner. If someone wants to give away his music (music that he created and owns the copyright to) on P2P, it's perfectly legal.

Other drawbacks of P2P

In addition to the dubious legality of sharing files, other problems can result from using P2P. Both the files exchanged and the service itself can cause problems.

Viruses and undesirables

You can't always be sure what you order from the menu of a P2P site is what you're going to get. You may get the song, but you may also get something much worse. Unscrupulous users have been known to mask viruses as audio files and turn them loose on P2P networks. Other undesirable elements, like pornography, can also be inserted into the network to look like songs. It's always a question of what you're going to get, and it may be better to be safe than sorry.

Spyware and adware

Both the service and the files may be responsible for putting software on your machine known as *spyware* or *adware*. This software can track what you do on your computer and where you go on the Internet, and use it to foul up your system. It can increase the amount of pop-up ads you see or change the home page of your browser. At its worst, this software can affect the performance of your computer by clogging the processor with unnecessary functions and tasks. This slows the system and increases your frustration.

Securing your system

You can take the following three steps to make sure that your system stays clean:

1. **Don't install P2P file-sharing systems.**

2. **Install virus protection on your computer, and keep it up to date.**

3. **Regularly update Windows XP with the security patches that are available through Microsoft's Windows Update system.**

Copying and burning files

And the debate continues to rage on. Many lawsuits against organizations and P2P users have resulted, and the matter is still being settled in the courts. Until it is settled, the law says that sharing these files is illegal, and it is best to avoid it. This doesn't mean that you can't make these files — it's just a matter of how you use them.

As a consumer purchasing a recording, it's still your right to make a backup copy. It's also your choice on what media you want to make that copy. If you choose to rip the CD to your computer and keep your backup copy on your hard drive, that's fine. Go ahead, and tell 'em I sent you.

Many copyright owners are also more than happy to allow you to transfer files to your portable media players or burn the songs to a CD to listen to elsewhere, if you want to leave the original at home, for example. A good rule of thumb is that as long as the recording stays in your possession, it's probably going to be okay.

The problem arises when you start making copies of songs or albums and giving the copies to other people. The purchase allows you to maintain copies, not to distribute them to others. Others may borrow them, but not make copies. This makes things like mix tapes (a collection of songs) dubious, but we haven't arrived at the day when the Recording Industry

File sharing: Should you do it?

I'm a little biased as far as file sharing is concerned, because I'm a musician who has recorded commercially available CDs. While I won't be making a living off of these CDs anytime soon, I'm still concerned with what happens to them. That being said, I can certainly sympathize with those who feel recordings are overpriced. I'm a certified recording addict, and I love purchasing and experiencing new music. If it were cheaper, I could get more. It's a simple equation. Still, I don't feel right violating the law to get my hands on recordings.

A great amount of debate continues over the business practices of the music industry, a field not exactly known for its adherence to ethics and fair business practices. Hopefully, that atmosphere will change soon. The Internet gives artists new distribution potential for their music. They can now reach their listeners (in theory) without the aid of a record company, keeping more profits to themselves. I'd love to see that happen, but that still doesn't make unauthorized downloading legal.

Okay, I'll step off my soapbox now. Gotta head down to the music store.

Association of America (RIAA) is going after Johnny Heartthrob for giving his true love a collection of romantic tunes that tells her *exactly* how he feels. It's the mass distribution of piracy, for profit or otherwise, that the copyright owners and the courts are concerned with.

Most download services are also offering the ability to share copies of songs legally among several sources. For example, you may be allowed to burn a certain number of copies of the song and transfer the file an unlimited number of times to your portable audio player. Hey, it's their dime. If these services give you permission, go right ahead. Again, it's illegal only if you're acting against your rights as a purchaser and against the wishes of the copyright owner.

Chapter 2

Wiring Your Computer for Sound

In This Chapter

▶ Understanding what makes a computer ready for audio

▶ Examining the computer's digital audio hardware

▶ Connecting the required audio hardware

▶ Networking your components

•••

I admit it — I'm a geek. Playing with new digital sound toys makes me a happy man, and I'm always willing to tinker around with a new piece of gear to see what I can get out of it. And I always have the instructions in case something goes wrong or I get stumped (it happens more than I care to admit). So I'm going to have a lot of fun with this chapter. This is where I look at the technical guts of the Windows XP system and see what it takes to make beautiful music.

Before I begin, this is one case where a familiar saying probably applies: "Bigger (or more) is better." You should pay attention to some of the numbers, and for the most part, higher is better. But I also look at how some components work better with others and how this interaction can make as much of a difference as the speed of your processor and the amount of memory in your PC.

But I'm getting ahead of myself. Look at the computer like your own minia-ture orchestra — a combination of parts and players working together to follow the score and make your music audible. Each plays its own role, and in concert, they create a whole that's bigger than the sum of their (computer) parts. And that's when the whole thing rocks.

Getting the Right Computer

My first computer was barely capable of emitting the beeps and clicks neces-sary to tell me it was on. Producing any decent sound wasn't even possible. And so it remained a data tool, capable of no entertainment beyond a game of

Battle Chess. In this day and age, however, just about any computer you purchase is more than capable of acting as a home stereo system (and so much more). The issues now are how much music can be stored and played, and how can that music be arranged and modified. The first component I look at is probably the one you've heard the most about (if only from an advertising jingle).

The minimum system requirements for using Windows XP on a personal computer are a 233-MHz processor, 32MB RAM, and 2.5GB free hard drive space. These are the bare minimums, so I assume that your computer has at least those attributes. As you'll read, though, you need much more than that.

Processing . . . processing . . .

In the orchestra of your computer, the processor is the conductor. This is where the commands are issued, the directives sent out, and the information routed. The processor is the centerpiece of your computer, and as such, it draws a lot of attention.

For a long time, the identifying characteristic of processors has been clock speed. This is probably the first statistic you saw when you bought your computer (or it will be the first thing you see when you go shopping). Most current processors are measured in gigahertz, or GHz. However, you may still have older computers running Windows XP that use processors measured in megahertz (MHz). This basically means that the processor can execute an amount of instructions or commands equal to its speed rating per second. For example, this means that one of my computers, with a 2.4-GHz processor, can execute a little over 2 billion basic instructions per second. (Every time I look at a sentence like that, I feel a little lazier and think about vacuuming my apartment.)

Your computer may also have more than one processor running. You can purchase some computers with a dual-processor setup. This allows the computer to use two processors to handle more instructions (and theoretically speed up the computer). It's a feature that's nice to have at times, but it's not something you should necessarily seek out if you're just going to be doing basic digital music duties (see the old story about bazookas and flyswatters here).

It's a virtual guarantee that any computer you've purchased in the last few years can handle playing audio files. You're going to be concerned with how many tasks your computer can handle in addition to the musical tasks you'll be doing. That's where the processor really plays its part.

While clock speed is an impressive number, the processor has other attributes. The way the chip is made can impact how it operates within your machine as well. In your search for your home entertainment computer, you'll run across two major types of chips, each with its benefits and drawbacks: Intel and AMD.

Intel and the Pentium processor

When I think of the Pentium processor, a very nontechnical thing springs to mind: that little jingle that Intel plays at the end of a computer advertisement (and there have been a lot of them). The fact that the jingle has been burned into my brain (I sometimes hear it in my sleep) shows just how ubiquitous these chips have become in the home computing industry. For a long time, these chips were a specific requirement for many pieces of software, precisely because they were built to be the fastest on the market. Intel's chips still rate very high in the speed department, although other manufacturers have managed to creep into its territory and challenge Intel's dominance.

Intel has introduced four generations of Pentium chips so far, and any computer you've recently purchased probably has the latest generation (logically named the Pentium 4) installed in it. This means that the system runs with a processor speed from 2 GHz to a little over 3 GHz. This is more than enough power to handle basic digital music duties.

However, speed isn't everything. Some of the more recent Pentiums come with a feature called *hyperthreading*. Without getting too technical, this basically fools the computer into thinking that two processors are operating inside the machine. As you can see in Figure 2-1, a Pentium 4 chip with hyperthreading is operating as two chips in one.

Hyperthreading allows the computer to process and handle multiple tasks occurring at the same time faster. (I think I want to get back to that vacuuming now.)

As with most name brands you've encountered, Intel chips often command premium prices. The company does make a "budget" line called the Celeron processor, which is available on lower-priced home computers. Still, these widely available chips are likely to be more expensive than their off-brand counterparts.

AMD and the Athlon processor

AMD processors have pulled into the race with Intel, attempting to make processors as fast as their competitors at a lower price. And some computer reviewers have noted that AMD's construction makes its processors faster than Intel processors rated at the same speed. Because of this construction style and lower price, AMD processors are a popular alternative to the Intel-dominated computer world. AMD manufactures two major names: the Athlon and the budget-line Duron chip. These are roughly comparable to Intel's Pentium and Celeron chips, respectively, although as noted before, construction differences can affect the chip's performance.

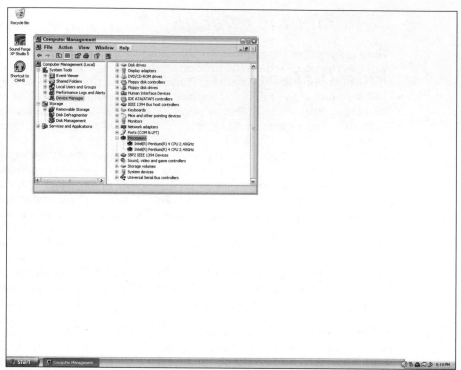

Figure 2-1:
A Pentium 4
processor
with hyper-
threading.

Breaking it down

It's good to know this information, but you're probably only concerned with
the computer's overall performance. If you bought a computer with one of
these processors installed, the system has likely been designed to accommodate what's included. You're most likely dealing with a processor speed of at
least 2 GHz — and maybe more if you purchase a computer designed specifically for multimedia use.

With those statistics, you can be more concerned with how many tasks you
can do at the same time. For example, you may want to be able to burn a CD
at the same time you're transferring files to a portable device and listening to
a streaming audio station. The higher your processor is rated (and the better
it's made), the better your computer can handle these multiple tasks.

However, the processor is only one part of the equation. It works in concert
with the memory that's installed in your computer to operate the programs
and make the system move faster.

RAMming it through

Here is the other big number for the computer. Random-access memory, or RAM, is the place where the processor stores the programs and the data that it's using to operate the system. Think of RAM as the players in the virtual orchestra. The conductor (processor) tells the players (RAM) what to load and when to execute its instructions. The more RAM you have, the faster the processor can get information and send out instructions to be executed.

Again, the minimum specification for running Windows XP on a computer is 64MB RAM. However, that's like driving the autobahn in a rusty Pinto. It's the minimum amount required to allow the operating system to function and to accomplish very basic tasks. Digital audio is one of the most demanding tasks a computer can undertake. Therefore, you need a great deal more RAM to properly handle both the programs you'll need to run and the files the programs will be playing.

I recommend at least 512MB RAM for proper digital audio playback. That should allow you to maintain a decent playback of audio while taking care of other programs you may be running, visualization effects from your media player, or other tasks. And the more RAM you have, the better. You should be able to get up to 1GB RAM without adding much expense.

Even if you're operating an older system with minimal RAM, you may be in luck. If you have the right type of memory chip available to you (you can buy chips at smaller computer stores or the large chain stores like Best Buy), it's just a matter of putting the right chip in the right slot and booting the computer. Most chips can only be installed in one way, so it's generally impossible to put the chip in the wrong place. Check your manufacturer's specifications, see what kind of RAM your computer requires, and determine the maximum amount of RAM that the system can recognize. For under $100, you could double or triple the memory that's installed in your computer and dramatically improve its performance.

Installing more RAM is just a matter of putting the right chip in the right slot. And it is one of the easiest ways to upgrade your system. However, unless you know exactly what the right chip is and where it goes, I suggest asking for help from someone who is knowledgeable about installing computer parts. You can damage something in the computer while you're installing the memory. If you think you're up to the challenge of upgrading your RAM, check out *Upgrading and Fixing PCs For Dummies,* 6th Edition, by Andy Rathbone (published by Wiley).

Static electricity is a huge danger to your system. If you're not properly grounded while installing these components, you could cause damage to the memory or other components in your computer. If you're not sure how to properly ground yourself, it's a good idea to leave it to someone who does.

Wanna go for a drive?

I'm going to continue to push the orchestra metaphor (as a former middle school violinist, I feel I'm honor-bound to do so) in talking about the computer's hard drive. If the processor is the conductor and the RAM is the players, then the hard drive represents the orchestra's repertoire, or library of songs. The hard drive is where the instructions and the data for each program and file are stored while not being used. When the processor calls for the information, it's loaded from the hard drive into memory and run.

The hard drive has two important attributes — storage space and rotations per minute, or rpm. Storage space for modern hard drives is measured in gigabytes, and most current hard drives can hold from 40GB to 200GB. Some computers can also be shipped with two hard drives to increase the amount of storage space. This is important because digital audio files tend to be rather large. Make sure you have at least a 100GB hard drive to store all of your programs and files.

One problem is that manufacturers and computer scientists tend to disagree about the definition of a gigabyte. Manufacturers generally define a gigabyte as 1000MB, whereas the tech folk point out that technically 1GB of memory is slightly more that 1000MB. (This makes much more sense if you're up on binary numbers, bits and bytes, and so on — don't worry if you're not.) Combine this argument with the formatting that's required for a computer to read a hard drive, and the actual storage capacity of a hard drive is somewhat less than what is advertised on the box.

The average song in MP3 format is about 5MB in size, and uncompressed WAV files can be ten times larger than that.

The hard drive's rotations per minute are important because a computer must be able to access information from the spinning platter of the drive. Because the hard drive is a circular drive, the computer reads the drive's information in a spinning fashion. The faster the drive can spin, the faster the information can be read and passed on to the memory. Most commercial hard drives spin at 5,400 rpm, although I recommend at least a 7,200-rpm drive for optimum digital audio playback. If you can spring for it, look for hard drives that speed along at 10,000 rpm.

You may also see hard drives that have a cache (for example, an 8MB cache). The cache allows the drive to store information where it is more accessible for reading in a quicker time. A cache may only shave a small amount off the access time, but the name of the game is speed. Getting more information faster ultimately improves the quality of sound that you hear.

Hard drives can also be located outside the computer. These external hard drives are most commonly connected to the system via USB or FireWire cables. They can have the same storage capacities as internal hard drives, although they come at a higher price. Because external drives generally take longer to access data, they are more suited for long-term storage, transport, or backing up of files as opposed to the day-to-day operations of an internal hard drive.

Heading to the Hardware Store

Everything I've talked about up to this point is standard in every computer. A processor and memory are on the motherboard, and a hard drive stores data. What changes at this point is where the other components are located. Some of the following components may be incorporated into the main circuitry of the computer or they can be added later as a modular component. Still, they're necessary for the operation of the computer and the playing of digital audio. I start with the most important audio component of all — the sound card.

Sounding off

The term *sound card* comes from a time when a computer's only audio component was a small internal speaker. This was suitable only for little beeps — good enough to signal a user that something just occurred with the main system or that something was wrong, but certainly not capable of playing any sort of recognizable music (beyond "Twinkle, Twinkle Little Star"). The audio component of the computer had to be added later, in one of the expansion slots on the computer's motherboard.

The main purpose of the sound card is to act as a gateway between the analog and digital realms. A good sound card can record audio from a microphone and a line in (such as from a cassette or record player) and send out audio to a set of speakers. Because all sound eventually becomes analog (your ears hear sound waves, not 1s and 0s), the sound card must include digital-to-analog signal converters. It must also include analog-to-digital signal converters to make the sound coming in from the microphone or line-in jack into a digital file.

The computer also has a digital signal processor, or DSP, which sends the digital audio information back and forth between the processor, memory, and storage media of the computer. You may see the DSP rated in a similar manner as CDs are rated. Whereas CD-quality audio is rated at 16-bit, 44.1-kHz sound (that's 16 bits of information sampled 44,100 times a second), current sound cards are capable of handling audio quality of up to 24-bit, 96-kHz sound and above.

Audio-in and -out functions are usually made available through *minijacks,* or ⅛-inch jacks. You've seen these jacks on headphones (and you could plug in headphones to the speaker-out jack for privacy's sake). Not only does this work for the 'phones, but it's also how most sound goes in and out of the sound card.

This may sound complicated, but most commercial sound cards are either labeled or color coded so that you can match component to component. It's just like Garanimals — the light green matches the light green, the red matches the red, and so on. In the end, you have your computer set up for sound with a minimum of fuss. With that in mind, Figure 2-2 shows a standard sound card.

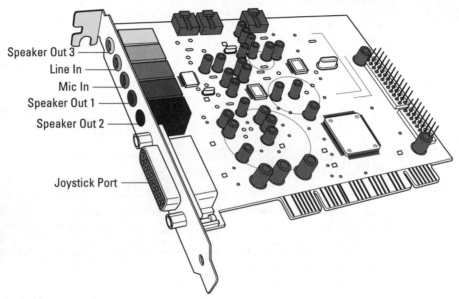

Speaker Out 3
Line In
Mic In
Speaker Out 1
Speaker Out 2

Joystick Port

Figure 2-2:
The stand-
ard PC
sound card.

The following types of sound cards are currently available:

- **Built-in or integral:** These cards are hard-wired into the main board of the computer, housed inside the computer's case.

- **Internal:** This card is plugged into an expansion slot on the main board of the computer.

- **External:** This card is plugged into an external jack on the computer and is placed outside of the computer.

Features of built-in sound cards

Built-in types are the most common sound cards currently available. An increasing number of motherboard manufacturers now incorporate the most-required components into their circuitry, eliminating the need to use the computer's expansion slots and saving room for something else. (However, I have yet to see a computer with all its expansion slots full, even with a sound card in place).

This design has advantages and disadvantages. The advantage is that you don't have to buy a sound card to go with the computer. You know that the card has been tested with the system, and you know it's going to work with the computer from the first startup. The disadvantage is that you're stuck with the card you have. You can't separate your system from the sound card, and you can't remove the card. If your sound card breaks or gets damaged, you would have to either add an internal or external sound card or install a new motherboard.

You can always override your internal sound card in favor of another device you'd rather use. Most computer's *BIOS programs* (the operating system you see on your system before Windows XP starts up) include a function that can disable integral sound devices. All BIOS programs have different options, so I can't point to any one surefire way to make this option happen. But, if you're feeling crafty, this is one possibility to investigate.

The easiest way to damage a sound card is to put too much strain on the external components by pulling the cords too tight. If you have anything plugged into your sound card, be sure that you have enough cord to allow some slack in the cords. Otherwise, you're looking at some time on the workbench.

Most built-in sound cards just have the basic inputs and outputs available. Manufacturers have begun to include digital or optical audio outputs on some motherboards, allowing users to send digital audio directly from the sound card to another device, like a stereo receiver or a wireless transmitter. The most common type of digital output is the S/PDIF (Sony/Phillips Digital Interface). This type of connection (developed by Sony and Phillips Electronics, as you might have surmised) sends all the audio information in digital format over a single cable. Not only do you get better sound quality, but you also reduce the amount of nasty cabling behind your electronic devices. This is a useful feature, but it's not widely available yet.

Keeping it all inside

The internal sound card is how it all began — a bunch of circuits embedded on a module mounted inside the computer. From the outside, though, it appears much the same as the built-in sound card that I talked about in the previous section. The internal card has the same basic inputs and outputs at the consumer level, but the additional space allows manufacturers to add more features, if desired.

The basics of a normal internal sound card include the microphone-in, line-in, and speaker-out jacks, as previously discussed. The speaker outputs can vary from normal stereo configurations to surround sound and 5.1 or 7.1 configurations. You may also find digital outputs for sending signals to other digital components, like the S/PDIF connection mentioned in the previous section.

In addition to those jacks, some older sound cards may have a joystick port mounted on them. Older veterans of video-game combat may recognize the joystick as a control that allowed you to deal death among many pixilated enemies or perhaps guide a hopeful young eating machine through a maze while avoiding paranormal enemies and picking up some tasty fruit along the way. So why was this feature added to the sound card, even though it has very little to do with audio? The first sound cards were developed to accommodate video-game players, and it made sense to combine all the features that were needed for gaming on one card (to save space and make sure that everything worked together). It sounds a lot like placing audio circuitry on a computer's motherboard, doesn't it? This probably won't make much difference to you, because most gaming devices plug in through a USB or FireWire port. However, some MIDI devices can function on this joystick port, allowing home recording buffs to record MIDI data on their computer. You can read more about MIDI recording in Chapter 12 or in the fine publication *Home Recording For Musicians For Dummies,* by Jeff Strong (published by Wiley).

Sound cards may also have components external to them, normally called *breakout boxes.* These boxes connect to the internal card (indeed, they require that card to function), but they put the jacks and controls closer to the user, instead of hiding them in the back of the computer. It's mostly a convenience factor. If you're going to be changing components frequently — for example, switching out speakers for headphones or changing the input for your sound card's line in — you may want to buy something with an external breakout box. Examine Figure 2-3 to see a typical breakout box.

As you can see, the main functions of the sound card jacks are transplanted from the dark, dusty forgotten realm known as the back of the computer to the light of day. This way, you can switch out components as necessary and make any needed adjustments. These boxes can also include volume controls, MIDI-in or -out jacks, and other options.

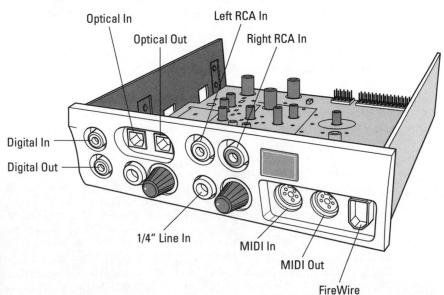

Figure 2-3:
A breakout
box.

Take it outside!

The faster data connections made possible by USB 2.0 and FireWire have opened a whole new type of sound cards — the external sound module. Instead of the modules built or mounted in the frame of your computer, these devices reside outside the case, as shown in Figure 2-4.

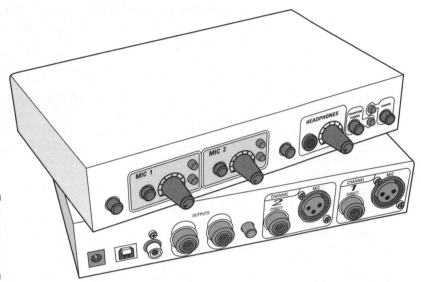

Figure 2-4:
An external sound module.

The module shown in Figure 2-4 is built for sound recording. That's why it has the specialized microphone-in jacks called XLR, a separate headphone jack, and other options. But the regular John Q. Digital may find a need for an external sound card, especially if he uses a laptop.

Because the circuitry is so compact in a laptop, both the speakers and the sound circuitry tend to be a little undersized. If you're interested in bigger and better sound, you need to add something to your little computer. By inserting this card into the laptop or connecting it via USB 2.0 or FireWire, you have the advantage of better sound circuitry and options. It may add a little weight to what you carry around, but that's the sacrifice you make for good sound!

Sound advice

Whenever you add a device to a computer — especially a duplicate of something that may be built into the circuitry of the computer, like a sound card — you have the potential for system resource conflict. As fast as the computer can be, it can have problems dealing with conflicting instructions. Imagine having one CD and being told to put it in two different CD players. You can't do both, and no other factor tells you which way to go. The computer has trouble dealing with this kind of situation, and it may either hang or not allow

Making the connection

Just about everything in this book that resides outside the computer case — from external hard drives and sound cards to portable audio players — benefits from the high-speed connections available through USB 2.0 and FireWire connections. These connections allow a device to communicate with the system at great speeds without mounting the device internally. Thus, the device can be quickly swapped out with other devices. You can have as many devices as you have ports connected to your computer (or with external hubs, up to 127 USB 2.0 devices or 63 FireWire devices — that's a lot of jukeboxes!) and switch out the devices as necessary. The ability to use a variety of devices operating from the same port is a huge advance in versatility. USB 2.0 is slightly faster than FireWire, although both achieve very high data-rate transfers. For digital media transfers, this means that a CD can be ripped to your computer in minutes, or an external sound card can be used instantly with your computer to produce music. Keep FireWire and USB 2.0 in mind — these are your data pipelines of the future.

the devices to function. If you have this kind of conflict (for example, you have a built-in sound card but have just installed an internal card because it has better features), it may be best to either remove one of the components or turn it off. This can be done either in the computer's BIOS or through the Windows XP Device Manager.

Before attempting such tasks, you should be familiar with this territory. If you have doubts, ask someone with experience to help you.

Same disc, different box

You probably already own a CD player, a DVD player, or a player that handles both. The part of your computer that handles CDs and DVDs is perfectly capable of handling those tasks (given the right software), and it's also capable of much more. These drives can play both songs and movies as a normal CD or DVD player would, but they can also read these files as digital media files, opening a whole new world of possibilities. CDs and DVDs can function as recordings, playing anywhere. They can also function as storage media, allowing you to transport many more songs as files and play them as normal music. The key is in how the disc is made. It's not important to understand the exact transfer methods and storage formats here. You should just know that CDs and DVDs come in two basic formats — music (or movie, for DVDs) and data.

The music and movie discs are formatted to play in stand-alone players, without the aid of a personal computer. The data disc requires the use of a personal computer to decode, but it can store hundreds of files. Whereas a CD burned in the standard format can hold about 80 minutes of music, an MP3

data CD with files averaging 4MB in size can store 150 to 200 songs. Some
newer DVD and CD players can now handle files, so look for these types of
recordings to become more prevalent.

Seeing the light

You can hear the computer, but you must be able to see what you're playing
as well. At the very least, you must be able to find your files. And then you
may want to see the music videos or visualization effects in some media players. Again, the term *video card* refers to a time when the circuitry was
installed separately from the main motherboard of the computer. Like the
sound card, the video card is often found on the motherboard of most current computers. Internal video cards are available for those who want better
graphics or maybe want to show live television on their home computer.
Because video isn't the focus of this book, I'll just say that the video card that
shipped with your computer is more than sufficient for your uses here
(although I revisit this topic briefly in Chapter 4 when I discuss Windows XP
Media Center Edition).

In fact, unless you're doing heavy-duty video viewing or gaming, it's probably
best to leave out the huge video cards, especially if you're doing any of the
audio recording that I describe in Part IV. "Why?" I can hear you ask.
"Wouldn't you want the best resources available to your computer?" At some
point, you can get too much of a good thing, and it can come back to haunt
your computer's performance. If a video card and a sound card are competing for processing power and memory resources, the performance of one or
both can be degraded. It's like being pulled in two different directions, and it
can cause just as much trouble to your computer as it can to the overworked
corporate cog sitting in the cubicle next to you. Cards that carry their own
memory and processing power (like many current video cards) lessen this
problem.

Speakers of the house

These are the boxes that go boom. The speakers could be the cheapest portion of your computer setup (a cheap pair probably came with your system),
or you could spend hundreds of dollars on either a pair or a greater number
of speakers that deliver high-quality sound worthy of a home theater system.
The line between computers and home entertainment is blurring, and many
speakers can be used in either setting.

The standard computer setup in systems shipped today is a pair of stereo
speakers plugged directly into the sound card. This can suffice for basic
sound reproduction for everything from system sounds to music playback.
Many gaming systems also include a *2.1 system* — the .1 refers to a large subwoofer that takes a line off of the main speakers and reproduces a sizable

The competition format

Remember VHS versus Beta? We're at it again with SACD and DVD-A. These audiophile formats are competing for the same market — the high-end audio listener. SACD is sponsored by Sony (who has a history of pushing its own formats), and DVD-A is an audio format sponsored by the engineering group that developed the DVD format that we use for home video. The nice thing about this format war is that because the discs each format uses are the same size, some hybrid players can handle both formats. That way, if one format eventually takes over the other, you aren't stuck with a bunch of useless hardware. Also, remember that you need special equipment to play these high-end recordings. You can't take advantage of the additional features that SACD and DVD-A offer if you're only using stereo speakers. The good news is that SACD can play in normal players, albeit at the standard fidelity.

quantity of bass frequencies. Whenever you're dealing with surround sound like 5.1 or 7.1, that .1 indicates the subwoofer. The other numbers refer to the number of speakers used in a circular array.

Surround-sound systems are great for movies, television, and other media specifically created for these kind of speaker setups. The amount of sound sent to each speaker creates an illusion of space within the sound — think of being in a movie theater. Unfortunately, a great deal of today's recorded music has not been created with those specifications in mind. It's still being recorded and delivered to the listener in stereo. You can get recordings that take advantage of these enhanced audio systems in formats like SACD (Super Audio CD) and DVD-A, which are designed for audiophiles who want to hear classic and new recordings in an expanded sonic atmosphere. Sounds pretty heady, doesn't it? Some players on the market can handle these formats, but they're not mainstream formats yet.

Seeing the light

The last component that I address is the video card. Again, the *card* part of the term refers to when this component was an addition you had to make to the computer if you wanted to see anything beyond black and white (or green, or amber, as the case may be). To see anything in any sort of color, you added the video card to the system (and prayed that it didn't cause system conflicts). The video card function has largely been built into the motherboard, although you can purchase separate cards that can be installed for additional capability. The devices can fit into the same slots that internal sound cards fit in, but special slots, called *AGP slots,* have been developed specifically for video. These connections offer faster refreshing speeds and higher resolution for monitors. For the nontechnical reader, this basically translates into more screen "real estate" and less video glitches than other connections may offer.

Having a great video connection sounds like a wonderful idea, especially if you're going to be watching television and video on the same computer (see Chapter 4 for information on this type of multimedia PC). Remember that audio and video are two of the most memory-intensive tasks a computer can handle, though. Make sure that your system can handle the strain that's associated with these activities. This memory requirement is why many currently available video cards carry their own memory directly on the card. This facilitates the quick refreshing and detail needed to power the monitors and to present a clear and strong signal.

Making the Connections

So you've decided to add some extra equipment to your machine, along with a nice set of speakers, to make it the blazing sound machine you've always wanted. At the start, you have a mess of wires, a bunch of jacks, and a few boxes. The challenge is getting them all together and functional. So where to begin?

First, computer and equipment manufacturers have felt your pain, and they've made the process relatively simply by following two simple rules:

1. Each connector can only fit in one place.
2. If that doesn't work, each connector is color coded with the jack that it's supposed to go in.

Some of the connections even have pictures next to them to facilitate the setup. The ultimate goal is to get everything set up in the shortest amount of time so that you can start enjoying your new toy!

Dealing a new hand of cards

The most complicated thing in this chapter is installing a new audio or video card, because it involves opening the computer and physically putting the card in one of the slots. Unless you're comfortable with the process or have done this type of installation before, it may be something best left to the professionals. Still, for those intrepid souls who want to press on, I show you the correct way to proceed.

The vast majority of cards follow the Plug and Play standard, or PnP for short. This process ensures that devices installed in the system are recognized and work automatically. Because of the myriad devices and the software required to run the devices — and the complications that can arise — this process has been renamed by many as "Plug and Pray." Still, the computer usually recognizes the new part. I assume that the new device is PnP compatible and proceed from there. Follow these steps to install your audio or video card:

1. **Read the instructions that came with the card.**

   This may seem like a no-brainer step, but it's an important beginning. Each device may have individual quirks or needs, like installing its drivers before you install the component, that should be addressed before going through this generic installation process.

2. **Unplug the computer, and open your case.**

   Again, this is an important step. Make sure that the computer is not receiving any electricity, and then open your case. (Each computer case is different, so refer to your manufacturer's instructions.)

   The computer *must* be unplugged, and you must not attempt to open the power supply casing. This could result in electrocution. See why this process may be something best left to the pros? Also, this is another step where static electricity may be a problem. Make sure you are properly grounded, and don't rub your feet on heavy carpet just before installing the card.

3. **Locate the PCI or AGP slots on the motherboard.**

   Remember, each component only fits in the slot for which it is intended. Figure 2-5 shows you a typical PCI slot and an AGP slot.

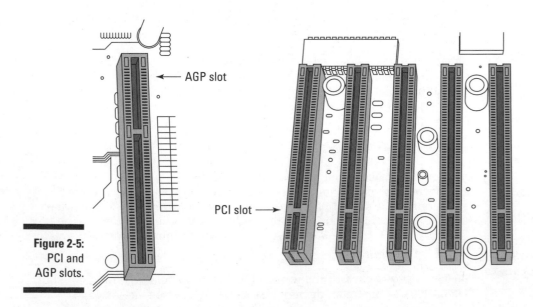

Figure 2-5: PCI and AGP slots.

AGP slot ←

PCI slot →

4. **Remove the slot cover from your computer, and install the component in the machine.**

   The slot cover is just a piece of metal that is removable when you install a component. Simply slide the cover out and put the component in. Installation may require a little pressure — press on the edge of the card until it's firmly seated.

   Don't leave unoccupied PCI or AGP slots uncovered. That hole in the computer chassis can allow dust to get in, causing parts to malfunction and the computer to overheat.

5. **Replace the computer's cover, and plug it back in.**

   You're ready to roll from here. Restart the computer, and follow the on-screen instructions to install the new device.

FireWire and USB

These external connections are probably the easiest to make. Although their individual speeds and connection shapes may differ, they share a common trait: You don't have to power down the computer to install or disconnect the device. This is called *hot swapping,* and it's a great timesaver. Also, these connections only fit in the slot that they're supposed to inhabit, so it's very easy. These connections can even supply power to some devices, so that's one less wire to occupy the spaghetti bowl behind your desk. The USB slot looks like a thin rectangular jack, while a FireWire connection looks like either a more-square jack with two corners edged off or a significantly smaller jack with two elongated edges. Figure 2-6 shows USB and FireWire jacks.

Figure 2-6:
USB and
FireWire
connections.

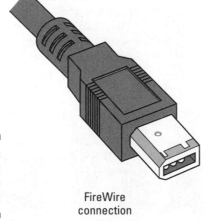

FireWire
connection

USB
connection

Because these devices can be powered by their attachments to the computer, you may need to "stop" the device before you unplug the cable. This is basically an instruction to the computer to discontinue using and powering the device so that the device can be safely removed from the computer. To stop a device, click the Unplug or Eject Hardware icon on the right side of the taskbar. This opens a menu of devices that are running on the computer, as shown in Figure 2-7.

Select the device you want to remove and choose Stop This Device. You can now safely unplug the device.

You can install up to 127 USB devices or 63 FireWire devices on any computer. You won't find enough jacks on the computer itself, but you can purchase hubs to increase the number of jacks on your computer.

Speak, Spot!

Speakers have standard jacks, too. However, they can vary widely depending on the set of speakers you've purchased. I start by showing you how to connect a simple set of stereo speakers (the kind that probably came with your computer), and then I work my way up through some of the more intricate setups.

The basic model

If you ordered your computer from a major manufacturer, you probably got a set of speakers along with the machine. These are likely to be two small speakers — decent enough to reproduce everyday sound and the dings and beeps that Windows XP uses to communicate basic functions to you. All you have to do is plug in the power for the speakers and then connect the speakers to the computer. Not only is this connection most often a ⅛-inch minijack like the kind you've seen on headphones, but it also most likely plugs into a light green–colored jack on the sound card (a holdover from the SoundBlaster color scheme). Turn on the speakers, and you have sound!

Expanded features

Some sound cards (like the more advanced SoundBlaster models or higher-end internal sound cards) have additional outputs for surround-sound applications. These can come in the form of additional jacks or a proprietary output.

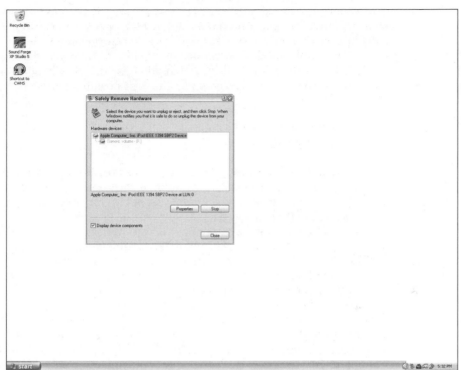

Figure 2-7:
Stopping
an external
device.

Analog connections

The additional jacks are for additional analog speaker connections. For example, the first speaker jack may be for the first two speakers, the second jack is
for the next two speakers, and so on. Just connect the speakers as designated, and you have surround sound. Remember that to take advantage of
this type of sound, you probably have to buy speakers that are made by the
sound card's company or designed with that company's setup in mind. Again,
because of standardized connections, this probably won't be an issue. Just
make sure that the two sets are compatible (it should say so on the speaker's
box) when you buy them.

Digital connections

These connections, like the S/PDIF jack that I talked about in the section
"Features of built-in sound cards," earlier in this chapter, rely on a digital connection to separate and pass off the audio information to the speakers. This
involves connecting the digital jack from the sound card into a receiver via a
digital connection cable. The receiver then passes the signal to the speakers.

The precise arrangement of these speakers can be debated by audiophiles for days, and it depends on the room in which you'll be listening as well. For the initial setup, set the speakers in a circular pattern focusing on a center spot, that spot being where you plan to sit and partake of the music. Put the speakers at ear level to make sure that you hear the direct signal, as opposed to any reflected sound. This gets you the best possible sound.

Networking

Networking connects you with the rest of the world — or at least its Internet representation. This is something that your Internet service provider (ISP) should guide you through when you first sign up for service. I just want to emphasize here that to use streaming media or download files or song information, you need a network connection. And to take advantage of the vast majority of music possibilities, you need a high-speed Internet connection. You can obtain a high-speed connection from a cable modem, a digital subscriber line (DSL), or satellite networking. The availability of these connections differs depending on your location, but one should be available in your area.

Regardless of the type of high-speed connection, it terminates at the modem and uses an Ethernet cable. This cable has a connector at each end that looks like a large phone jack. To connect this cable to your computer, you need a network interface card, or NIC. Simply plug the Ethernet cable into the NIC (like many of the cards, it can either be integrated into the motherboard or mounted internally), and you're ready to go. Each ISP has its own setup requirements — be sure to follow the setup directions. Alternately, more cable modems can use FireWire to get a network connection to the computer.

After all these connections have been made, you're ready to explore the world of music in Windows XP. This is the blank canvas — the music you use to color it is up to you.

Chapter 3

Basic Operations

In This Chapter

▶ Knowing where the sound controls are

▶ Controlling the basic volume operations in Windows XP

▶ Mixing up the media you can use

I'm probably just like most people who have just received a new toy: My brain immediately flashes the command that it's time to *play,* with no regard to any meaningless bits of paper marked "Instructions — read before you use this device." In some instances, I am successful in the venture, and a few clicks is all I need to get everything running. At other times, I fail miserably and am forced to crawl back to where the piece of paper lies discarded, mocking me with its silence. Hey, it happens sometimes.

Why do I tell you this? It's probably possible to figure out the basic volume controls of Windows XP if you give it some time, especially if you've had any sort of experience with audio mixing before. I'm not going to assume that, though, and this chapter saves you the time it would take to wonder where you put the instructions.

Getting Sound Out of Windows XP

You can play sound from several different sources in Windows XP. Sound can come from files stored on your hard drive or external media, like CDs or DVDs. Flash memory or external drives can also contain audio data that can be played in this operating system. Finally, you can get sound from network sources, like Internet radio or remote servers.

All of these sources require some sort of control to play well together, so to speak. Without some sort of control for each source, they could blend together into an unlistenable mess (much like a bad Las Vegas lounge performer). Windows XP provides a series of controls that allow you to work through the mire and get everything sounding the way you want.

Finding the Controls

Windows XP is a menu-driven way of managing your computer. Instead of using it to order breakfast (which, by the way, I would pay good money for the ability to use), Windows XP uses a series of lists that you navigate with the mouse or keyboard to get where you want to go. To get the whole thing started, Microsoft has kindly presented you with the Start button. To find the volume controls, follow these steps:

1. **Look at Figure 3-1, and find the Start button in the lower-left corner.**

2. **Click the Start button.**

   The Start menu pops up, as shown in Figure 3-2.

Figure 3-1:
The Start button in Windows XP.

Start button

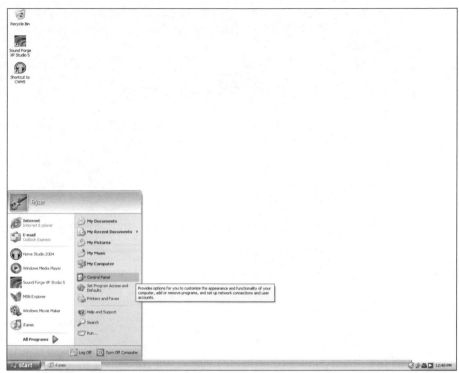

Figure 3-2:
The
Windows XP
Start menu.

3. **Click the Control Panel option.**

   The Control Panel is where you can find the controls for most of the Windows XP functions. It's a good idea to know where this is for future reference.

4. **Select the Sounds, Speech, and Audio Devices category from the Control Panel menu, as shown in Figure 3-3.**

   This is where all the audio controls for Windows XP reside.

   Because some manufacturers use different sound cards and some proprietary software for their sound functions, you may find some additional audio controls, depending on the equipment that your computer maker installed. Look at the lower-right corner of Figure 3-1, and you can see a small blue square with a white triangle in it. That's an icon for the proprietary audio software that my manufacturer installed.

5. **Select Adjust the System Volume, as shown in Figure 3-4.**

   This brings up the main audio controls for your computer.

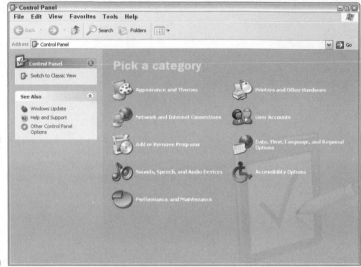

Figure 3-3:
Choose the
Sounds,
Speech, and
Audio
Devices
category.

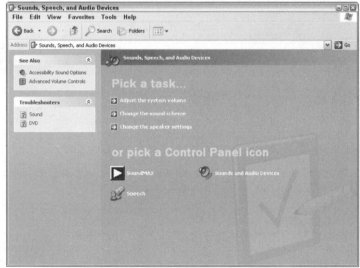

Figure 3-4:
Opening the
main audio
controls.

The other options on this menu appear as tabs under the main audio controls. Instead of backtracking, you can use the tabs to switch views and save yourself a step or two.

6. **As shown in Figure 3-5, adjust the slider to an acceptable audio level.**

I define "acceptable audio level" as one where I don't have to crank up the physical volume knob of the speakers past the eight or nine o'clock position and no distortion is coming through the speakers when audio is played. Generally, the level shown in Figure 3-5 is acceptable.

Figure 3-5:
Adjusting
the overall
system
volume.

To avoid going through these steps again, select the Add a Volume Icon in the Taskbar checkbox. This places a small icon in the lower-right corner that looks like a speaker. By clicking the icon, you are returned to the Windows XP Audio Mixer immediately, and you skip the previous process.

You can take care of the overall system volume using this slider, but part of the usefulness of a computer is that it can regulate the volume of several sources individually. That is, you can make one type of audio louder than the other, depending on what sounds best to you.

In the Device Volume section (refer to Figure 3-5), click the Advanced button, and a separate window containing the Windows XP Audio Mixer appears. This window (shown in Figure 3-6) allows you to individually raise or lower the volume of different types of devices that are hooked to your computer.

Each device has the following basic controls:

- **Balance:** The Balance control slides from left to right and determines the amount of signal present in each side of the stereo field. If you move the control to the right, that source is in the right speaker. If you move it to the left, the source goes to the left. Leave the control in the center, and the source comes equally from both speakers.

- **Volume:** The Volume control is on a *fader,* that is, moving the control fades the volume up and down. This controls the volume of that sound source in the overall "mix" for your computer. The fader on the left controls the overall volume for the computer's mix, and the rest of the faders determine what goes into that mix.

✔ **Mute:** The Mute control works exactly like it sounds. Select the control, and that source is silenced — no signal is sent to the computer's mix. The Mute switch for the fader on the left silences the entire computer, and the other Mute switches control the individual sound sources.

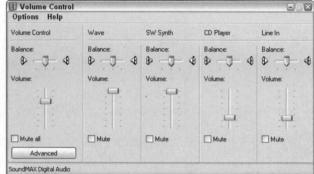

Figure 3-6:
The
Windows XP
Audio Mixer.

Each of the individual sources has its own label, as shown previously in Figure 3-6. The following is a brief explanation of what each of the sources does:

✔ **Wave:** This is the control for sound from things like audio or video files stored on your hard drive. This also controls the volume for sound sources coming across your Internet connection.

✔ **SW Synth:** This is the control for the synthesizer that's stored on current sound cards. This synthesizer receives instructions from MIDI data and reproduces them as sounds.

✔ **CD Player:** This is pretty self-explanatory. This control makes the CD player louder or softer.

✔ **Line In:** Most sound cards have a jack to accept signal from an outside device, like an analog cassette or record player. This control raises and lowers the volume coming in from that source. This isn't important now, but I explain this control in more detail in Chapter 6.

Keep the volume controls as high as possible without getting any distortion for the best signal, or lower the controls to reduce their presence in the mix.

By clicking the Advanced button in the Volume Control window, you can add or remove controls from the Windows XP Audio Mixer. Look at Figure 3-7 to see how this works. For example, if you have a microphone that you've connected to your computer, you can add it to the mixer and control its volume from here.

Figure 3-7:
Adding and
removing
controls
in the
Windows XP
Audio Mixer.

Look back at Figure 3-5 to find the Speaker Volume button in the Speaker Settings section. Click this button, and you can adjust the volume for each speaker, as shown in Figure 3-8.

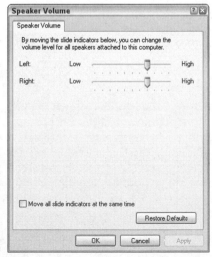

Figure 3-8:
Adjusting
the individual speaker
volume.

How useful is this? Well, if you have some speakers that have inconsistent volume between the pair, you could adjust the volume here. Otherwise, this control may not be that useful during normal play.

The previous steps have assumed that you're using a normal set of speakers, like the kind that are shipped with any newly purchased computer. If you have another type of setup, click the Advanced button in the Speaker Settings section (refer to Figure 3-5). As you can see in Figure 3-9, a ton of other options are available to help configure your system.

Figure 3-9:
Selecting
another
speaker
setup.

Click the Performance tab at the top of the window shown in Figure 3-9 to view the performance settings of the Advanced Audio Properties window. The two faders determine the amount of system resources to devote to reproducing audio. These faders should default to the fastest level possible, as shown in Figure 3-10. Unless you start noticing problems with your computer's audio, like scratches, pops, distortion, or an unexplained dropping out of sound, it's best to leave these faders at their default settings.

Exit from the speaker settings, and return to the window shown in Figure 3-5. You can see four more tabs in this window, but you should know going in that they won't affect your enjoyment of sound on your computer as much as the first tab. Figure 3-11 shows the sound scheme controls for Windows XP. This setup controls the sounds your computer makes when certain events occur, like the music that plays when you first sign in to Windows XP and the little bells and whistles that go off occasionally. If you install themes (files that change the appearance or sounds of Windows XP) on your system, this setup can change. You can also change the individual sounds of certain events.

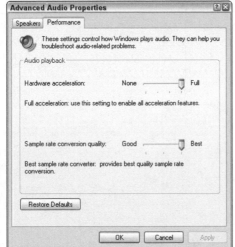

Figure 3-10:
Your
computer's
audio per-
formance.

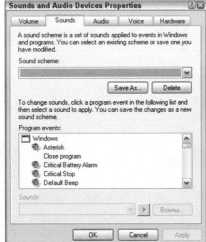

Figure 3-11:
Windows XP
sound
scheme
controls.

Figure 3-12 shows the Audio tab; use this tab to select which audio device plays sound on your computer. Unless you have more than one sound card installed, just leave these controls where they are.

In Figure 3-13 you see the voice controls. Again, unless you have a voice recorder or microphone installed on your computer, you can leave these controls alone.

Figure 3-12:
Windows XP
audio
controls.

Figure 3-13:
Windows XP
voice
controls.

Finally, the Hardware tab (as shown in Figure 3-14) shows the physical and virtual audio devices you have installed on your computer. These devices should have come installed on your computer and operating system in perfect working order. If you have problems with any audio devices, you can click on the device and examine the message box to see what's wrong and how you can fix it.

Unless you feel comfortable working with drivers and the inner workings of Windows XP, it's best to leave work like this to an experienced computer technician. Putting the wrong files or drivers on a system can cause additional problems.

Types of Usable Media

So what can you control with these menus? Most sound comes on one of the following types of media:

- ✔ Optical media
- ✔ Internal or external memory
- ✔ Analog sources

Optical media are the CDs and DVDs that you're already used to. Most newer computers come with a drive that recognizes both formats, and some computers may even be able to burn both types.

Internal and external memory refers to the hard drive that's already in your computer. This could also include any hard drives connected to your system via a FireWire or USB connection, or a Flash drive that's connected to your computer.

You can even connect analog devices to your computer and listen to them using the computer's speakers and mixer. This can be a little complicated. Most commercially available sound cards accept a line in through a ⅛-inch minijack, and analog devices could range from that type of connector to RCA connections, ¼-inch tip-ring-sleeve connections, or other plugs. This may require a trip to your local electronics store to make sure that you can make the connection. Most of the time, this type of connection is made to record analog sound to the computer to get it into the digital realm. Refer to Chapter 6 for more information about making this transfer.

Chapter 4

Windows XP Media Center Edition

*I*t's a beautiful thing when everything and everyone work together. The focus changes from several individual parts to one larger whole, the separate units working in concert to make something happen. This may sound like the rhetoric of a corporate middle manager or the motivational speaker whose show you passed over last night on your way to watching that sequel for the 37th time. It also describes what happens when your computer and your media center merge to work together.

The Media Center Edition (MCE) of Windows XP is still a full-featured version of Microsoft's operating system. On startup, you don't notice much of a difference between this and any other Windows XP startup. A few significant hardware and software differences make this system more suited for your living room. With these tools, you can experience your digital music in new and different ways.

What Is Windows XP MCE?

The first difference you'll notice about Windows XP MCE is where and how you can purchase it. Virtually all computer systems arrive with an operating system already loaded on the hard drive, ready to be used. But Windows XP's standard versions (Home and Professional) are also available by themselves. If you want to upgrade your system from an earlier version (provided your hardware can handle it), you can just go out and buy the disc. A quick install later, and your system is ready to go.

Windows XP MCE is a little more finicky, mostly at the insistence of Microsoft. You can only buy it as part of a computer, and it's not available to the general public as stand-alone software. The systems it is available on must also include hardware like a TV tuner card, entertainment-center-quality audio, and a remote control that allows you to change and choose the additional functions available in this operating system. Because of the additional hardware requirements and the fact that MCE is not available to the general public as a separate program (Microsoft insists that it be bundled with certain approved pieces of hardware to ensure that the program functions correctly), expect to pay a great deal more for this type of computer system compared to a standard Windows XP machine. Most of the systems I saw while researching this book were priced at about $1,500, and that was without a monitor. You need either a monitor and a television or a high-quality television to use Windows XP MCE, because a standard TV cannot handle the resolution and video demands placed on it by Windows XP MCE.

The similarities

Windows XP MCE shares the look of its compatriots, Windows XP Home and Professional Editions. The menus and file structures are the same, and the requirements of maintaining a computer system (defragmenting your hard drive and performing system and virus software updates) are still there. Furthermore, you can load all the programs you would normally put on a Windows XP machine, like Adobe Photoshop, Microsoft Office, or any of the multitude of games available today. In virtually all respects, this is just like the computer on which you check your e-mail, surf the Web, and make your eBay purchases.

The differences

In addition to the hardware changes that I discussed, Windows XP MCE carries with it a software package that enhances what your system can do with digital audio and video. This control panel, accessed via the Start button, brings up the additional features that MCE provides. Windows XP MCE handles all sorts of media, including video and images, but in this chapter, I focus on those features specifically associated with digital audio. For additional information on the entire system, check out *Windows XP Media Center Edition 2004 PC For Dummies,* by Danny Briere and Pat Hurley (published by Wiley).

My Music

The main screen in the Media Center Edition gives you several choices, as shown in Figure 4-1. Right now, you should only be concerned with the My Music choice. The rest of the choices tackle areas like television and DVDs.

Selecting My Music opens the choices shown in Figure 4-2. This essentially duplicates the functions that are already present in the Windows Media Player that comes with all versions of Windows XP, but MCE integrates it in the larger program and allows you to access other functions without leaving the program.

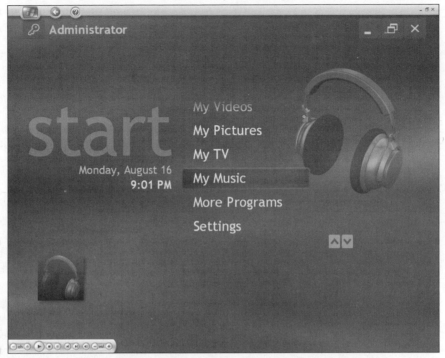

Figure 4-1:
My Music in
Windows XP
Media
Center
Edition.

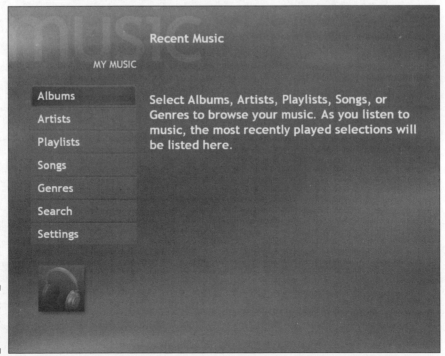

Figure 4-2:
My Music's
choices.

The Media Center Edition's library catalogues all the music and other media on your hard drive and presents it according to the choices you see in the left column of Figure 4-2. Choosing Albums shows the music subdivided by the album title, while selecting Genres aligns the tracks according to how the music is classified, for example, Rock, Funk, or Classical.

Unless you've been buying a lot of files online (something I take a look at in Chapter 7), you'll probably get a lot of music onto your system via the Copy CD function (see Figure 4-3). Insert an audio CD of your choice into the CD player. Media Center recognizes the recording and begins playing it; this is also shown in Figure 4-3.

Select the Copy CD function in the left column, and follow the instructions. Your files will be ripped in the WMA format to your hard drive following a few decisions on your part, including an agreement not to illegally copy songs and the choice to copy-protect anything you rip to your hard drive, as shown in Figure 4-4. Choosing copy protection makes sure that your music isn't illegally moved from your computer to another source.

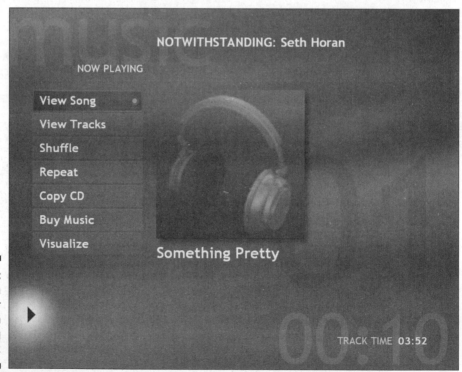

Figure 4-3:
Media
Center
Edition
playing
a CD.

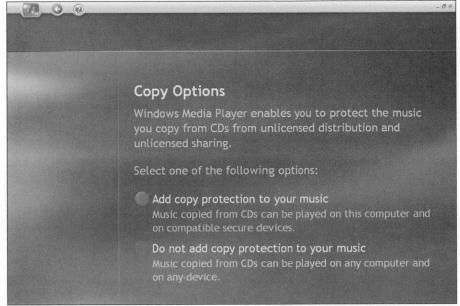

Figure 4-4:
Copy-
protecting
your files.

After you've ripped the files, they are catalogued and present on the system at a moment's notice, as shown in Figure 4-5. You can keep the discs as a backup and not worry about scratches or sticky little fingers.

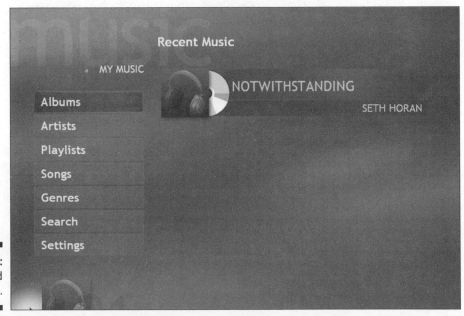

Figure 4-5:
The finished
rip.

Also notice the Buy Music button on the menu of options (refer to Figure 4-3). This opens a menu of Web sites where you can purchase music similar to what you're currently listening to — just remember that having a record store in your living room could be detrimental to your wallet.

My Radio

Depending on the equipment included with your computer, you may also be able to listen to radio on your system. Media Center Edition gives you the option of tuning in to either FM on-air broadcasts or Internet radio. If you have the appropriate equipment, from the main screen, select My Radio. You can tune in broadcasts from there using the numeric keypad. My Radio also allows you to set nine presets.

Getting What You Want

Digital audio plays only one part in the MCE package. Remember, this device is intended to not only replace the computer in many homes but also to take the place of the television, stereo system, cable box, DVD player, digital video recorder, and photo albums (I've always found this emphasis on digital images a little odd). That's a lot of duties to take on, so it's understandable that not all of MCE's resources are devoted to playing and recording digital audio. Windows Media Player can handle the audio functions present in this system, so you have to decide whether the extra functions you get with MCE are worth the extra money you'll be shelling out.

If you decide to get the MCE machine, you need several things to make sure that you can get the most use out of it for digital audio.

Hard drive

You need an even bigger hard drive than what normally comes with a Windows XP machine. In addition to the extra software going onto the drive, you'll probably end up with a great deal more audio and video files than you would with a standard computer system. Look for machines with at least 200GB of hard drive space, and get more if you can.

Memory

Again, this system deals with a great deal of memory-intensive functions. These kind of computer systems are also prone to multitasking, such as recording a program while surfing the Internet or typing an e-mail. One gigabyte of RAM is a good amount for an MCE machine, and you should get more if you can.

Processor

Speed is of the essence for real-time functions like audio and video, so having a fast processor is essential to keeping things moving along. Don't settle for less than a 3.2-GHz Pentium 4 (or its AMD equivalent) in an MCE system. You're paying enough — you should get something fast in the process.

Shop around! Because you can only get this operating system along with systems or certain pieces of hardware, it's more important than ever to check out all your options. Major manufacturers like Dell, Gateway, and Alienware build these machines, but smaller builders can also create them. Evaluate all your choices before you buy.

Part II
Making Windows XP Your Digital Jukebox

The 5th Wave   By Rich Tennant

LEGAL music
downloads
$1.50 per MIN.

In this part . . .

There are so many pieces of software available for getting and listening to music that it can seem a little intimidating. These next few chapters take a look at the current media players in the market and break down their features and functions.

You'll also learn how to use these players to make digital copies of your already-existing music collection and listen to Internet radio stations. After all, you'll need to get ideas on what to add to your collection next, right?

Chapter 5

Stalking the Wild Jukebox Software

*T*his may be revealing a little more about myself than I care to admit, but I remember just about every musical device I've been given as a special thing. My first Walkman was truly a joy — finally, I could take my music anywhere. My first boombox was also a wonder, because I could now create mix tapes to listen to on said Walkman. And it had detachable speakers, so I could arrange the sound the way I wanted to. And I loved the Program and Random functions on my first CD player. No longer was I confined to the structure imposed on me by the order of the songs. I could toss in a CD and just see what came up.

Needless to say, the fact that currently available jukebox software can do all of this and more is fascinating. Now you can organize, control, and manipulate how you listen to your music like never before. When you understand how to use this software, it can replace all the devices in your stereo with ease and add features you may not have thought of. And it can do it all without requiring a degree in programming or database engineering. Windows XP has all you need on your computer right now, and free alternatives are out there if you find something you like more.

Something in Common

Forgive me for devolving into a sports metaphor here, but quite a few people I know have a favorite team. They cheer and brag and sometimes cry (I know,

Cubs fans, it's okay) about their respective teams, and they've grown accustomed to the personality and appearance of their team. Yet, an outsider looking in may see that all the teams have the same number of people, they all wear uniforms, and they're all playing basically the same game. Some players just function better or differently than others.

And so it is for media player software. Each has its own look and individual features that make it stand out from other players in the field (or on your computer, as the case may be), but they all perform basically the same task. I outline those basic functions here so that you should know what to expect from any software you run across and can evaluate it on its own merits.

Playback

All media players can play music. It just depends on what file formats the player can accept. Think of it as trying to play a CD on a record player. It's just not going to work, despite your best attempts to carve grooves into the CD or to make the turntable the same size as the disc. That said, the number of file types most media players can handle is huge. It's just a matter of what they've been programmed to handle.

For example, MP3 files are an accepted standard, and just about every media player out there gladly handles them. When you start getting into formats developed by commercial interests like Microsoft or Real Player, things get a little hairier. These players use proprietary technology or technology that is owned and licensed by the companies in question. The persons or companies that create the media players must pay for the rights to play this file format. And so if you want to play a file in Real media format, you must use a version of the Real Player. Only certain players can handle the Windows Media File format, while others (most notably iTunes) cannot play this type of file.

You can approach the playback factor for media players in one of the following ways:

- ✔ **Catch-all:** Get the media player that handles the most types of media formats and shows them all without giving error messages or unrecognizable playback. This is helpful if you're drawing media in from several different sources, like multiple Internet download sites.

- ✔ **Specialized:** This player specializes in one type of file format. It doesn't handle everything well, but it does its specific task very well.

I review several different types of media players later in the chapter and identify each one for its usefulness in this area.

Musical databases

By now, you should notice that the information tags attached to these music files are vital to the function of the media player. However, unless you're terribly in love with the thought of performing data entry for every music file you create (a strange and twisted idea to me, but I'll go along with whatever works for you), this can be a long and tedious process. Thankfully, with the help of an Internet connection, you should be able to avoid this task by using an online database of musical recordings. The player can take the file or CD, contact the musical database via the network connection to compare the information, and automatically add any tags it finds to the files.

The most popular database that provides this service is Gracenote CDDB (Compact Disc Database). It has an exhaustive collection of information about modern recordings, and there's an excellent chance that any commercially released CD or music file purchased online will be found. This service does not recognize any CDs you create, like a mix of music. By burning such a CD from your media player, though, the information should be transported with it and the information will be recognized the next time you put the CD in the player.

Other services, like FreeDDB, can also provide this information. More than likely, however, you'll run into Gracenote when you use a major media player.

Organization

I have a lot of CDs, and I wouldn't give them up for anything. The problem is that I'm not the greatest when it comes to keeping them in an identifiable order. I had them alphabetized when I first moved into my apartment, but months of transferring them from home to car and work have left them in a disheveled mass with little resemblance to what they had been earlier.

Media players should alleviate this problem by keeping your music files organized and well labeled. If there's one thing computers can do better than anything else invented by humans, it's keeping things organized. Given the right information, a media player should be able to present your music files in any order you want based on the information with which your files have been tagged. Be it the artist name, the song title, the genre, the year it was created, or anything else placed in the file's tag, your media player should be able to read and identify that information. For MP3 players, this is known as the ID3 tag, where the information on each file is stored. Other formats have proprietary tags attached to them that carry this information.

Playlists

This generic term refers to a specific way to organize your music that allows the media player to play specific songs in a specific order determined either by you or the player itself (more on that in just a moment). This depends on the information present in the file's ID tag.

A standard playlist is one you create yourself. Using the media player, you add files to the playlist, give it a name, and save it. The media player remembers the order and brings it up on command. If you choose to randomize the playback of these files, the player only randomizes the files within that list.

A smart or automatic playlist is based on simple database instructions. This list compares the files against a list of instructions (like "The song title includes the term *Green*" or "The artist name does not include the words *Wang Chung*" — a smart idea indeed) and allows in any songs that meet the correct conditions. The advantage to this is that the structure of this playlist can change every time you add a song — if the song meets the criteria, it goes in the list. Thus, you have a new and dynamic way of listening to your music. They are the same songs, but you never hear them the same way twice.

Ripping

If you've organized a playlist of files in just the right way and you want to take it to the car, or you want to burn a backup of a playlist in case your hard drive crashes, most media players can accommodate that need. A CD or CD/DVD burner is standard equipment on most current computers, and it's an easy addition if you want to put one in your system. The media player can work with that equipment to make CDs playable in regular CD players.

The reverse also applies — most media players are able to rip music from CDs and store it as a digital music file on your computer's hard drive. Again, this is a good idea if you want to put your songs into a playlist on your computer or back up your music to your hard drive in case of a lost CD. I've ripped more than one CD to my computer because it's a hard-to-find or out-of-print recording.

You need to take a few variables into account. The first one is the file format that the media player creates during the ripping process. Depending on whether the music is to stay on your system or be moved to a CD or portable audio player, it's important to know whether it will be recognized. The second variable is the size and resolution of the file. Digital audio files are usually measured in kilobits per second. A good media player can give you control over the amount of data contained in the file.

A file sounds better as you increase the amount of kilobits per second at which it plays, but this also increases the size of the file and decreases how many songs you can fit on your hard drive, CD, or portable audio player.

Burning

Most media players are capable of burning audio CDs from playlists or single files. A simple built-in function can convert the audio formats the player handles into information that can be burned to a normal audio CD format. It's easy, but keep one thing in mind: If you're converting audio from compressed audio files (like MP3, WMA, and so on), the sound quality will not be as good as that of a normal CD. You can only get out of it what you put into it. Still, this is a very simple and easy function to use. Simply select the file or files to be included, insert a blank CD, press the required button, and you're burning a new CD.

Visualizations

We know that the media player can handle audio — if it doesn't, it needs either serious reprogramming or a new purpose in life. But many people add an optional visual component to the music being played. Think of it as your own miniature planetarium laser light show, minus any outrageous admission fees and with the ability to listen to something other than Pink Floyd.

This really isn't an important feature of the media player. It's a simple gimmick or add-on that most seem to have included just to give the monitor something to do while the speakers do their own thing. The optional visual component is separate from the video function that most media players handle — it's just a light show synchronized to volume increases or decreases in the music.

Player appearance

Like everything else in Windows XP, you can affect how the media player appears on your monitor. The choices can range from color changes to radical redesigns of the player's appearance. If you don't like the way the basic media player appears, someone has probably designed a new appearance for it. This is commonly known as a *skin*. Some player manufacturers have made it exceptionally easy to create new skins by allowing amateur programmers access to their basic code. This allows owners to rework the controls and appearance of the player while maintaining its functionality. Other manufacturers are more protective and only allow certain skins to be distributed.

The appearance of the player is up to you, although the size and look of the player can affect how you use it and other programs. If a player is too big, it may block your mouse access to windows below it. It can also cause problems if the skin slows the operations of the computer. This shouldn't be much of a factor, because the size of these skin files is extremely small. If the skin is poorly coded, it could also cause problems. Given these considerations, the appearance of the player is up to you.

Other features

Most media players also include additional features, including connections to Internet radio stations or other media services, both free and subscription. You may also find views for files now being played and other screens, depending on what media player you're using. Feel free to experiment with the different players to see what makes the most sense to you. I take a look at the different features that each major media player offers later in this chapter.

Playing Your Files

I'm going to start with the fun part first — listening to your music is why you and I are here in the first place, correct? I start with Windows Media Player (currently in Version 9) and a track located in Windows XP's default music location.

Windows Media Player 10 is currently being tested, and a beta version was released to the public in the fall of 2004. However, new software tends to be a little buggy, and you may want to stick with Windows Media Player 9 while any significant bugs, errors, or "unintended features" are corrected. You can play a song by following these steps:

1. **Select Start⇨Programs⇨Windows Media Player.**

   This is the default way to start Windows Media Player. If you have shortcuts on your system, you can also use those that are located on the desktop or a toolbar.

2. **Select File⇨Open.**

   As shown in Figure 5-1, this opens your default music folder. You can also browse to any other location where you may have stored sound or music files.

All the controls in Windows Media Player are visible in Full Screen mode. However, if you shrink the size of the player, Windows Media Player 9 hides the menu bar unless you put the cursor just above the media player itself. This can be frustrating, so you can always press Ctrl+M to make it appear without moving your mouse.

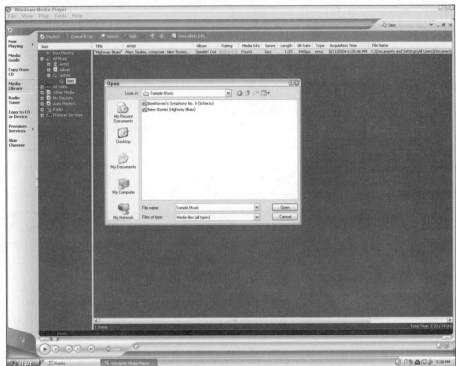

Figure 5-1:
Opening
an audio
file with
Windows
Media
Player.

Try placing your music in folders named after the artists or albums you keep on your computer, and keep those folders inside the My Music folder that's automatically created by Windows XP. This keeps your music centrally located, but it also allows you to easily differentiate between the songs in that main folder.

3. **Select the song you want to play, and click the Open button.**

   You can open multiple songs by holding down the Ctrl key, highlighting their names and then clicking the Open button.

If you have Windows Explorer open to your My Music folder, you can double-click any file or files to open them. This triggers your default media player — in this case, Windows Media Player.

This is fine if you only want to open a select number of files at any one time, but more convenient ways of playing your music using Windows Media Player are available. The first step is getting your collection organized.

Getting Organized

The bane of my existence is trying to find the music I want if I haven't somehow organized the music in my CD collection (or if someone has rummaged through them and thrown my intricate plans out of whack). Luckily, Windows XP makes it possible to track where your files are and pull them up at a moment's notice. Your computer always knows where your files are (and it doesn't accidentally put them in the wrong case, either).

Hitting the library

Windows Media Player can seek out any audio you have on your computer and keep a list of what's available. Appropriately enough, this function is known as the Media Library. Access the Media Library by selecting the tab with that label on the left side of the Windows Media Player, as shown in Figure 5-2.

Notice that the left column of this window shows a collapsible list of types of media. Unless you've used this before, you probably have nothing but a couple of sample files there. You can change that now — select Tools⇨Search for Media Files (or press F3). This brings up the window shown in Figure 5-3.

Figure 5-2:
Opening the
Media
Library.

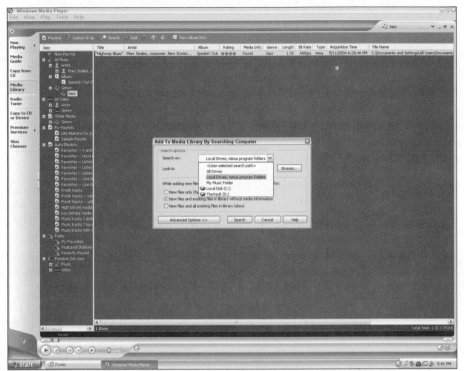

Figure 5-3:
Adding new
media to
Windows
Media
Player.

The drop-down menu shows the available locations in which you can search for media. The default choice is Local Drives, Minus Program Folders. This is an excellent choice, because searching the local drives indiscriminately could place the sounds that Windows XP normally uses (the beeps and chimes used for system alerts) in the playlists next to your music. You can also search just your My Music folder or other locations you choose. This search can also add media information from outside databases like Gracenote or CDDB for better organization. Click the Search button, and you're off!

This search picks up any sound that's located in the folders you search. Even if you don't want to include them in your library, a search like this can add these sounds. Be prepared to delete them once the search is done, or narrow the focus of your search.

After the search is done, you see a list of audio files in the right column of the media player. These are your files, and you can organize them however you want at this point. You can move these files around using any of the following methods:

✔ Clicking the Artist, Album, Genres, or other buttons in that row causes the files to align in the direction of the arrow that appears. The order is alphabetical, numerical, or quality, depending on the button you clicked.

- ✔ The collapsible folder on the left allows you to view only the files that fit into that category, such as All Music, My Playlists, or other choices.

- ✔ Use the blue arrow keys to move selected files up or down in the order of the library.

- ✔ Right-click the file and select Move Up or Move Down from the shortcut menu that appears. This can be a lot of extra effort, though.

I've already mentioned the blue arrows at the top of Windows Media Player. You can also find the following additional controls there to help you manage your Media Library:

- ✔ Clicking the Playlists button gives you the option to create a new playlist or add a file to an existing playlist, as well as copying that playlist to a CD or portable audio player. (I review making playlists in the section "Writing Your Playlist," later in this chapter.)

- ✔ Clicking the Search button allows you to search for files using a keyword or number. This can be handy if you have a great deal of files and want to find one quickly.

- ✔ Clicking the Add button brings files into the Media Library from a variety of sources, including a computer search, a folder, a Web location, or other user-selected areas.

- ✔ Clicking the red "X" deletes any selected files from the Media Library. Note that this does *not* delete the file from the computer, just from the Media Library selection.

- ✔ Clicking the Album Info button gets you information on any album you're listening to, depending on what's available in the database.

Labeling your music

Organizing your files in the library works great if all the information on your song is current. However, this may not always be the case, especially if the song is coming from an out-of-print CD or your own creation. Luckily, adding information to your audio files is a right-click away. Follow these steps to label your music:

1. **Select the song you want to edit, and right-click it.**

   This brings up the menu shown in Figure 5-4.

2. **Choose the attribute you want to change, and select Edit from the menu.**

   This makes the text editable. Type in anything you want.

3. **Click outside of that song.**

   Your changes have been made.

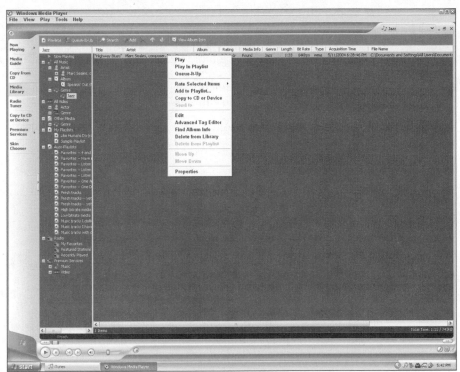

Figure 5-4:
The pop-up
menu in
the Media
Library.

Other organizational commands

The buttons to the left allow you to switch between different views of
Windows Media Player, giving you access to different commands. Think of it
as different channels on your television. Each of the following buttons gives
you different information and options:

✔ **Now Playing:** Shows you the file that's playing now, along with any visualization effects you've chosen. If you're just interested in letting Windows
Media Player run from file to file, this is the view to use. Upcoming tracks
are shown to the right, so you can choose what's coming up next.

✔ **Media Guide:** Takes you to Microsoft's available digital media for that
day, if you're connected to the Internet. Microsoft updates content daily
and gives you access to upcoming movies or songs, along with features
and other gimmicks.

✔ **Copy from CD** and **Copy to CD or Device:** Accesses the ripping and
burning/transfer functions of Windows Media Player, respectively. I
cover these buttons in the section "Ripping Your Files," later in this
chapter.

- **Radio Tuner:** Allows you to choose from various Internet radio stations that Microsoft has deemed fit to link to its player. Should you find a different location you want to listen to, choose File⇨Open URL to connect to that radio station. Premium Services operates in much the same way, but that button accesses any subscription services you've ordered to view through Windows Media Player. Remember, this is not free. You must use your credit card to access these services.

- **Skin Chooser:** Allows you to choose what skin you want to use to alter the appearance of Windows Media Player. Skins are discussed in the section "Skinning the Player," later in this chapter.

Writing Your Playlist

The Media Library shows you every file on your computer. When you exceed a couple hundred files, though, searching through them can get a bit tedious. And what if you only want to listen to your Marvin Gaye tunes, without sifting through your sizable Celtic Frost collection? That's where the playlist comes in.

Select File⇨New Playlist to begin the process. This opens the window shown in Figure 5-5, which allows you to copy files from the Media Library to the New Playlist, from the left side to the right side.

The drop-down menu on the left side gives you access to the Media Library files in a variety of configurations, including the standard suspects Artist, Album, Genre, and others. When you see the files you want, just click them and they are on the list. Type the name of the playlist in the upper-right corner, and click the OK button. Your new playlist is available for use. You can either play the songs from the left column or the drop-down menu in the upper-right corner.

To change a playlist after you've created it, just right-click the playlist in the left column and select Edit from the shortcut menu that appears. You're sent back to the window shown in Figure 5-5, where you can move, add, and delete files as necessary.

Notice the listing in the left column for auto playlists; these are the playlists I mentioned earlier that add files automatically based on certain criteria. Select the playlist titled Favorites — 4 and 5 Star Rated, and you see all the files that have a high star rating. (You can change each file's star rating by mousing over it in the Media Library view and selecting the amount of stars you give that song — take that, Ebert and Roper!)

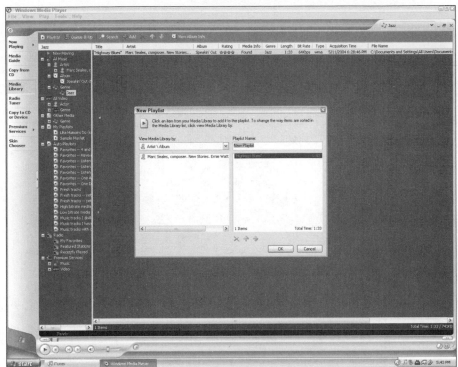

Figure 5-5:
Creating a
new playlist.

Microsoft has already provided some playlists, but software giants aren't always the best at anticipating the needs of the regular user (as has been painfully proven time and time again). You can create a new auto playlist by clicking the Playlists button in the upper-left corner of the screen. This time, select New Auto Playlist, as shown in the menu in Figure 5-6.

You can add as many conditions as you want to these auto playlists. Windows Media Player can search through all the available media files and keep only those that match the conditions you've set. For example, perhaps you're a huge fan of Neil Diamond, but you don't care for the "Jazz Singer" soundtrack. Just set up two conditions — one includes all artists named Neil Diamond and the other excludes all songs from the album named "Jazz Singer." Follow these instructions to set up this playlist:

1. **Click the Playlists button, and select New Auto Playlist.**

   This brings up the menu shown in Figure 5-6.

Figure 5-6:
Setting the
rules for a
new auto
playlist.

2. **Select the first drop-down menu, and choose Artist.**

   This sets the parameter for the rule you're creating.

3. **Select the next drop-down menu, and choose Contains.**

   This command ensures that the command includes the information that
   is entered in the Artist field.

4. **Select the last drop-down menu, and type in *Neil Diamond*.**

   Every song with Neil Diamond in the Artist field is now selected.

5. **Choose the Create New Rule command.**

   You can have as many new limitations or rules as you need here.

6. **Repeat this process for the rule Album Title Does Not Include Jazz
   Singer.**

   Entering this rule filters out any Neil Diamond songs from the Jazz
   Singer album. Your playlist is now complete.

These steps show exactly why it's important to keep as much information about your audio files as possible. You can manipulate and organize them with great ease if all the fields are filled. And you can set up your music exactly the way you want it. Such are the wonders of the digital age in which we live.

Feel the Burn

Storing your music on the computer is great, but it can be a hassle if you're not around your computer. If you're going for a drive and want something for your car's CD player, you can use Windows Media Player 9 to burn songs to a CD that's playable in standard CD players. The process is quite simple, and it's built around the playlists you've already created. Follow these steps to burn the CD:

1. **Insert a blank CD into the CD burning device.**

    This is an important first step — otherwise, there's nothing to burn.

2. **Select Copy to CD or Device on the left side of your Windows Media Player.**

    This brings up the view used to burn files to CD.

3. **Use the left drop-down menu, shown in Figure 5-7, to select the playlist to burn.**

    The files included in that list show up below it.

4. **Select the device to be used for burning from the right drop-down menu.**

    This defaults to the CD-burning device in your machine.

5. **Click the Copy button.**

    This activates the Roxio burning applet screen, as shown in Figure 5-8, and creates the CD. When the burning is done, you have a CD that's ready to play in any CD player.

Figure 5-7:
Burning
tracks to a
CD in
Windows
Media
Player.

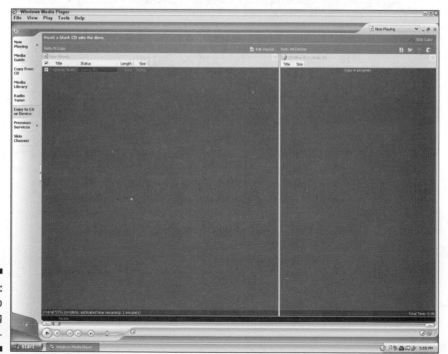

Figure 5-8:
The Roxio
burning
applet.

Ripping Your Files

It sounds violent, but ripping is a relatively simple process. The first step is deciding the quality and format of the files you're going to create. In Windows Media Player 9, start by selecting Tools➪Options and clicking the Copy Music tab, as shown in Figure 5-9.

Figure 5-9: Selecting the file format and quality in Windows Media Player.

Here you have a choice of Windows Media Audio or Windows Media Audio (variable rate) on the drop-down menu. The two formats are similar, but the variable rate selection allows you to save some room. By reducing the amount of information recorded about the song at times where it's not needed (like a second's pause of silence at the beginning or end of the track), you can shave some data off of the file size (other players encode in different file formats).

When you've selected your file format, it's time to make the decision between file size and audio quality. The slider runs from smallest file size to largest (with the subsequent rise and fall in audio quality). The standard for near-CD quality sound is 128 kilobits per second (Kbps), and Windows Media Player 9 gives you room on either side for altering the sound quality of the file.

The check boxes above the slider allow you to choose whether the music comes with copy protection when it's ripped and how the computer behaves when a CD is inserted into the computer. After you've made your choices, click the OK button. You're ready to rip!

This tabbed menu is full of options that can customize how you interact with Windows Media Player. Most options are set for standard playback when the player is installed, so you shouldn't have to make many additional changes here.

Ultimately, your ears are the final judge of how something sounds. Try out both formats, and see what you think about the music. If you can save some hard drive space in the process, that's great. But remember to make it sound good first.

Windows Media Player 9 rips files from CDs under the Copy From CD view that's available on the side of the player. Follow these steps to rip a file:

1. **Click Copy From CD to bring up that view.**

   If you have an audio CD in your CD or DVD player, the tracks show up here.

2. **Deselect the check boxes to the left of the songs you don't want to keep.**

   All the boxes are checked by default.

3. **Click the Copy Music button to begin the ripping process.**

   This brings up the screen shown in Figure 5-10. Decide whether you want your music to be copy protected (any copy-protected files have a license that must be present for the files to be played) and select the check box indicating that you won't steal music.

4. **Select your file format, and click the Next button.**

   This gives you the choice of sticking with your default setting or choosing something different for this one-time ripping process.

5. **Click the OK button.**

   Your files are ripped following this command.

Figure 5-10:
Ripping music from a CD in Windows Media Player.

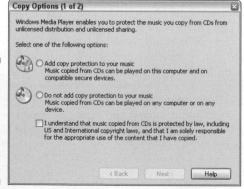

Visualize the Music

This is where the light show begins. The visualizations are programs designed to create intricate designs in time with the music to create an entertaining visual display. In Windows Media Player 9, you activate the visualizations by selecting the Now Playing view of the player. Follow these steps to choose the visualizations:

1. **Select View⇨Visualizations from the media player toolbar.**

   The menu shows a list of choices to choose from.

2. **Select the visualization you want from the menu.**

   You can also choose to have no visualization or to download other visualizations from Microsoft.

3. **Press Alt+Enter to make the visualization full screen, or leave it as is to keep the player controls visible.**

   By mousing down to the bottom of the player, you can bring the controls up while the full-screen visualization stays up.

In the regular view, you can also cycle through the visualizations using the arrow keys in the lower-left corner of the player, as shown in Figure 5-11.

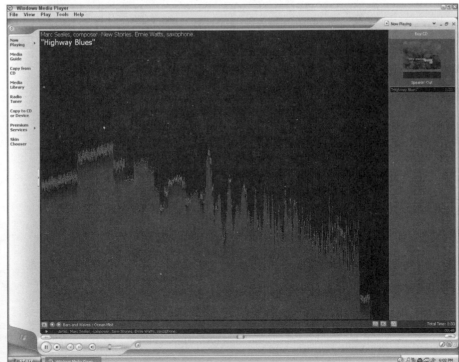

Figure 5-11: Choosing visualizations in Windows Media Player.

Skinning the Player

You know how to make Windows Media Player work now, so it's time to mix things up and change how the player itself looks. You can choose various looks for the player from the Skin Chooser view of Windows Media Player. Follow these steps to add or remove a skin:

1. **Cycle through the choices on the left side of the player.**

   The appearance of the skin is shown on the right side of the player.

2. **Select View⇨Skin Mode, Apply Skin or press Ctrl+1 to put the skin into effect.**

   This changes the appearance of the player on the screen.

3. **Press Ctrl+2 to go back to the full-screen mode.**

   Each skin has a button so that you can return the player to the Full-Screen mode, but it can move around depending on the design of the skin. Look for the button in Figure 5-12 for an easy back-and-forth switch.

You can download more skins for Windows Media Player by clicking the More Skins button in the upper-right corner of the Skin Chooser view. Your browser opens to the section of Microsoft's Web site with available skin downloads. Select the one you want, and it will change the player automatically.

Figure 5-12:
The Full-Screen Mode button in Windows Media Player.

Switch to full-screen mode

Other Features

Windows Media Player 9 has a lot of other features lurking about in the menus that could enhance your enjoyment of the player. Many of them can be found in the View menu of the Windows Media Player 9 toolbar. Some of these features are as follows:

- **Plug-ins:** These are additional bits of code that allow you to change the way Windows Media Player looks and sounds. Select View⇨Plug-Ins⇨Download Plug-ins to get the additional features, or select Options to return to the tabbed menu section and activate the plug-ins. Remember that DSP stands for digital signal processors. These types of plug-ins affect the general performance of the player, whether it be through audio or video processing. You can also change the background, the window appearance, and other visual effects.

- **Graphic Equalizer:** This is the virtual equivalent of a common stereo component. Select View⇨Enhancements⇨Graphic Equalizer to bring it up. By moving the faders, you can boost or cut that frequency in the audio being played. If you want more bass, move the faders on the left side up more. If you want more treble, adjust the faders on the right.

- **Media Link for E-mail:** If you're partaking of something you think someone should see, select View⇨Enhancements⇨Media Link for E-mail. This sends a link to a clip found on the Internet to the person you want. You can set start and end points for the clip as well.

- **Video Effects:** Selecting View⇨Enhancements⇨Video Effects brings up a series of controls (Hue, Brightness, Saturation, and Contrast). Adjust these to make the screen look its best for you.

- **SRS WOW Effect:** This plug-in (located at View⇨Enhancements⇨SRS WOW Effect) is a stereo enhancement effect. Slide the TruBass to add more bass to the audio, or use the WOW effect to add or subtract more "space" in the stereo field.

Players on the Field

So far, I've focused entirely on Windows Media Player 9, and for good reason — it's a versatile player that is automatically included with every version of Windows XP on the market today. But other media players are available, and many have become popular. In the following sections, I take a look at four other common players and compare them with Windows Media Player 9.

iTunes

The popularity of the iTunes online music store (discussed in Chapter 7) makes this a common player, although a great deal of these users are on Apple machines. Still, iTunes is available to Windows XP users, who can now access the iTunes music store. While this is the primary purpose of the interface, it does act as a full-featured media player, including the smart playlist functions and organizing capabilities similar to Windows Media Player. It can also rip music to AAC, Apple Lossless Audio Format, MP3, and WAV. It lacks the skinning capabilities of Windows Media Player, but like its counterpart, it's available as a free download at `www.apple.com/itunes`.

Winamp

This popular media player is available for free as a download from `www.winamp.com`. It's similar in function to Windows Media Player, and it can handle Windows Media Format files in addition to a great deal of other files. If Winamp can't handle it, something's probably wrong with the file (with the exception of Real media files). Because the code for Winamp is available to the public, a vast amount of skins and plug-ins are also available for it. Winamp is probably the most customizable player available today. The main drawback is that the free version is not capable of ripping or burning files (you must buy the premium version for that capability). Otherwise, Winamp is a capable media player.

Real Player

This media player is quite similar to the previously mentioned players, although it is the only player authorized to play files in the proprietary Real format. It's available as a free download at `www.real.com`, although many have complained that it's too difficult to sift through the ads for the premium version. Otherwise, it's capable of everything Windows Media Player can do, with the addition of being able to record audio from the line-in or mic-in section of your sound card. It is not capable of adding skins, but it recently achieved an extra level of versatility when it was made compatible with the Linux operating system, an open source alternative to Windows.

Musicmatch

This jukebox software is a popular alternative to Windows Media Player and iTunes, and the basic version is available for download at `www.musicmatch.com`. The ripper can handle WAV, MP3, and Windows Media Format files and it can burn CDs, and the organizing and identification features are similar to Windows Media Player. A Plus version is available with enhanced features. The software has no skinning capabilities.

These are all free downloads at the basic level, so feel free to shop around, try them out, and see which one you like the best. You can always remove the ones you don't like by using the Add/Remove feature of Windows XP (located in the Control Panel) to get rid of the excess players.

Chapter 6

Ripping Music Files from CDs, DVDs, and More

*I*n Chapter 5, I review the popular media players, most of which could rip and burn music in addition to their other functions. These are basic functions, and you can get by using them. However, you can achieve much more advanced functions using other types of software. This can give you a finer level of control over how your music is taken from disc and burned to your choice of media.

If you bought a computer with a CD or DVD burner, you probably received at least a basic version of burning software included with your computer. Like any other piece of software, you can purchase advanced functions for a higher price. I take a look at the basic features common to all the software and show you how to use them. I also compare some popular brands and show you what to look for.

What Can I Make, and Where Can I Use It?

The CD is a universal carrier for all sorts of information. I know it sounds like it's diseased, but that's a good thing. You can put just about anything on a CD and have another computer recognize it. (This is in theory — you may find problems between some drives, but for the most part, these glitches have been worked out.) CDs are formatted as two main types of CDs — data and music.

Music CDs

This is probably the first kind of CD you ever experienced. This recording medium is popped right into anything capable of playing a standard CD, and the music's on! This type of disc can be played in a computer, but the information isn't available as a standard computer file. It must be ripped first. This is an important consideration when you're talking about transferring the music — the ripping format that's used decides how much of the CD quality the music will retain.

Data CDs

This CD carries files only. These files can be anything from your big business project (*please* don't lose that disc!) to slides from your uncle's foot surgery (ugh, just toss that over there; no biggie). A CD can also contain a huge amount of music files. These files can't be played in normal CD players (although some newer CD and DVD players can recognize and play these audio files from both CDs and DVDs), but a computer with a media player can play these files as if they were coming off of a CD.

Keeping It In-House

Windows XP has a couple of tools already included its basic operating system that can help you burn CDs. I describe burning CDs in Windows Media Player 9 in Chapter 5, but that process produced music CDs.

For other functions, Windows XP can burn basic data CDs with no additional software. And, in traditional Windows XP simplicity, it's as easy as dragging and dropping files from one open window to another. Follow these steps to burn a CD:

1. **Put a blank CD in the CD burner.**

   This first step makes the process much easier — trust me.

2. **Choose Start⇨My Computer⇨*Your Burner Name*.**

   This is where you drag your files for burning.

3. **Drag the files you want to burn onto the CD burner.**

   Windows XP burns the files in alphabetical order.

4. **In the left column of the CD burner window, select Write These Files to CD.**

   This brings up the CD Burning Wizard.

5. **Follow the CD Burning Wizard instructions to burn the CD.**

   This completes the process and burns your CD.

So now you have a CD that can transport data wherever you go (and, depending on your DVD or CD player, one that can play music files as opposed to standard CDs). Between this and Windows Media Player, you have the tools to create the basic burned CD. So why would you need additional software? As always, it depends on what you want to do.

Bigger and Better Tools

Roxio and Nero are two examples of full-featured burning software. Not only can they handle the burning tasks I described earlier in this chapter, but they are capable of doing much more. The newer versions of burning software also create DVDs, manage other media (like photos and video), and create and edit video. These are full media-production packages, not just the music burning programs of old.

So, if you're just concerned with creating digital audio, this may be like taking your Porsche around the corner for groceries (although that does sound like fun occasionally). You don't have to have all the tools contained in these media-production suites to fulfill your digital music needs. Nevertheless, a few functions in these software packages are useful.

Ripping

These programs rip songs from CDs to most major formats, like MP3, WAV, and WMA. Of course, Windows Media Player also accomplishes this task. Burning software just offers more options, such as the WAV. This is especially important if you're burning CDs. Remember that formats like MP3 compress data — that may be fine if you're just putting it on a hard drive, but you could lose fidelity if you have to burn that file back to a CD. Using these programs to rip to WAV and then burn the file to a music CD can preserve the quality of the recording.

Making a single backup copy of your valuable media is considered legal, but making a bunch of copies for other reasons is still copyright infringement. Also, these burning programs cannot copy music that's encoded with copy protection. As of this writing, it's illegal to use technology to defeat digital copy-protection measures. How does this manage to coexist with the consumers' right to make backup copies? Hopefully, a court decision will soon make that clear.

Burning

Making CDs is how brands like Roxio and Nero got started. The Roxio burning engine is even integrated into Windows Media Player 9 to allow burning of playlists. These programs handle the burning of both data and music CDs, and these programs can also handle the copying of one CD to another without copying the disc to the hard drive first. This is exceptionally useful if you're making a backup copy and you want to save time.

Depending on what you want, you should also be able to burn both CD music and data to the same disc. This was popular in the '90s as "Enhanced CD," although the format never really caught on in popularity (some of the enhanced features were clunky or useless, while others just couldn't fit enough information to make it worthwhile). You may still come across these types of CDs, and they can give you ideas if you want to have a CD that is both playable in standard players and capable of delivering data to your computer.

Recording

This is where the third-party software stands above the standard media player burning fare. Programs like Roxio and Nero are capable of recording audio from outside sources and either keeping it on the hard drive of your computer or burning it to your backup disc collection. The following items are included in this package:

- ✔ A recording program that can convert the analog audio to a digital music file
- ✔ A sound editor that allows you to copy, paste, and edit the audio to fit your needs
- ✔ The standard burning software to put these files on CD as music or data

This is a lifesaving function if you have a large collection of analog audio (like cassettes or vinyl) that you want to preserve or listen to without further damaging the analog source. In the section "Analog to Digital," later in this chapter, I show you how to perform this and save that priceless collection of Englebert Humperdink 45s.

CD labeling

Labeling may seem like a function that's better left to a word processor or graphics program, but it's a feature that's commonly bundled into programs like Roxio and Nero for the convenience factor. In combination with the printer you may have, this program can print labels for your CDs. Templates are included, or you can design your own. After you place some labels in the printer tray, you have labels to put on your recordings. This is usually a good idea, because nothing is more frustrating than searching through a pile of unlabeled CDs looking for something. The constant switching and searching of CDs has driven at least one man mad, I'm sure.

That's what you get

The previously mentioned software can produce any CD you want, and it has so many more features that may be of interest to you. My advice is to think about exactly what you want to do, and whether the additional expense of doing that is worth it. The bottom line is this: If all you want to do is burn CDs or back up your files, you're not going to need something like the full versions of Roxio or Nero. If you need something more advanced, like copying CDs from disc to disc for backup, you may want to look into getting a program like this. And if you're doing any sort of analog recording, a program like this (or a stand-alone audio recorder) is a must. Finally, other features are available with the full-version programs. If these seem useful or attractive, you may want to invest in Roxio or Nero. Just make sure that you plan to use what you're buying.

Analog to Digital

I want to take a special look at converting analog audio to digital audio, because it's something that quite a few people could benefit from using. While the CD is the dominant musical media, and digital downloads are quickly gaining acceptance in the marketplace, plenty of cassettes and vinyl are still out there that could be transferred to the digital realm without much trouble. Also, as I mentioned earlier in the book, analog media degrades with each playback — transferring it to digital format could give your songs extended life.

This is not meant to imply that digital media is immortal. More studies show that optical and magnetic digital media can degrade or fail years from now. Still, copies can be made much easier after the material is in the digital realm, so it's easier to keep ahead of time's inevitable destruction. Sorry to sound so gloomy — that's just the way it is.

Making the connection

The first step in converting analog music to digital form is to connect your analog playback device to the computer. This assumes that you have a record player or cassette that's capable of connecting to outside devices. To use your player in conjunction with your computer to make digital recordings, you should look for the following items:

- ✔ Line-out jack
- ✔ Headphone jack
- ✔ RCA stereo-out jacks, as shown in Figure 6-1
- ✔ Male minijack cable, as shown in Figure 6-2
- ✔ Stereo RCA cables, as shown in Figure 6-3
- ✔ RCA-to-minijack adapters, as shown in Figure 6-4

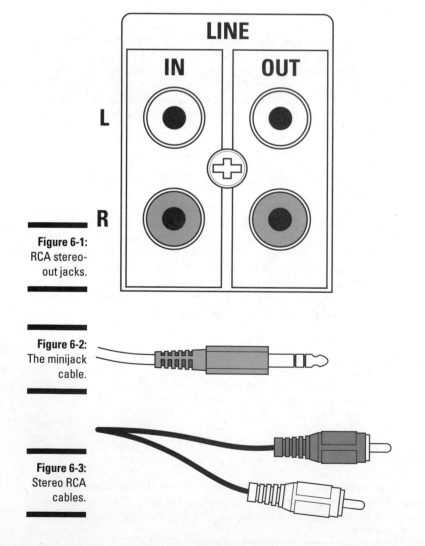

Figure 6-1: RCA stereo-out jacks.

Figure 6-2: The minijack cable.

Figure 6-3: Stereo RCA cables.

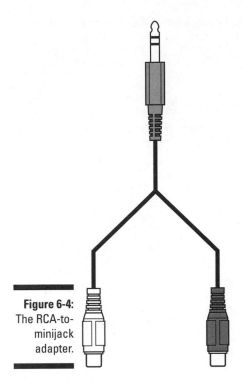

Figure 6-4:
The RCA-to-
minijack
adapter.

Your analog player must have one of the jacks shown in the previous figures to send a signal out to the computer. If you're recording from a headphone jack or line-out jack that uses a minijack, pair it with the minijack cable. RCA connectors can also function if you use the RCA-to-minijack adapter. All of these parts are available at Radio Shack or similar stores for less than $20. It's a small price to pay to have digital backups of your precious analog recordings, isn't it?

It's better to use a line-out jack as opposed to the headphone jack, if possible. Headphone jacks are designed to drive the small speakers you wear on your head, and not much else. It's possible to send out a signal from the head-phone jack, but be sure that the volume control is eased back from the loud-est possible setting. A high setting could introduce distortion into the sound you're sending to the computer. Try to send a decent amount of sound with-out making it too loud.

Any record player or turntable you use must have a *preamp* between the device and the computer. The signal coming off of a record player requires a boost to get a decent volume level. Many modern record players have a preamp built into them, although it's best to check your manufacturer's liter-ature to make sure you have the right equipment. Otherwise, you may have to take the signal from the receiver or put an external preamp between the record player and the computer.

The sound card has a minijack in for the line-in slot — this is where you send the signal from your analog device. Connect the device to the computer using the appropriate cord and adapters, as illustrated in Figure 6-5. You're ready to go!

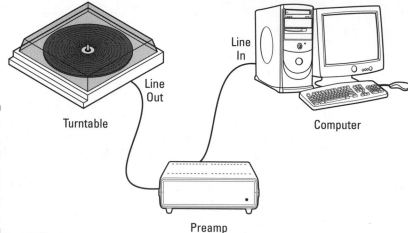

Line
In

Line
Out

Turntable

Computer

Figure 6-5:
The
complete
analog-to-
digital
recording
setup.

Preamp

Checking the line

After you've made the physical connections (with or without the assistance of Chuck Woolery) of the computer and the analog device, it's time to test the audio signal and make sure that you're getting something into the line-in jacks. Press the Play button on the analog device, and see if you can hear anything. If you can, you're ready to record. If not, follow these troubleshooting tips to make sure that everything is hooked up properly:

✔ **Make sure that all the connections are seated tightly.** This is a common cause and easy solution to the lack of audio signal.

✔ **Make sure that the analog device's volume control is raised to a sufficient level.** Anything between 60 and 80 percent should be fine. The goal is to make it loud without getting distortion.

✔ **Make sure that the line-in volume is set high enough.** In Chapter 3, I explain where to find the audio mixer in Windows XP. Make sure that the fader for the line in isn't muted and has been raised to a good audio level (again, about 60 to 80 percent should be enough to get you started).

✔ **Make sure that your analog device is functional.** If you aren't getting an audio signal out of the analog device, plug it into a receiver or another sound source and make sure that it's functional.

Make sure that you not only have enough audio cord to connect the devices, but also that you don't strain the jacks by pulling the cord too tightly. You can severely damage or disable the jack by putting too much tension on it. More than one speaker or line-in jack has met an untimely demise through this kind of torture.

Leveling it out

The sound is flowing easily into your computer now, and you're ready to capture it to your hard drive. The first step is making sure that the audio-recording program is getting the signal from the line-in jack. You can use Roxio, Nero, or any other media program capable of recording audio for this process. For this discussion, however, I've chosen to go the free route and use an open source program called Audacity. You can find this program at `www.sourceforge.net.`

Open source means that both the program and the underlying code are distributed freely to the public. Donations are always welcome to support their effort, however.

Using a program like Audacity is a good way to introduce yourself to the world of digital-to-analog recording without spending a lot. If you later decide to move on to a program with more features, you haven't lost a thing.

Download Audacity and follow the instructions to install the program on your machine. Open the program and make sure that it's active, as shown in Figure 6-6.

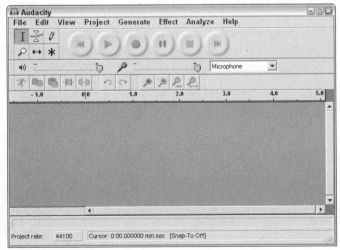

Figure 6-6:
Audacity's program window.

First, make sure that the audio file is recorded in stereo. Select File⇨ Preferences, and click the Audio I/O tab. Select the option "2 (Stereo)" in he bottom pull-down menu to record in stereo, as shown in Figure 6-7.

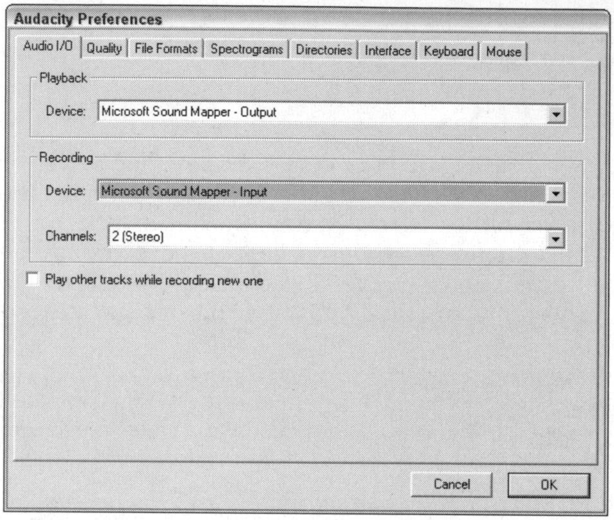

Audacity Preferences

Audio I/O | Quality | File Formats | Spectrograms | Directories | Interface | Keyboard | Mouse

Playback

Device: Microsoft Sound Mapper - Output

Recording

Device: Microsoft Sound Mapper - Input

Channels: 2 (Stereo)

☐ Play other tracks while recording new one

Cancel   OK

Figure 6-7:
Audio I/O
options.

Also make sure that you've selected the correct sample rate for your project. The recording should default to the CD-quality rate of 44.1 kHz. Note that unless you're running professional-level audio equipment, you aren't likely to get the same quality as you would from a factory-duplicated CD. That's just the nature of the equipment you're using. However, the recording should still retain virtually all the quality. If you record at a lower sample rate, you'll lose sound quality. Figure 6-8 shows how you choose the default sample rate.

I like Audacity for its simple interface. You have straightforward controls that are easy to understand and use. However, you can't check the audio level of the file before you begin recording. Therefore, it's important to start low on the volume and raise it using test recordings to get a decent level (a higher-level recording program would have some kind of meter to show the volume of the audio being recorded).

To check the volume levels, press the Play button on your analog device and click the Record button in Audacity (it's the large circular button with the smaller dot on it, as shown in Figure 6-6). A visual representation of the audio being captured scrolls across the screen, as shown in Figure 6-9.

After you've recorded a bit of the audio, click Stop, move the cursor back to the beginning by clicking where you want it on the visual representation of the audio, and click Play.

Figure 6-8:
Sample rate
options.

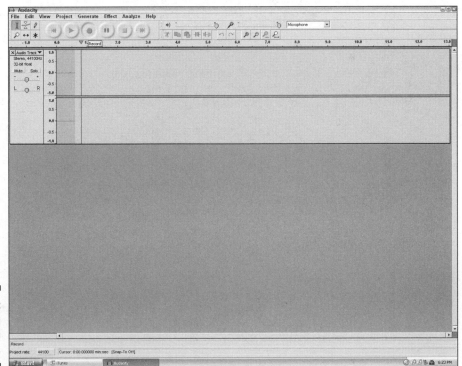

If the volume levels are too high, the audio will distort and you'll get a dirty recording. Digital distortion is bad — very bad. It's full of glitches and static that's unusable, and you want to avoid this at all costs.

Figure 6-9:
Recording
with
Audacity.

You know your audio is too loud if you notice either of the following things:

✔ You can see a peak in the audio (part of the visual audio representation touches the top of the recording audio track).

✔ You can hear an unpleasant distortion or glitchiness during playback of the file.

Again, your goal is to make sure that you have as much volume as possible without encountering distortion. You can adjust the signal level going into the player by opening Windows XP Audio Mixer, selecting Options⇨ Recording, and making sure that the Line In check box is selected. Then click the OK button to open the mixer. Start with the fader at about 25 percent and move it up or down, depending on your volume needs.

When you get the best possible audio level, it's time to make your recordings.

It's always a good idea to start the digital recording before the analog audio recording to make sure that you get everything from the original recording. Otherwise, you could chop off some of the analog audio. You can always go back and edit out the unused digital audio at the beginning or end of the track.

Start the digital recording, and then start the analog device. You should notice the audio wave shown by Audacity as the sound is recorded. When you get to the end of the song, click Stop, and you should see a window that is similar to Figure 6-10. The audio is temporarily held in a file associated with Audacity, and it's now time to export the audio.

Select File⇨Export as WAV. (You can also export to OGG Vorbis, or to MP3 with a plug-in called a LAME encoder, which is available at `http://source forge.net`.) You're now ready to save the file, as shown in Figure 6-11.

You've successfully recorded your analog song to the digital world — Congratulations!

Cleaning up

You should know that simply recording your records or cassettes to the digital realm does not automatically make them sound better. This process just makes a digital representation of how the analog source sounds. However, you can clean things up a bit.hearing the audio you want to keep.

Figure 6-10:
The
recorded
audio file.

Making the cut

First, I show you how to take out the silence at the beginning of the song you just recorded. Highlight the section of the audio file you want to eliminate, as shown in Figure 6-12. You can make sure that it's the section you want to remove by clicking the Play button and hearing only silence, as opposed to

Press Ctrl+X, and the silence is removed from the audio. You can do this to any section you want. Remember to reexport the file when you're done. Saving the project remembers and reproduces the changes you made to the original audio file, but only reexporting the file permanently makes those changes to that audio file.

Eliminating pops and scratches

To eliminate unwanted noise, the audio file is run through a filter that searches for certain noises, like the pops and scratches that often accompany the aging of vinyl records, and eliminates them. Newer versions of programs like Nero and Roxio have these functions built in, and open source equivalents are available as well.

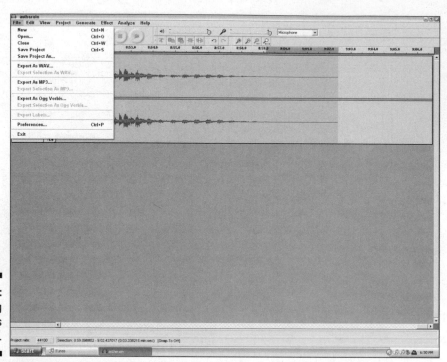

Figure 6-11:
Exporting
the song as
a WAV file.

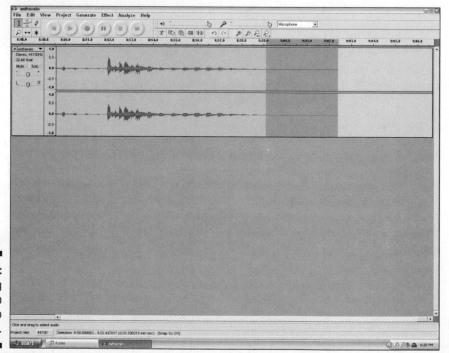

Figure 6-12:
Removing
silence from
an audio
file.

Apples and Oranges

So how do these programs stack up? Table 6-1 compares some of the more important factors, such as the files they can create or the programs' sound-editing capabilities. However, you find a weird intersection with these programs. Five years ago, the burning programs and the sound-editing programs would never have invited comparisons. Simply put, they did two very separate things. However, time and the inevitable desire for programmers to add more bells and whistles to their product have made aspects of these programs very similar. The burning programs have limited sound-editing capabilities, and the sound-editing programs can perform limited burning functions (or work in concert with Windows XP's burning capabilities).

Table 6-1		Burning and Sound-Editing Programs		
Software Name	*Edit Sound?*	*Export File Formats*	*Burn Files?*	*Other Features*
Roxio	Yes	WAV, WMA, MP3	Yes	DVD, video, and photo-album production features, vinyl restoration plug-in
Nero	Yes	WAV, WMA, MP3	Yes	DVD, video, and photo-album production features, vinyl restoration plug-in
Screenblast Sound Forge	Yes	WAV, MP3, AIFF, WMA, Ogg Vorbis, QuickTime	Yes	Vinyl restoration plug-in, audio level meters
Audacity	Yes	WAV, Ogg Vorbis, MP3 (with external plug-in)	No	It's free!

All of these programs look fairly similar, don't they? They have similar functions, and they could all handle your recording needs. However, Roxio and Nero arose from burning and media-production tools, while Sound Forge developed from pro-level audio production. Audacity stands alone as an example of open source programming. Costs range from free to $300. Ask the following questions as you make your purchase:

 ✔ Do you want to spend that much?

 ✔ Are you buying functions you don't need?

 ✔ Are there additional functions you would like to use?

Keep these factors in mind when you make your purchase, and you'll be okay.

Chapter 7

Buying Songs at the 99-Cent Store

In This Chapter

▶ Checking out the available online stores

▶ Browsing the selection of a typical online store

▶ Downloading the music you want

▶ Examining the unique qualities of each store and the files they sell

▶ Knowing where to find free digital music

This moment is just like the time you slid behind the wheel of your first car. Your Windows music machine is primed and ready to go, and now's the time to take it on the road. So where will you go? Plenty of outlets are available from which you can purchase the music you want. Some of them have unfamiliar names, and some of them are common household names.

A great many stores are out there, but not all of them sell the same thing. When you go to a traditional music store, you can count on being able to buy a CD or DVD and knowing how the disc will work. With online music, you need to know what kind of file works on your computer and your portable device, how you can use that file, and whether the store even has the song you want. In this chapter, I help you sort out the details as you search for the latest hit or a comfortable classic.

As of this writing, most of these download services are available only to residents of the United States. Although the Internet allows access worldwide, copyright and trade legalities have yet to catch up with the technology.

Choosing the Best Virtual Record Store

Before the Internet, buying a recording was based mostly on whether you liked the artist. You went to your store of choice (based on size or location)

and made your purchase. You probably had a decent stereo, and you knew that any recording you brought home would play well. All you had to do was sit back and enjoy the music. Then the Internet came on the scene.

While buying music became a little more convenient (you can purchase and listen to your music at home seconds later, even in your "comfy" clothes), you have to be more aware of what you lay down your money for. From file type to licensing to whether it can transfer to your portable media player, you have to be careful. I now take a look at these factors and help you understand what you should expect.

File format

To keep your Windows music machine running smoothly, you have to put in the right fuel. Just like you have different types of gasoline, you have different file formats for different players. You must be careful about purchasing the right type of file, or your player may not run smoothly (or at all). If you're the proud owner of an iPod, you'll be spending most of your time (and money) at iTunes. However, taking trips anywhere else may be problematic, because the iPod doesn't handle copy-protected WMA files, which seem to be the format of choice for many stores. For a more in-depth description of the many types of digital music file formats, check out Chapter 3. A brief overview of the most common formats follows:

- **AAC:** Also known as MPEG-4 AAC, this is a relatively new format that's supported mainly by Apple and iTunes.

- **MP3:** Probably the most widely known audio file format, this format became popular because of its small file size and relatively good audio quality.

- **WMA:** This is the proprietary audio format for Microsoft and Windows Media Player. Some retailers choose it over MP3 because of enhanced digital media rights management.

- **WAV:** These files usually have the best sound quality of all the available sound files. However, these files are quite large and not really feasible for download, even over high-speed connections.

These format letters can make a huge difference in where you buy your files.

You also need to know where the file is when you purchase it. Some services put the file on your computer, while others stream it from their servers to your system. You can hear the file, but you can't use that file anyplace that doesn't have a computer with a network connection. The stores will announce what kind of files they sell when you sign up for the service. Carefully read any information they give you. It makes a difference in how you use your files.

File protection

Not only do you have to worry about whether the file can play on your computer, but you also have to know where you can use the file after you get it. As online music stores use more digital-rights-management coding with audio files, how you can listen to your files can vary from store to store. Consider the following issues about file protection:

- ✔ **Copying:** This determines how many times you can make a copy of your download.

- ✔ **Transferring:** This indicates how many systems or portable devices you can legally put the file on.

- ✔ **Burning:** This is important if you want to copy the file to a CD or DVD and listen to it in a standard player.

If you're only planning on listening to your music at your computer, you'll probably be comfortable shopping at any of the available stores. If you want to burn files to a disc or put them on a portable player, however, you should make sure that your files and portable players are compatible. Read the fine print for every store and portable player you consider to make sure that it fits your needs.

Selection

Selling digital audio online is still a relatively new process compared to the more traditional music sales of record stores. Customers could count on most large record stores to have a decent selection of popular music, and more discerning customers could go to smaller boutiques that catered to more specific tastes. If a store didn't have a specific recording, it could probably order it. This type of purchase is not necessarily the case on the Internet. The recording industry has yet to fully embrace online music sales, and some of the most popular music is not available online at the time of this writing.

Right now, for example, if you're a Beatles fan looking for online music, you're out of luck. As time goes on, the selection will likely get better. A great deal of new music is being released on both CD and DVD and online at the same time, and the Internet is also a great way to get new music out to listeners before traditional recordings are available.

Not only do popular music selections vary from store to store, but you can also find a wide variety of outlets for music not available on the major labels. While these aren't household names, it's possible to find some hidden gems among the vast quantities of downloads available on these sites. The price is also right — most of these selections are available for free download.

Software

Your computer most likely came with a media player already installed, and it's probably Windows Media Player. Plenty of other music players, such as Winamp or the RealOne Player, are also available for free on the Internet. Even with these choices available, some online music services require you to download software that plays and manages your media files.

Napster, iTunes, and Rhapsody require you to install their software before you can use their services. An online store like eMusic allows you to use any player you want to listen to downloads from its site, but you have to install software from the online store to start downloading its MP3s. If you're not attached to a particular media player and you have plenty of room on your computer, this may not make a big difference to you. However, to avoid potential conflicts between media players and to keep your hard drive space free, you should look at this requirement closely.

Price

Just like most things in this world, a choice can often come down to the bottom line. One of the attractive aspects of shopping for music online is the fact that it's often less expensive than buying CDs or DVDs. You don't usually get the fancy packaging or the actual disc, but you get the music itself (and isn't that why you purchased the song in the first place?). But, just like everything else in this chapter, it's something that can vary from one online store to another. Despite the differences, these stores usually fall into one of the following categories:

- **Per-song pricing:** These stores are strictly pay-as-you-go. You pay a flat price per song (currently between 79 and 99 cents) or per album (currently around $10), and the money is collected each time you make a purchase. Pay attention to the digital rights management on these types of files — you should know what you can do with this file after you've purchased it.

- **Subscription:** These stores usually assess a monthly charge for the privilege of listening to the music they provide. Think of it as a service, like cable or satellite radio. In most cases, the music provided on services like this is streamed from servers and not downloaded to your computer. Even if the music is downloaded to your computer, you may want to check the fine print. There's usually a limit to the amount of music you can download every month, and the files may be taken away if you stop paying the monthly fee.

As with everything else mentioned in this chapter, knowing how you want to listen to your music can help you determine what you want to pay for it. The promised iTunes price of 99 cents per file could add up if you're using it to rebuild the music collection you had as a teenager. However, that $10 a month you spend on another service isn't worth anything if you can't listen to the songs when you're away from your computer.

Shop 'til You Bop

As of this writing, there are approximately five major online music stores, with several smaller ones and at least two other large services on the way. They all provide basically the same thing — songs and albums. However, they all have individual quirks that could either trip you up or enhance the way you listen to your music.

iTunes

This 800-pound gorilla of the online music world can be found at `www.iTunes.com`, although you must use the iTunes media player to actually buy and listen to music from this store. The company's model has earned it strong customer loyalty and a few imitators. Its details follow:

- **File format:** AAC
- **File protection:** Can be shared on five computers, burned to CD, and transferred to an iPod
- **Selection:** Carries both independent and major-label releases
- **Software:** Requires proprietary software
- **Price:** Usually 99 cents a song or $9.99 an album

Music.MSN.com

Microsoft recently introduced this service as a competitor to iTunes. You can find it at `www.music.msn.com`. The prices and selection are similar to iTunes, but Microsoft promises that its files will be compatible with more portable audio players than iTunes (which sells files only for use on the iPod). Its details follow:

- **File format:** WMA
- **File protection:** Can be shared on five computers, burned to CD, and transferred to several types of portable audio devices
- **Selections:** Carries mostly major-label releases
- **Software:** Can be played with a variety of players, although it's designed for use with Windows Media Player
- **Price:** Usually 99 cents a song or $9.99 an album

Napster

This name used to be synonymous with illegal downloads. However, it's been given a quick corporate makeover and a new business model — only the name remains the same. Surf over to www.napster.com. Otherwise, it looks a little like iTunes, but using different software and file formats. It's also based on a subscription model, where the company charges a monthly fee for access to the Napster music library. Napster Light allows users to purchase tracks and albums a la carte. Napster's details follow:

- **File format:** WMA
- **File protection:** Can be shared on three computers, burned to CD, and transferred to a portable media device
- **Selection:** Focuses mostly on major-label releases
- **Software:** Requires proprietary software
- **Price:** $9.95 a month, plus an extra fee for transferring songs to your hard drive or burning them. Napster Light charges 99 cents per track and $9.95 or more per album.

Rhapsody

This is a streaming service (www.listen.com), because the files always remain on the company's servers. Think of it as a radio station based on subscriptions. You can access music from any computer with a network connection and the Rhapsody software. Its details are as follows:

- **File format:** Real Media
- **File protection:** Unlimited streaming of files, or the songs can be burned to CD for an additional charge
- **Selection:** Focuses mainly on major-label releases
- **Software:** Requires proprietary software
- **Price:** $9.95 per month for the All-Access full service (you can also burn tracks at 79 cents apiece) or $4.95 for RadioPLUS (streaming only)

eMusic

eMusic charges a subscriber fee, but the downloads you get from this service are yours. Check out www.eMusic.com. You're limited only by how many downloads you order.

- **File format:** MP3
- **File protection:** Open MP3 — this file can be moved, burned, and transferred at will. You can only download a certain number of files a month.

- ✔ **Selection:** A mix of independent and major-label artists

- ✔ **Software:** Uses your choice of media player in conjunction with the eMusic Download Manager

- ✔ **Price:** Between $9.99 and $19.99, depending on how many files you want to download

Wal-Mart

This conglomerate sells everything else, so why not leap into the digital music world? Visit www.wal-mart.com. Wal-Mart offers downloads from many popular artists, if you're willing to put up with some possible family-friendly editing. Wal-Mart's details are as follows:

- ✔ **File format:** WMA

- ✔ **File protection:** Digital licenses are needed to transfer files between computers and portable media devices

- ✔ **Selection:** Major-label artists. In keeping with its corporate policy, music may be edited for content to keep it family-friendly

- ✔ **Software:** Uses your own media player

- ✔ **Price:** Currently 88 cents a song

Musicmatch

The popular jukebox software (www.musicmatch.com) has been expanded into a music download service. Other than the software and the file format, the service bears some resemblance to the successful iTunes business model. Its details are as follows:

- ✔ **File format:** WMA

- ✔ **File protection:** Can be played on three computers, burned to CD, or transferred to a portable device

- ✔ **Selection:** Major-label artists

- ✔ **Software:** Requires proprietary software

- ✔ **Price:** Usually 99 cents a song and $9.99 an album

BuyMusic

This service, which you can visit at www.buymusic.com, doesn't require any software downloads or installations. It focuses mostly on popular singles, skipping album cuts and exclusive offerings. BuyMusic's details are as follows:

- ✔ **File format:** WMA

- ✔ **File protection:** Can be played on three computers, burned to CD, or transferred to a portable media player

> ✔ **Selection:** Major-label artists, focusing mostly on singles
>
> ✔ **Software:** Uses your own media player, but make sure that it's up to date to handle the company's digital-rights-management software
>
> ✔ **Price:** Usually 79 cents a song

MusicNow

MusicNow (www.musicnow.com) combines downloadable files and streaming music into a unique offering. Just be sure of what you're buying from this service. Make sure that your music doesn't go away if you stop paying your membership fee. MusicNow's details follow:

> ✔ **File format:** WMA
>
> ✔ **File protection:** Some files are permanent downloads that can be burned or transferred to portable devices, while others can only be listened to while a membership fee is paid
>
> ✔ **Selection:** Major-label artists
>
> ✔ **Software:** Uses Windows Media Player and proprietary software to access your account
>
> ✔ **Price:** Usually 99 cents per song, with an expanded premium service for a monthly subscription fee

Music Rebellion

Music Rebellion allows artists to post their own work and splits the profits with the service in exchange for the "storefront." Look for an eclectic blend of music on this site at www.musicrebellion.com. Its details follow:

> ✔ **File format:** MP3 or WMA
>
> ✔ **File protection:** WMA files require digital licenses to play or move between computers; MP3 files are open
>
> ✔ **Selection:** Independent and major-label artists
>
> ✔ **Software:** Uses Windows Media Player or your preferred media player
>
> ✔ **Price:** Per-song or per-album price, depending on the artist being downloaded

A summary of the features of these services is shown in Table 7-1.

Table 7-1			Comparison Of Major Services		
Service	*Format*	*Protection*	*Selection*	*Software*	*Price*
iTunes	AAC	Share, burn, and transfer	Major-label and independent	Proprietary	Per-song or -album
Music. MSN.com	WMA	Share, burn, and transfer	Major Label	Windows Media Player	Per-song or -album
Napster	WMA	Share, burn, and transfer	Major-label	Proprietary	Subscription and per-song or -album
Rhapsody	Real Media	Streaming and (for an extra fee) burning	Major-label	Proprietary	Monthly subscription, per-burn fee
eMusic	MP3	Share, burn, and transfer — limited downloads	Major-label and independent	Your media player, proprietary Download Manager	Monthly subscription
Wal-Mart	WMA	Share and transfer	Major-label	Windows Media Player	Per-song or -album
Music-match	WMA	Share, burn, and transfer	Major-label	Proprietary	Per-song or -album, premium subscription
BuyMusic	WMA	Share, burn, and transfer	Major-label	Windows Media Player	Per-song
Music Now	WMA	Some permanent downloads, others are streaming only	Major-label	Windows Media Player, proprietary account software	Per-song or optional premium subscription fee
Music Rebellion	MP3 or WMA	Share, burn, and transfer	Major-label and independent	Your media player	Per-song or -album

Okay, so which one do I prefer? Maybe it's just because I sometimes cross into the world of Macintosh, but the ease of use and selection offered by iTunes has ensnared me as a customer. The company's smartest move was making its software and hardware available to the Windows community, taking its highly regarded product and opening it to the largest computing market in the United States. Apple also understands that users want to have flexible access to their music, and it provides the choice to change computers, burn the files, or place them on an iPod. It even uses a file format noted for good musical fidelity. The only drawbacks are that you have to use the company's software (I like keeping my hard drives clean) and you can't transfer the files to other players, like the Dell or Nomad brands. Still, I think the selection and exclusive material offered by iTunes outweigh these concerns.

Signing your name on the dotted line

So, you've checked out all the stores and decided which one makes sense for your needs. Now you have to become a member. One store won't give you six albums for a penny, but you're also sure that you're downloading exactly what you want instead of getting a Yanni disc in the mail every month. You can also browse the selection of the store, examine its special offers and exclusive tracks, and check out quickly (without having to reenter your credit card information or address every time).

Be prepared to give each of these services some common information. To streamline the purchase process, the companies store as much data about you as possible. This could include everything from a username and password to more detailed financial information. Look for the following common fields when filling out your membership application:

- **Username:** This is just the identifying name by which the online service can identify you. More than likely, you'll use your real name as it appears on your credit card.

- **Password:** This is a common feature of doing business on the Internet. You'll probably also be asked to provide a counter-question like "What is your pet's name?" in case you forget your password.

- **E-mail address:** This is the service's primary line of communication with you. This is how you receive important sign-up information, receipts, or promotional offers.

   If you don't want advertisements coming to your main e-mail account, sign up for a Webmail account (such as those available at `www.hotmail.com`) and use it for your e-mail correspondence with the online music service.

- **Credit card information:** If you've shopped online before, this should be familiar to you. The service will ask for the credit card type (MasterCard, Visa, American Express, and others), number, expiration date, and any additional security information.

Many current music download services require the user to download software to purchase music. iTunes was one of the first services to take this approach, and it remains the most popular (partly due to the overwhelming success of its partner device, the iPod). So, look at the service and see how it brings music to the masses. To use the iTunes service, you must download the software provided by Apple. There's no way around it — buying from iTunes means using its software. To download the iTunes software, just follow these steps:

1. **Type** `www.itunes.com` **in the address bar of your Web browser.**

   You come to the iTunes main Web page, as shown in Figure 7-1.

2. **Start the download process by clicking the Free Download button shown in Figure 7-1.**

   This downloads the iTunes software from Apple's servers to your computer.

3. **Fill in the text boxes shown in Figure 7-2 (note that you only have to provide your e-mail address), and deselect the check boxes at the right if you don't want to receive additional information.**

4. **Click the Download iTunes button.**

   Your download starts automatically.

5. **Save the setup file to your computer, and double-click it to install iTunes.**

   Note that this file is almost 20MB in size — the download could be a long process over dialup Internet connections.

Figure 7-1:
The main
iTunes Web
page.

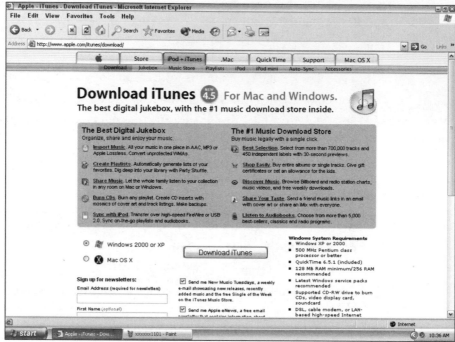

Figure 7-2:
The iTunes download page.

6. **Click the Next button, and follow the directions to install iTunes.**

   If you don't want iTunes and QuickTime to become the media players you'll use by default, be sure to deselect the check boxes shown in Figure 7-3.

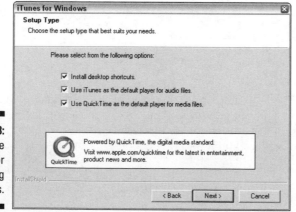

Figure 7-3:
Some options for using iTunes.

7. **Click the Next button a couple more times, and iTunes will install on your computer.**

   iTunes searches your computer for music to catalog and put into playlists. After that, you're ready to use iTunes.

Checking Out the Selection

Time for some shopping! The following sections cover a few things you should look for in every store to help you decide what you need.

The search engine

Nothing is more convenient than going to the store, typing in the artist or song you're looking for, and heading directly to that section. And you won't be embarrassed by the hipper-than-you record store employee if your selection doesn't meet their approval. Type what you want to look for in the engine to find a list of potential matches. Be as specific as you can — searching for "Tiffany Alone Now" is more likely to turn up the Tiffany song "I Think We're Alone Now" than searching for just one of those words.

Listings

Whether you're looking for something under the heading of Sixties Pop (where did that Melanie song go?) or exploring the new releases, these headings can help you narrow your search or explore a genre of music that fascinates you. Many of the storefronts (the first page you see when you reach the site) have sections that show genres of music, special pricing deals, and other offers.

Radio

Think of this as a driving companion who always knows what song is on the car radio. If you hear a song you like on the streaming broadcast, some services tell you information about the song and tell you how to buy it. It's a service that not only exposes you to new music (and potentially new purchases), but you also get the chance to listen to the music before you buy it.

With that in mind, I describe the shopping process using iTunes as an example. Follow these steps as you shop:

1. **Click the Sign In button in the upper-right corner, as shown in Figure 7-4.**

Figure 7-4:
The iTunes
front page.

You have to enter the information shown in Figure 7-5 to continue. Again, be sure to deselect the check boxes at the bottom of the screen for any information you don't want to give or receive.

2. **Click the Create New Account button.**

3. **Enter your credit card information.**

   This is where iTunes gets to the bottom line. The information is stored in its system and used each time you make a purchase.

Use a credit card and not a debit card to access iTunes. If your information gets in the wrong hands, it's easier to cancel a credit card transaction than to try to put money back into your bank account. This is a basic rule of shopping on the Internet.

4. **Type "Loretta" in the search field at the top of the store, and click the Search button.**

   You're looking for a favorite band of mine. There, tucked among famous country artists and some other references, is a selection of tunes from the band, as shown in Figure 7-6.

5. **Click the Buy Song button for the track "1000 Lbs."**

   When the selection is confirmed, the song is downloaded and you can listen to it whenever you want.

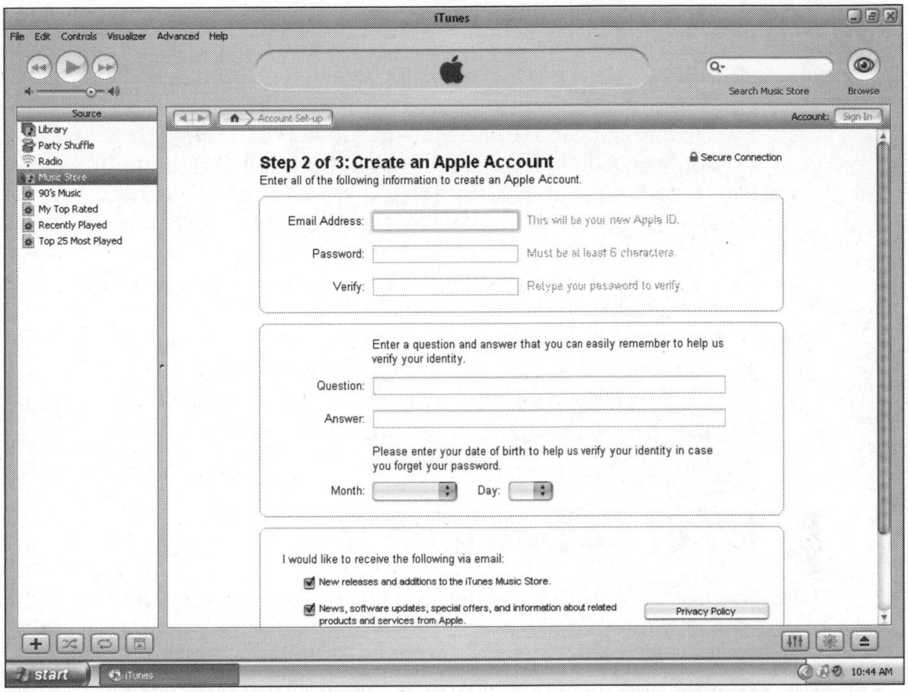

Figure 7-5:
New iTunes
account
information.

Figure 7-6:
Finding a
band in
iTunes.

You should preview the music before you buy it. Just like record stores have listening stations set up for you to hear the CD, online services should have at least snippets of the recording available for your listening pleasure before you buy the file. Imagine wanting to buy "Don't Stand So Close to Me" by The Police, and instead ending up with the horrible remix they made years after the original recording. Or, if you're a hip-hop fan, you may not want a Snoop Dog track that's so heavily edited that it sounds like sonic Swiss cheese. Look for a Preview or Listen button by each track so that you can hear before you buy.

Now that you've downloaded a single track, you can turn your attention to buying full-length albums. Find the Top 100 albums link in the lower-right corner of the store page, and select it to see some more popular choices. If you want to look a little deeper, you can search for albums or artists as I described before. When you've found what you want, just click the Buy Album button, and the buying process runs again. It's that simple.

What do I do with it?

So after you've downloaded the file, it's time to face the music. Assuming you've done your research, this should be a simple process. Still, it's worth a closer look to see exactly what you can do. First, I look at playing the file on your computer, and then you see what you can do to take your music outside the box on your desk.

Saving your music

When you're downloading a file, always be sure that you know exactly where it's going on your computer. Many services have a default folder for music — iTunes places it in a preexisting My Music folder, for example. However, you may want to store your music somewhere else, such as a dedicated hard drive that you've set aside for audio. You should be able to establish exactly where your music is headed when you first download it. In Figure 7-7, you're given a choice of where you want to save the file.

Simply navigate your folders until you find the right location, and then click the Save button. Your file is headed right where you want it.

Burning your music

Depending on what store you went to, you may be able to burn your music to CD as either an audio track (to be played in standard CD players) or as an MP3 or WMA CD (to be played on your computer or some CD and DVD players). The advantage of the audio burn is the ability to work in older CD players, while newer players allow you to burn more and smaller files on one disc. Assuming that you have a CD burner, this should be an easy process.

Players like Windows Media Player have an integral burning function built into them. Select the playlist of the music you want to burn, click the Copy button, and you're off, as shown in Figure 7-8.

You can also use third-party burning software like Roxio or Nero to burn your music CD. You probably got a free or limited-function version of this type of software when you bought the burning drive on your computer. Here, you must create the playlists again manually, but the software can give you more control over how you burn your CDs. The software can also allow you to burn other files to discs.

When using third-party software, make sure you specify that you're burning a music CD or a data CD. That way, you'll know exactly what you're getting and you won't be surprised by a nonplaying CD.

Transferring your music to your player

You have to crawl out from behind the computer at some point. Luckily, you can take your music with you. If you shopped at the right store, you can transfer your files to a portable device. Most of the these services have preferred devices, like iTunes and the iPod. However, some services allow you to use a variety of players with their service, as long as the file formats are compatible. See where this can get complicated? This is why you have to pay attention.

Figure 7-7:
Saving a song to your preferred location.

The process of transferring files is much like burning. Make sure that you have your device linked to the computer, most likely with a USB or FireWire connection. In Windows Media Player, for example, change the drop-down menu on the right that shows G: in Figure 7-8 to the device you're using.

Select the playlist you want to transfer, and click the Copy button. The files make their way over to the player, and you'll be listening on the road in no time (that is, if you haven't exceeded your maximum transfer rate).

As I noted previously, some services only allow you to move a certain number of files. Keep a count so that you don't accidentally run out of transfer allotments. You should also make sure that you have enough room on your player. It may be hard for you to fill a 30GB hard drive with MP3s at first, but they do add up. If you don't listen to certain songs anymore, be sure to delete them to make room for more music. I take a closer look at this topic in Chapter 10.

Free samples

The pay services I cover in this chapter are like traditional record stores in one aspect — they charge you money to listen to music. Just because you've moved the point of sale to the Internet doesn't change the basic business equation. The only thing missing is the actual disc and the jewel case (and maybe the files themselves, if you stop paying the subscription fee to the service).

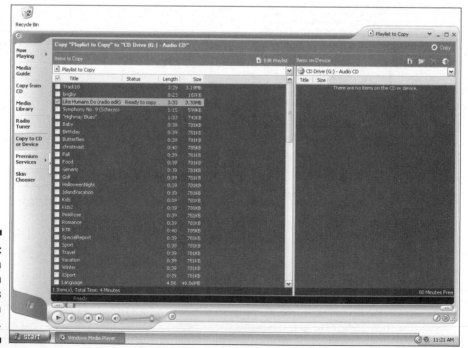

Figure 7-8:
Burning a
playlist in
Windows
Media
Player.

But the birth of digital music did not arise from pay-per-song or -album services. You (and most consumers) probably heard about music on the Internet as a giant trading site of music. Legal or not, this is how trading music across the Internet first became popular. So a long-standing tradition of free music exists on the Web. While the most popular service (Napster) has been closed and rebranded, you can still find the Internet's equivalents of the supermarket's free samples in the digital music world. Increasingly, they fall into three main categories: record labels, artist sites, and third-party sites.

Record labels

The record labels are in the business of making money off of recordings, but occasionally these labels give out singles or sample tracks from some releases. These often take the form of additional tracks that are available to those who purchased the album as an incentive to keep the fans following the artists and shelling out for their albums. Select fans may also receive advance MP3s of upcoming releases, or the company can stream an upcoming single from its site.

R.I.P. MP3.com

The most famous third-party music-hosting site was probably the now-shuttered MP3.com. It was a story that symbolized the growing pains of the Internet and a new way of doing business. Originally, MP3.com billed itself as an online music locker, where people who had bought a CD could access their music through pre-recorded tracks on the MP3.com servers. This raised the ire of the recording industry, who believed this violated the copyrights attached to that music. After settling a multimillion dollar lawsuit with the major labels, MP3.com focused its energy on becoming a promotional service for all sorts of musicians, from local garage band recordings to sneak previews of megastar albums (I first heard a new Billy Corgan track there, for example). The site would host tracks from bands and allow the bands to choose whether to allow downloads or streaming-only tracks. Like most things on the Internet, it was advertising driven, although MP3.com adopted a subscription model for hosting music in its final days. However, the company was forced out of business in 2003. The majority of the content and software was purchased by CNET, and the site reopened as `http://music.download.com`, although the company has other plans for the MP3.com name. Much like Napster, it will probably be given a new identity and sent back into cyberspace for a second chance.

Although individual rules may differ from site to site, the general gist is that bands can upload their tracks to these sites and allow others to download the tracks from the previously mentioned sites (with perhaps some banner ads or pop-up windows along the way). Bands get the benefit of limited Internet distribution, and the sites get the benefit of increased traffic and advertising revenue. You can find some hidden gems while searching these sites, but be ready to sift through a great deal of files. The sites usually make this job a little easier by categorizing these tracks into genres (rock, funk, pop, and so on), but you still find quite a few entries. Bands that use these sites usually just provide direct links to their files and bypass the general search function.

Artist sites

Most of the time, the artists give out samples in the same manner as the record companies. However, they may be willing to take it a step further. For example, Billy Corgan put the majority of the last album that Smashing Pumpkins recorded on their Web site for free download. Check out the home sites for your famous artists to see what they're giving away.

Third-party sites

This is usually an option for artists who don't have a label yet and/or can't afford to host large files on their Web site. In exchange for the advertising revenue they get for hosting free content, these sites place music on their site for downloads.

It's difficult to list all the services that host music download files for bands, but a sampling of what's available is as follows:

- http://purevolume.com
- http://garageband.com
- http://soundclick.com
- http://radiotakeover.com

Why would bands give it away for free?

Consider the example of a fictional band called Truck Stop Sushi. After spending eight months in their road-worn van touring the tristate area, the band finally piles into a recording studio and manages to eke out an album in between arguments and cheesecake runs. They've built up a decent-sized following during their time on tour, and the fans are clamoring to hear what they've come up with. It's going to be a little while before they can go back on tour and sell CDs (girlfriends and boyfriends are angry, and the van needs serious attention to the transmission before they can risk another road trip). Suddenly, the drummer proposes the idea of allowing listeners to partake of the band's sound from the Web site that they paid a friend of theirs to put together.

After much discussion and more cheesecake, the band decides to stream two tracks from its Web site. Assuming that most folks are using Windows XP over at least a 56-Kbps dialup connection, the band has its Web site friend save their tracks in streaming WMA format and put them on the front page of the site. By clicking the appropriate link, Windows Media Player is automatically activated, and the song streams from the band's server to the user's PC.

Now, the fans can listen to the advance tracks, and the band can have a welcoming and friendly audience when they finally get back out on the road.

The strategy works well for Truck Stop Sushi, and they expand their touring radius beyond the greater tristate area. Their tireless efforts earn them a major-label contract, and the band records another album in a more posh studio, with cheesecake of a much higher quality. The band and the label are happy with the recording, but they want to add some incentive for people to purchase it. The drummer's idea of placing small plastic whistles inside the CD is quickly dismissed in favor of allowing those who buy the CD to download a special track from the band's Web site. By recognizing a special code on the CD via the Internet, the Web site can verify an actual factory-produced CD (versus one that was burned) and allow the user to access a special section of the site where he or she can download that special drunken jam the engineer recorded when the band thought they were just messing around. The band gets its share of the profits from the album sales, the fans get something extra from their purchase, and everybody continues to love the magic that is Truck Stop Sushi.

Chapter 8

Radio Station WNXP

· ·

In This Chapter

▶ Understanding the basics of Internet streaming radio stations

▶ Knowing where and when you can use Internet radio

▶ Setting up your own Internet radio station

· ·

Radio stations (along with the record collection of a parent or older sibling) probably helped to form your musical tastes and the way you listen to music. I used to obsessively tune the dial on my clock radio, trying to find something new and different to listen to. Regardless of what you think of modern broadcast radio, it's been an important force in shaping today's musical trends. It brings you something new and lets you try it before you decide to purchase the recording.

Of course, broadcast radio stations still rule the airwaves (and the cash flow), but the discriminating listener now has the opportunity to choose something different, something closer to his or her own tastes. Internet broadcasters are opening a new frontier of possibilities for radio programming. They aren't bound by having to be in the broadcast range of the station — you can tune in a station from North America to Albania, depending on the speed and stability of your Internet connection. And because you're accessing the station over your computer, you have so many more possibilities as to how you can use the music.

Gently Down the Stream

Internet radio depends on streaming media technology to make its broadcasts listenable. Your computer just wouldn't be able to handle regular downloads of all the music and the need to play it in real time. It's also not dependent on file-by-file access. The server that is streaming the radio station provides a constant flow of encoded music (along with any chatter or advertisements it may want to include — this is a form of radio, after all) to your computer.

The main difference between this type of radio and regular broadcast radio is the variety of available formats and the way the broadcaster formats and sets up the broadcast. Because these stations don't require the federal license that the broadcast radio station must have, you generally find many more of them. It's like the difference between the broadcast networks and the exponentially larger number of cable channels. This allows for broadcasters to more narrowly target their audience with specialized music formats. Dub reggae? Check! The heaviest of the heavy metal? Check! Lawrence Welk? Well, I haven't gone looking for it, but I'm sure one is out there somewhere.

These songs are also sent out over the "airwaves" of the Internet in a variety of ways. You may find a disc jockey playing songs live over the Internet, just like broadcast radio (it's most likely a machine spinning the tunes on broadcast radio right now, but that's a whole different story). This is most likely the case when broadcast radio stations are converting their on-air broadcasts to Internet streams. However, most Internet broadcasts are labors of love and not professional ventures. Therefore, you're probably getting either a live DJ for a little time and taped broadcasts the rest of the time — or a glorified media player playlist. You can even get "smart" radio stations that take your preferences and convert that information into a radio broadcast that's tailored to your desires.

A few factors are associated with streaming broadcasts. They involve the quality of the broadcast, the format of the broadcast, and what software you have to use to access the broadcast. Notice that I didn't mention the type of network connection that you need to get the broadcast. In this case, I'm afraid that dialup networks over telephone modems are simply not an option. Even at the highest rate possible over regular phone lines (around 52 Kbps — unfortunately, you can't use the full potential of your 56K modem), audio dropouts and backed-up streaming audio are bound to occur. Just think of it as a radio station that's just out of range of your car stereo. You'll likely just become too frustrated with the intermittent sound. A DSL (digital subscriber line), high-speed cable, or Ethernet connection (available at most businesses and schools) is required for listening to streaming Internet broadcasts.

Running it through the pipeline

The quality of a radio broadcast depends on the amount of audio data being sent over the Internet at any one time. As I explain in Chapter 1, the quality of the audio depends primarily on the amount of data being sent per second in the stream. (The quality of the song depends entirely on who's performing it, and technology has yet to find a way to perfect that.) Therefore, a song that's being streamed at 128 kilobits per second (Kbps) is going to sound better than the same song streamed at 96 Kbps or lower. The amount of times the song is sampled per second also makes a difference. A song sampled at a rate of 44.1 kHz (the standard CD rate) sounds better than the same song sampled at 22 kHz.

The sample rate of the song is the amount of times per second information is gathered about the audio being encoded. More samples equal more detail, which equals better sound.

The station's format

Just like you must have a radio (or a set of braces set on your teeth just right) to listen to any broadcasts, you must have some sort of media player set to receive the Internet streaming broadcast. The trick here is that, due to the various formats in which audio can be encoded, you'll run across several players in your search for the perfect station.

Most stations have several options available to you. For example, a radio station may offer three different formats — Windows Media Player, Real Player, or streaming MP3 (which can be used by most any media player). From there, the radio station could break it down into high-, medium-, and low-speed broadcasts so that you can tailor what you hear to your system.

While you should still pay more attention to the speed of the broadcast than the format, the type of encoding used still plays a role in how you listen to the station. At this point, it becomes a matter of the software you have available.

Tuning in your software

Most radio stations offer options to default to your standard media player. Just navigate to the broadcast's site, select the right logo, and you're on your way. Windows Media Player, iTunes, and the other major software players even have specific views written in to them that allow you to access Internet broadcasts directly from the player itself, as illustrated by Windows Media Player and iTunes in Figures 8-1 and 8-2, respectively.

However, some radio stations may require you to download either their own proprietary software or a plug-in to use with your software to allow listening to their broadcasts. This type of download is most often tailored to that station's specific needs and isn't of use to you for listening to other stations.

Be careful when downloading software from a source with which you're unfamiliar. You may get more than you bargained for. Programmers can include additional information in the software, from cookies that anonymously track your listening preferences to full-blown viruses, without your knowledge. The best way to protect yourself is to keep your virus protection up to date (you *do* have virus protection, right?), heed Microsoft's warnings to load its latest security patches, and only download software that you're sure you want and has proven to be safe.

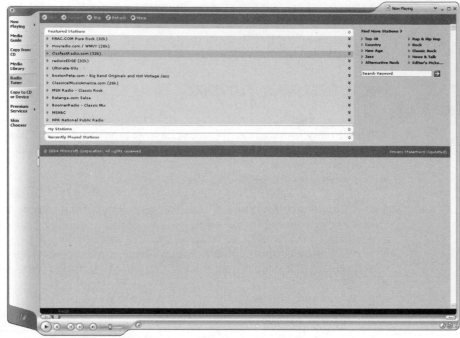

Figure 8-1:
Internet
radio in
Windows
Media
Player.

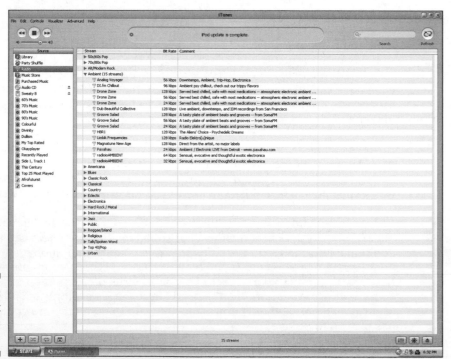

Figure 8-2:
Internet
radio in
iTunes.

But Wait, There's More!

Because of the technology used in streaming Internet broadcasts, more information is available to you than just the name of the song, the weather, and a wacky DJ's take on those lovable scamps in Congress. At the very least, you may be able to get the name of the song and the artist while you're listening to the song. No more suffering because you don't know the name of that catchy new tune (I searched incessantly for one song's title every time I heard it for six months — true story). One of my favorite radio stations used to keep a running tab of songs that it had played in the last half-hour or so.

Some stations also have ordering information or additional information about the artist. This is especially the case for those Web sites that are trying to sell music or downloads and are using Internet radio to preview the music. Broadcasts can also link to the artist's Web sites, associated fan sites, or similar artists you may enjoy. Basically, depending on how much programming the broadcaster wants to attach to the media player, it's possible to convey just about anything along with the Webcast.

Turn Up the Radio

So what are you in the mood for? The Internet has a tremendous amount of options available for the curious radio listener. Use the following steps and start with Windows Media Player to begin hearing what the Internet has to offer:

1. **Open Windows Media Player from the Start menu and select Radio Tuner from the menu along the left side of the screen.**

   This brings up the broadcast view.

2. **Type in the genre or artist you're looking for in the Search box on the right side of the player window, and click the Search button.**

   Alternatively, you could choose a station from Microsoft's featured list on the left. In this case, I'll test my statement from earlier and see if I can find a Lawrence Welk radio station (I'm a glutton for punishment).

3. **Select a radio station from the list that's returned by Windows Media Player.**

   Well, what do you know? In Figure 8-3, you see several stations that cater to your schmaltzy polka needs.

Figure 8-3:
The past
meets the
future in
Windows
Media
Player.

If you can't find what you're looking for, try entering different keywords and see what you get. You're more likely to find popular acts than obscure treasures, but anything is worth a shot. Be aware that in some cases, you may have to register with a site or pay a membership premium to get access to the station. You may also have to sift through advertisements that help pay for the maintenance and management of the site. Nothing is totally free, even on the Internet.

So what if you can't find anything in your media player? You always have the old standby of Google — surf over to www.google.com and enter what you're looking for along with the keyword "radio" or "broadcast."

One-Stop Radio Shopping

So far, I've covered how to find Internet radio broadcasts via your media player or the station's individual Web site. You may want to investigate the other available services that consolidate several stations into one site. This is usually the domain of large corporations and businesses, so it may seem counter to the independent spirit of the Internet. Still, it's possible to find some gems.

Microsoft, Yahoo, AOL, and other companies offer sites that host several different music streams that appeal to a more massive audience. Instead of seeking out a single station, you use one of these services to find what you're looking for. After the service's search engine has returned the results, you "tune in" that station and listen to your heart's content.

Again, these services can cover several genres of music, making it more likely that you'll find what you want. But you're also more likely to run into membership registration requirements or even monthly fees. After the bloom fell off of the late '90s Internet rose, very little is free anymore.

In the following sections, I take a look four major services. Three are owned by major Internet companies, and one services more independent listening options.

Live365

This service (`http://live365.com`) also spans the globe to bring you almost every imaginable Internet broadcast. It does require a player download, which can be inconvenient. You also have to put up with some advertisements, because this service picks up the costs of broadcasting many independent radio stations on the Internet. You do get variety, though, and that should keep you more than entertained. Live365 also provides the ability to set up your own Internet radio station. I discuss this topic in the section "Making Your Own Internet Radio Station," later in this chapter.

Paying the piper

Internet broadcasts have to put up with some of the same costs that regular radio stations do. To play music, broadcasters have to pay licensing fees to groups (like ASCAP and BMI) that collect and distribute money to the artists who created the music. It's a great benefit to artists (who deservedly collect on their creative effort), but it also puts a chilling effect on many of the smaller Internet broadcasters who were unable to pay the licensing fees after the courts decided to enforce collection. Consequently, you find fewer radio stations on the Internet today than in the heyday of the late '90s. Many larger stations pulled their broadcasts off the Web to avoid dealing with additional licensing fees, and smaller Webcasters just turned off their computers. However, companies like Live365 have begun to pay these costs (turning over some of the additional fees to their members) and continue broadcasting over the Internet. It's more expensive, but Internet radio is still going strong.

Radio@Netscape

If you're an AOL customer, you have unlimited access to this service (`www.netscape.net`). It provides over 150 channels devoted to artists, genres, and other musical conglomerations. It does require a player download, however, so don't expect it to interface with your media player of choice. If you're not a member of AOL, you have to deal with limited listening time. You also have to put up with some advertisements. Still, if you're looking for a large variety, this is a good place to start.

Shoutcast

Despite the similar name, no association exists between this and Yahoo's broadcast service. Visit Shoutcast at `http://winamp.com`. This service operates through the Winamp media player, but it operates more like a network of stations than just the offerings you can find through most media players. Shoutcast acts as a clearinghouse, not only for radio stations but also for anyone who is set up to transmit audio over the Internet. You can find just about anything here from around the world. It's like a much cooler version of HAM radio, and you don't have to isolate yourself in a booth with all kinds of whirring gadgets to hear it.

Yahoo Launchcast

This service (`http://yahoo.com`) is a little more interactive than AOL's radio offering. You can listen to the channels and rate the songs as they're played. This allows the service to track your likes and dislikes and tailor a radio broadcast to you. It's certainly easier than trusting that wacky lunchtime DJ who's allegedly taking requests. Launchcast has several basic channels, and an additional membership fee allows access to more-obscure offerings. It also doesn't require the download of any player. You do get advertisements, though.

Making Your Own Internet Radio Station

Yes, I once made a crystal radio out of a kit purchased from a children's museum and was quite happy when I finally got it working, hearing the sound of the local AM radio station coming over the headphones that I had connected. I even worked briefly for that radio station later in life, handling its Sunday morning broadcasts of religious programming while I was in high school. It was fun, but I never got to play what I wanted to. And it's a dirty little secret of broadcast radio that the DJs don't get to pick what they play — it's more likely determined by a radio consultant or corporate team far away from the actual radio station.

So for those of us who have always wanted to program our own radio station and share the music we love with the world, the Internet is the chance of a lifetime. By setting up your own Internet radio station, you call the shots — aside from any advertisements that may get inserted by broadcast services or hosting companies you use. As I note in the sidebar, "Paying the piper," costs have to be paid, and someone has to pony up the dough. If you're willing to pay up, though, you have the opportunity to make your own radio station.

Several services can provide streaming radio services for a price, but I'm going to concentrate on using Live365 here for one simple reason: It's a legal service that keeps all the loose ends tied up for you. If you follow its membership agreement, you don't have to worry about straying outside the bounds of legal broadcasting. From licensing fees to being compliant with government regulations, you have a lot of stuff to keep track of. This service allows you to concentrate on the fun part of broadcasting — playing the songs.

Getting started

The first step is getting over to the Live365 site and selecting Create Your Own Broadcast from the front page. This takes you to the sales area, where you can choose the broadcast package you want to purchase (again, everything has its price). Unless your name ends with Clear Channel, you should probably consider the individual packages over the professional variety. At the time of this writing, the basic individual package was $9.95 a month, and the advanced packages started at $14.95 a month. The level you want depends on a few factors, which I describe in the following sections.

Server space

You have to upload your music to the Live365 servers to broadcast it over the Internet. The basic package starts with 100MB — that's about one-seventh of the size of a data CD. While that doesn't sound like much, remember that you're required to use MP3 files encoded at 56 Kbps, or files encoded at 64 Kbps with the MP3Pro format (a proprietary form of MP3 that includes digital-rights-management encoding). At an average of 3–4MB, that's about two to three hours worth of programming — a decent-sized radio show. As you pay more, you get more space.

Number of listeners

Regular radio stations don't have to worry about how many people are listening to their stations. The signal is strewn out to the ether, and the number of people listening doesn't affect the quality of the sound. The more listeners, the better.

Unfortunately, this is not the case for Internet broadcasting. The more listeners your station has (meaning the more computers that are drawing information off the Live365 server), the more Internet bandwidth is used, and the more cost is incurred. Therefore, Live365 puts a cap on the amount of listeners you can have at any one time. When this limit is reached, no more additional listeners are allowed until someone disconnects.

Is it live?

As you can imagine, it's much easier to handle a pre-taped radio playlist than it is to transmit something in real time. Live365 has proprietary software that allows a live broadcast, but it's more demanding on the company's resources. Therefore, the more basic packages don't allow live broadcasts, and those that do have a more restrictive limit on the number of listeners who are allowed to tune in.

Advertising

Even on the Internet, you can't get away from advertisements. To pay the bills, Live365 inserts advertisements into your broadcast to reach your listeners. As an individual broadcaster, note that you can't sell your own advertisements, either — this is strictly your amateur hour. Be prepared to deal with it.

Repetition

The Digital Millennium Copyright Act (DMCA) passed by Congress was meant to block the illegal transmission of music and other digital media over the Internet, among other things. Live365's attempt to comply with these regulations includes restrictions on how often you can repeat songs or play tracks from the same album or collection of songs. This is meant to keep broadcasters from transmitting an entire album or anthology and allowing others to tape or otherwise copy the material. You are also prohibited from playing songs within an hour of a listener contacting you with a request. ("I'm sorry, Bob from Topeka, we'll get to 'Wichita Lineman' as soon as Congress says it's okay!")

Pay close attention to the membership agreement, and follow those directions closely. The Live365 software helps prevent this occurrence. Note that this may limit the amount of times your broadcast can play, if you're using one of the small-bandwidth broadcasting packages.

Programming

For simplicity's sake, I'll assume here that you'll be uploading a playlist of songs to the Live365 servers. You can choose to do a live broadcast if you want — and if you have a fast and hardy computer. Remember that sending out audio playback in real time over a network is a demanding activity. You must have a system that's capable of handling the strain. Still, most of the tips I present here are useful regardless of whether you broadcast live or submit a playlist. The playlist is just for simplicity's sake.

Picking your material

The important factor here is figuring out what you want to share with the small segment of the masses that connect to your station. Before you begin, think about what you want to play. Does a common theme run through your choices? For example, if you like country music, you may want to start with songs from your favorite artist that folks don't get to hear that often. Or you may want to choose songs around a theme — love, an upcoming holiday, songs that remind you of the color green, or whatever you think is appropriate.

Take your listeners into account as well. Unless you become the next Internet sensation, the people listening to you will probably be those you know or those who just happen to wander in. Either way, think about what they want to listen to as well. The Internet allows you to be quite self-indulgent ("I love Britney Spears, so I'm going to play nothing but her love songs for the next *18 hours!*"), but people will only read or tune in to something if they find it interesting or entertaining. The same old thing probably won't attract many listeners.

Encoding your material

Live365 requires you to upload your music in MP3 format at 56 Kbps or lower. You can alternately use music encoded with MP3Pro at 64 Kbps or less. Most audio experts place 56-Kbps files somewhere near FM radio quality — not as good as the original recording, but better than AM. Not only does this save space on the Live365 servers, but the lower encoding rate also discourages unauthorized recording.

Don't think that you have to upload only music, though. If you want to say something about the music in between songs or introduce your broadcast, just use a microphone plugged in to your sound card and record what you say with one of the audio programs that I describe in Chapter 6. (You're probably going to have to use one in any case to convert your files into MP3 format, because Windows Media Player doesn't encode to MP3 without the use of a software plug-in.) You can convert your voice recording into an MP3 file and put it in the playlist with your music. You don't even have to use an annoying broadcasting voice.

Uploading your files

When you have everything ready to go, use the Live365 software to put everything on the server. Live365 has made this as easy as possible, but one sticking point is that you must sign a licensing statement for each track you put on the servers. This just ensures that you're not putting illegal or bootlegged material up for broadcast. Everything you play should either be yours (that is, you wrote and created it, and by default gave yourself permission to use it) or licensed through ASCAP, BMI, or SESAC to ensure that the correct royalties are paid to the artists.

Adding the details

You should give your station a title and some descriptive details. This ensures that people who run across your station know what they're getting into when they click the Play button. Be complete and accurate in the fields that Live365 provides for your station. Remember, a database performs better with more information. It allows better searching and categorization. Most people will search for your station based on name or genre, with the bandwidth being a secondary concern.

The future of the Future of Rock and Roll

One radio station exemplifies both the lessening of choice in traditional broadcast media and the rise of Internet broadcasting. I used to live close to a radio station called WOXY (best known for having its tag line of "97X – BAMMM! The Future of Rock and Roll" repeated ad infinitum by Dustin Hoffman in "Rainman") that featured alternative artists in a regular rotation with specialty weekend programming that covered everything from reggae to techno. Best of all, it was owned locally and it managed to steer clear of the major battles fought over big radio playlists. It was a source for hearing great new music that may not otherwise be broadcast on commercial radio.

Although I moved out of WOXY's regular broadcasting range after a few years, I was still able to listen to the station over the Internet. The station transferred its on-air broadcast to the Internet in a variety of formats, including WMA, Real, and MP3. It quickly earned a reputation, and soon its on-air dedications went from towns around Oxford and Cincinnati, Ohio, to all over the nation and the world.

Unfortunately, economics caught up with the station's independent owners, and they decided to sell their license to another company. However, they retained the rights to the Web site, their slogan, and most importantly, their entire library of music. After some uncertain times and much demand by the station's faithful followers, a pair of sponsors emerged to help finance the transfer of the station and its image from broadcasting to Internet streaming. By the time this book is published, 97X – The Future of Rock and Roll is back up and broadcasting to a virtual world, keeping its identity intact and still providing a valuable introduction of music to its loyal listeners.

To hear what I'm talking about, check out www.woxy.com.

Part III
Goin' Mobile: Taking Your Songs on the Road

The 5th Wave   By Rich Tennant

"Why can't you just bring your iPod like everyone else?"

In this part . . .

When you're ready to take your music out of the house, you'll need a portable digital audio player. These next few chapters show you similarities and differences between portable audio players. By the time you're done, you'll be able to pick the portable player that's best for you.

You'll also learn how to transfer and organize your music. By using playlists, you'll be able to get the most out of your music.

Chapter 9

Choosing an Okay Player

I think if I'm separated from music for longer than an hour or so, I may go through withdrawal. It's just such an important part of my life that I like to have it available wherever I go. You may not share my addiction (it's probably best if you don't — it's not healthy), but being able to take your music along with you is a benefit that most people are looking for.

The Sony Walkman first made such personal music transport possible, and the portable CD player upgraded the personal music experience with both the convenience of quickly selecting tracks and the better sound quality. Still, the device was limited to carrying one recording at any one time. You could pack around more than one cassette or CD, but that bulk could add up quickly. You could also lose your recordings. (Can you imagine the heartbreak of losing a huge binder of CDs, both in the cost and the time and effort needed to replace them, and dealing with that hassle?) In short, these devices were convenient, but you still had to deal with some problems.

Enter the portable audio player. These devices take the audio files you've already been introduced to and take them off your computer, putting them into a small box you can carry around with you and listen to whenever you choose. This allows you to protect your original recordings and use safe and legal copies, carry around a lot more music than was possible before, and put all of that in a package much smaller than the devices that preceded it. You also get many more benefits, including the ability to categorize and organize files and a readout of all the information pertinent to the song. It's a new way of making your music portable.

I should also note here that I'm using the generic term *portable audio player* to describe these devices. You may have gotten used to hearing these devices called *MP3 players* when that was the dominant form of audio file in use. However, these devices can now handle more than just the MP3 standard. In fact, the dominant music download service at this writing (iTunes) uses the AAC format; this is the audio layer of the MPEG-4 standard, which offers higher audio quality than MP3. Most players can also handle formats like WMA, Ogg Vorbis, and so on. Therefore, I'll use the term *portable audio player* as a generic catchall to include all the variations of devices that follow the same mission — to take digital audio and put it in a small, portable playback device.

One, Two, Three Types of Players

Although they perform the same basic function, media players come in three distinct types. These players all have different benefits and drawbacks due to their construction and the memory type used for storing the media. In the following sections, I take a look at the three types of players and explain what makes each one unique.

Hard drive players

So far, you've only dealt with hard drives as a component of your computer. They are the massive storage devices that reside inside the computer's tower (or are connected to the tower by a FireWire or USB cable) and hold all the data on your computer while it's not being used. It's basically a huge filing cabinet.

Remember that manufacturers are always trying to make things smaller and more functional, however. One expression of this is the hard drive portable audio player. This device takes a miniature hard drive and places it inside a case that also includes *firmware memory* (the memory that carries the instructions for how to operate the player and find the files on the hard drive) and *audio playback hardware* (the circuits that feed the audio signal to the headphones). The iPod, as shown in Figure 9-1, is a popular example of a portable hard drive audio player.

Benefits

The major advantage of this is the sheer amount of data you can pack into such a small package. No other portable audio player can hold the sheer amount of data that a hard drive player can. These devices usually measure memory in gigabytes; at the time of this writing, portable hard drive audio players can handle from 5GB to 60GB worth of material.

Figure 9-1:
The iPod
media
player.

Again, it's important to remember that manufacturers and computer scientists measure gigabytes in different ways. Because the computers are built on the theories of the computer scientists, this basically means that you end up with slightly less data than what was listed on the box. Formatting the hard drive also takes up some of its space. As an example, just after my personal 20GB iPod was formatted but before I loaded any music, it showed 18.5GB of usable space.

Hard drive players are also capable of taking information from your computer in the form of playlists and the information tags attached to the audio files. The player can organize the files according to the same tags the media player uses, and you can select files by artists, genres, or other identifying tags. Again, this sounds simple, but hard drive players can accommodate thousands of songs — you should be able to find your songs with a minimum amount of hassle.

Many hard drive players also carry additional features like computer games or the ability to show basic information like calendars, notes, or contacts. You can also use these devices as portable storage drives. Most of them can handle documents, pictures, and other files as well as digital music. Connect one to a computer, and you can read and transfer files like any other storage device. This function takes up storage space as well, and some players cannot play digital music that has been loaded as a file instead of through the media player.

Drawbacks

The primary difference between hard drive players and the other classes of portable audio players is price. Because of the technology involved and the size (small hard drives with a large capacity are more expensive), these devices start at around $200 and can cost as much as $500. This can be cost prohibitive for some budgets. Unless you need to carry around a huge amount of music with you, the cost could make you want to look elsewhere. Just remember that the cost per GB of hard drive memory is much lower than the cost per GB of flash memory.

Hard drives can also be very sensitive. Obviously, the manufacturers took this into account when building their products and took every opportunity to shockproof these devices. Still, an excessive amount of jostling or dropping could make the hard drive skip (if that doesn't damage the unit first). And if the hard drive gets damaged, it's time to get a new player. Hopefully your warranty will cover it, but this isn't the case for older hard drive players.

Battery life has been a sticky point of contention for some hard drive players. Most notorious has been Apple's iPod, which attracted attention for having defective batteries that aren't user-replaceable. These are the same type of batteries that are used in cell phones, personal digital assistants (PDAs), and other rechargeable devices. Still, six to eight hours may not provide enough play time if you're going to be away from an electrical outlet or computer without an opportunity to recharge the unit. Some devices have logged up to 15 hours of battery life, but such limits depend on how often you use the unit and what functions you use while playing it — for example, setting playback to random or frequently using additional features on the device.

Who this player is made for

If you have enough money and want to carry a wide variety or large quantity of music around with you, a hard drive player would be a great choice. You should also look into the additional features a hard drive player offers and see if those would be beneficial as well. As more online music stores are tying their services to the use of hard drive players, this is a good choice if you're planning to buy music online.

Flash media players

This category of players uses a different type of memory than the hard drive players. As opposed to using a spinning magnetic disc, this device uses stationary media similar to RAM to store the files. The player accesses the songs from this memory and plays them back. The memory can either be stored in the device or added to the player via an external card.

In some respects, these types of players are similar to hard drive portable audio players. You connect them to a computer via a USB or FireWire cable, and you transfer files to them via either your media player or the portable audio player's proprietary software. That's about where the similarities end, though. In many other aspects, these are totally different animals. A flash memory audio player is shown in Figure 9-2.

Figure 9-2:
The Rio
Chiba flash
memory
portable
audio
player.

Benefits

These are usually the smallest players available on the market. Because they don't use memory that takes up a large amount of physical space, it's possible to condense the players to a couple inches in size. If you don't want to worry about carrying something large around with you, this type of player could work for you.

Flash memory is also very durable. You should be able to move the player around and jostle it without fear of it skipping or getting damaged. Computers can also access it like any other memory. If the player allows it, you can put files on it in a manner similar to the hard drive portable media players. Finally, flash memory can easily be increased. If the player allows the use of smart cards or other removable memory, you can put over 1GB of additional memory on the player and carry around that much more music.

These players also cost less than the hard drive portable audio players. Whereas hard drive players usually start at around $200, flash players begin at less than $100. If you're just concerned with getting into portable digital audio for a smaller amount of money, this type of player should work for you.

Drawbacks

While the flash portable audio player is small and portable, it also offers the least amount of built-in memory. At this writing, the internal memory of a flash player tops out at about 512MB, and most players start out with 64–128MB. Some have the expansion slots I talked about earlier, but even with those slots, this type of player pales in comparison to the storage space offered by the hard drive players. This is okay if you only want to carry around a few albums' worth of music with you, but you'll be disappointed if you digitize your entire collection.

Because they're small and compact, flash players may be a little harder to control than the larger hard drive players. The controls and screens are smaller, and it could be a difficult go for those of us with poor vision or big sausage fingers (like me). They can also feel a little less stable than the hard drive players just because they are made more inexpensively.

These players tend to offer fewer features than the hard drive players. Don't expect to find any calendar functions or games on this type of player. This is a device devoted only to playing music, and space allows for little of anything else. The small size also means that you probably won't get an internal recharge able battery with the player. You'll have to keep buying AA or AAA batteries to power your device.

Who this player is made for

Flash players are a natural marriage with the active lifestyle. The small size and weight make it perfect for those on the move, and because it's likely to be used for only a couple hours at a time in those situations, the smaller memory isn't likely to be a factor. You spend more time shuttling files back and forth between the player and the computer, but that's a small price to pay for the other benefits.

MP3 CD Players

You've seen a portable CD player before, and these types of portable audio players look like their regular counterparts. However, this type of player has additional capabilities beyond the standard player. The MP3 CD player can still play regular audio CDs, but it can also play data CDs that carry digital audio files. At 700MB per CD, you can hold the entire catalog of some artists on one CD. This vastly improves the amount of music you can carry with you at one time.

Some players (mainly those made by Sony) use a format called MiniDisc, or MD. These discs are significantly smaller than CDs and use a different encoding scheme, but you can still store a great deal of music on these discs. It's also easier to carry a larger number of small discs around.

MiniDisc is a proprietary format of Sony. You might see small CDs floating around that play in regular CD players — these are not MiniDiscs. They're just smaller CDs that hold less data and are often distributed as novelty or promotional items. If it doesn't say MiniDisc on it, it's not playable in a Sony MiniDisc player.

Benefits

The MP3 CD player can be the least expensive portable digital audio player. Models start at under $40, and even the most expensive models usually top out at about $100. If you're comfortable with portable CD players and want to get going with digital audio at the smallest price, this is the way to go.

You also don't need to install proprietary software on your computer to use the MP3 CD player. Just burn the files to disc and you're ready to go. You're also only limited by the amount of CDs you can carry around with you. Put 20 CDs in a binder, and you have 14GB worth of storage.

These players can also handle either audio or data CDs. You can carry around a data CD full of digital audio, but you also don't have to wait until you get home and digitize an audio CD to listen to it. This is a versatile player when it comes to dealing with CDs.

Drawbacks

These are the largest players on the market, simply because they have to accommodate a CD or MiniDisc to function. This size is coupled with the fact that to gain the benefits of increased variety, you have to carry around more discs. This can get bulky, and you can still lose music that you don't have backed up on some other source.

These players often offer skip protection — that is, the player reads ahead and stores music so that if the disc starts skipping, it can continue playback uninterrupted for a minute or two. Still, if you're very active or in a place where a lot of vibration exists, this could be less than adequate. This type of player is more likely to skip or stall than the other players.

CDs can also be easily damaged compared to flash or hard drive storage. Normal use can result in scratches or smudges, which can cause playback problems. Unless you're careful, you may end up cleaning the CDs or skipping scratched tracks. MP3 CD files can carry song information with them, but it's more difficult to transmit the playlists or other track configurations with them. You're pretty much stuck with the order the files are burned in, coupled with a shuffle or random play function.

Who this player is made for

If you don't mind size or carrying around multiple discs, this is an inexpensive way to listen to digital audio files. Also, if you're already familiar with portable CD players and want to stick with that design, you can retain that familiarity with these players.

A Three-Album Tour

Aside from the difference in storage media, flash and hard drive players share characteristics that are common to all portable digital audio players. I'm going to use one of the most popular players to illustrate these functions, but you should know that most of these features are standard on all the players. With that said, I'll start the tour of Apple's iPod, the most popular portable digital audio player on the market today.

Playing your song

Turn on the iPod, and you're greeted with a menu that shows your initial choices for what to play (see Figure 9-3). You can start with playlists you've generated on the computer (the iPod even features a playlist you can create on the go for additional selection while you're away from your computer), you can browse the songs you've loaded, or you can work with the extra functions or change the settings.

Figure 9-3:
The iPod's
opening
screen.

Check out the Browse function, where you can choose from all the songs you've loaded. The iPod lists songs by artist, albums, songs, genres, and composers. Other players may use similar categories, or they could use other identifying labels like bit rate, file format, and so on. You'll probably use the first four characteristics most often, although you could find the Composer field very valuable if you're a fan of classical music and want to find your library of Bach recordings. Browse by genre, as shown in Figure 9-4, and see what you can find.

Okay, you've decided you want to listen to some go-go music. Remember "Da Butt"? That's go-go music. The iPod allows you to choose from all the tracks listed under that genre (see Figure 9-5), or it allows you to pick any artist that has songs listed under that genre. Any old track is fine with me, so select All and go to a list of songs. The iPod plays that list of songs and then returns to the main menu for further instructions.

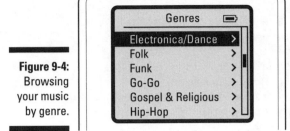

Figure 9-4:
Browsing
your music
by genre.

This process is similar to playing music from any field or playlist, so you should be able to follow a similar path to get what you want. The iPod uses buttons and a thumb wheel to navigate these menus, but other hard drive players may use a rotary wheel or a joystick to move around and find files. These controls also allow you to fast-forward or move back through tracks, go to a specific point in a song, or open menus to make additional selections.

Figure 9-5:
Choosing a
song from
the song list.

Changing your settings

Hard drive portable digital audio players include similar features, like a shuffle or random play function, screen settings, and sound equalization (EQ) functions. Again, I'll illustrate this on an iPod, but these functions are similar on most hard drive and flash players. Select Settings from the main menu, and you see the screen shown in Figure 9-6.

You have your EQ set currently on Jazz, but you're getting ready to listen to some dance music, and you want your EQ settings tailored to that genre of music. Therefore, select EQ and change the EQ setting to Dance, as shown in Figure 9-7.

Most players have EQ settings tailored to a genre music or a specific function, although others go with a more traditional five-band EQ setting that you can adjust manually. It all depends on the player you choose. You can follow this process to change any setting on a flash or hard drive portable audio player.

The Lineup of Players

I use this section of the book to take a look at specific players and their advantages and drawbacks. I'm taking the time to look at these features and point them out because this can represent a major investment, more than everything in this book except for the Windows XP Media Center Edition computers. It's important to understand the features you'll have and the drawbacks you may encounter.

Instead of tackling each player individually, I'm going to address each aspect of the portable audio player and then make recommendations based on the best in each category. That way, you can choose what features are important to you and go from there.

Hard drive players

Because storage and battery life are key for hard drive portable audio players, I address those concerns first. I cover these issues and some additional features in the list that follows:

- ✔ **Storage space:** If you're trying to pack your entire music collection onto one player, it's important that you have plenty of room. The size of the files also plays a part — I prefer to have my files encoded at least at 128 kilobits per second (Kbps), and preferably higher. Using lossless codecs, like the varieties pushed by both Apple and Microsoft, can eat up even more disc space. In this case, bigger is better. For that reason, I recommend the 20GB or 40GB iPod, the 20GB Dell Digital Jukebox, or the monster size of the 60GB Nomad Jukebox Zen Xtra from Creative Labs.

- ✔ **Battery life:** Eventually, all rechargeable batteries will die. It's just the nature of the beast. The question is how much life you get from them in their life spans, and how easy they are to replace when they finally do poop out. The iPod doesn't get high marks in this category. The battery carries a six- to eight-hour charge, and it's not as easily replaceable as models you can find in other devices, like cell phones. Therefore, if you're concerned about being able to play music away from a stable power source for a long time, consider players like the Creative MuVo2 or Dell Jukebox (15- to 16-hour battery life) or the Zen Xtra, which uses a disposable battery that you can easily replace.

- ✔ **Software:** Most players require some sort of proprietary software to transfer digital audio between your computer and your portable audio player (as opposed to the simple hard drive function I mentioned earlier). The integration of iPod and iTunes, along with the iTunes music store, is seamless. The Windows XP version has overcome earlier bugs and integrated everything into a neat package of ripping, transferring, and buying files. It's so easy that I may well put myself into debt using the music store. Many users also report good luck with MusicMatch software.

- ✔ **File formats:** Not every file you may want to put on your portable player will be of the same format. Converting a file to another file format can also be problematic. If you make an MP3 file out of a WAV file, you'll probably get an acceptable conversion, because you're going from a lossless audio format to a lossy compression scheme. However, if you rip files to a Windows Media format from an audio CD that were originally created from MP3 files, you can run into problems.

A *lossless* audio format doesn't lose any data when it's encoded. A *lossy* audio format sacrifices some audio data in favor of smaller file sizes — the trick is not to lose so much that it severely affects the sound of the file.

Therefore, you're going to want a player that can handle a variety of formats. MP3 and WAV formats should be a given, and AAC, Windows Media, and others are helpful add-ons. The iRiver IHP-20 and Rio Karma are favorites in this case. Both can handle the normal selection, while the iRiver also uses ASF and the relatively rare Ogg Vorbis format. The Rio uses Ogg Vorbis and FLAC (Free Lossless Audio Codec). The iPod also comes through by using AAC and Apple Lossless Codecs, which present higher audio quality than normal MP3s.

✔ **Transfer speed:** Unless the player uses USB 2.0 or FireWire to move songs and files back and forth, you're going to be sitting around for a long time. Stay away from players that still rely on USB 1.1. The iPod (which can use either format) is a winner in this category.

✔ **Ease of use:** If you have to press a lot of buttons or scroll through a lot of confusing menus, it's going to get in the way of listening to your music. You want simple controls that allow full control of your music with the minimum amount of effort. Every player has some sort of learning curve, but the iPod's interface has been universally acclaimed as a good, clean way to access and play your music. The iPod also shows up instantly when it's plugged into your computer for use as an external hard drive, whereas some other players require the use of external software that you must install before transferring files. The Dell Jukebox should also be noted for its effective controls.

✔ **Sound:** Nothing about the player matters if you don't like listening to it. This attribute is a combination of the file formats a player can use (discussed earlier) and the actual hardware that's built into the player. The iPod has received attention from normal users to audiophile experts for its quality sound. However, note that just about any portable audio player's sound can be improved by upgrading the quality of the headphones you use.

✔ **Size:** Size matters — but in this case, smaller is usually better. While you definitely want a durable player, keeping it compact can make a difference if you're moving around while listening — and isn't that what portable is for? The iPods (especially the iPod Mini) are the smallest and lightest in this category. (The Mini is almost the size of flash memory players, with about four times the storage capacity.)

✔ **Price:** Sometimes, the bottom line receives the most attention. You must be able to afford it. You should know going in that the price range for hard drive portable audio players is $200–$500. The iPods lead the portable audio players in just about every other category except this one. For buyers on a budget, look instead to the Dell Jukebox. You also get the extra feature of a built-in voice recorder.

Flash players

The main advantage of the flash memory portable audio player is size. This is the type of player to choose if you're looking for easy portability. Given the size, make sure that the user interface is easy to use and not just crammed onto the device. Storage space is also an important consideration. Consider the following items when buying a flash player:

✔ **Size:** Most players in this category are going to be tiny — it's just a question of how small the manufacturer can get it. The iRiver players are quite small, as are the key chain–style players from Creative and Phillips. The Rio Chiba is one of the wider players in the category, but it does have a shape that fits easily into the palm.

✔ **Ease of use:** Most players in this category use some sort of rocker switch or joystick to move between songs. The iRiver and Rio controls are quite easy to master, and both feature a softly glowing screen that's easy to read under all conditions.

✔ **Storage space:** Most of these players max out on memory between 256MB and 512MB, so you can't expect too much out of the on-board memory. That's why I like the Rio Chiba, which carries an expansion slot for memory cards that can expand the memory up to an additional 512MB. That goes a long way in putting a good variety of songs on your player.

✔ **Battery life:** Most of the players in this category don't rely on rechargeable batteries — instead, they use the traditional AA or AAA replaceable battery. Therefore, the battery life depends mostly on how often you use the device, as opposed to what functions you use. Buying more batteries is always a hassle, but it does have a benefit: You don't have to replace the entire unit when the battery goes dead.

✔ **Software:** You have a little more wiggle room with software on the flash memory portable audio players. If you prefer to just drag and drop files to your player without using any specific software, consider buying the Gateway DMP-310. Alternately, you may want to look at a player that interfaces directly with Windows Media Player or MusicMatch, like offerings from Phillips or Rio. The latter requires installing some additional software to make the Windows Media Player interface work, but the interface also works with the iTunes and Real players.

✔ **File formats:** This is a wash — all the players I could find handled MP3 and WMA formats with ease, but not much else. This is to be expected, though. The storage space prevents the use of WAV files or the lossless codecs.

✓ **Transfer speed:** None of the flash players I found worked off the FireWire interface, so you're looking at USB interfaces only. Again, make sure that you get one that has a USB 2.0 interface, as opposed to the older 1.1 interface. The Rio Chiba is saddled with the slower connection, whereas the iRiver iFP-390T zooms along with USB 2.0. The iRiver has the added benefit of being able to record audio through an analog line-in jack or directly from the built-in FM radio.

If your player uses USB 2.0 and the computer only supports USB 1.1 (or vice versa), your transfer speed only matches that of USB 1.1. You must have new equipment on both ends to take advantage of the additional speed that USB 2.0 provides.

✓ **Sound:** Because of the player's smaller size, you can't get very many large files on it. The sound quality will suffer accordingly. Remember, this unit is built for portability, not audiophile quality. Concentrate more on the quality of your headphones than on the player.

✓ **Price:** The price for flash memory players lands between $100 and $200, with most of the players, like the Rio Chiba and iRiver, priced squarely in the middle. Expect to pay that much for a decent model.

✓ **Extras:** Most of these players have a built-in FM radio, and some include features like a clock or stopwatch — it's handy, but not musically useful. One benefit to look for is the storage drive function. Much like hard drive players, you can put files on some flash players (like the Rio line) and use the player to transfer content between PCs.

MP3 CD players

So many players are available with this function that to address specific models is a little daunting. Furthermore, the size and functions are going to be about the same — a CD is a CD, and these players rely on buttons instead of wheels or joysticks almost universally. Instead, I'm going to give you some tips on what to look for when you're shopping for these kind of players. These tips are as follows:

✓ **Information readout:** Most CD players provide only the track number and the time. Look for one that can give you additional information, like the artist and the track name of the song you're listening to. This can be especially valuable for MP3 CDs, because you can pack quite a few files on a single disc.

✓ **Skip protection:** Nothing is more frustrating than listening to a skipping CD — given enough time, it may drive someone insane (just a personal theory; Freud doesn't back me up on that). Look for at least 45 seconds of regular audio skip protection (MP3 files should be even higher).

✔ **Price:** These portable players are priced at about $80 to $100, so you're not going to be shelling out a lot of money in any case. You can find a player as cheap as $30. This technology is easily being integrated with regular audio-playing hardware, so it doesn't add much cost to the standard portable CD player.

Common Pitfalls and Problems

People make a few common mistakes when they're dealing with hard drive and flash memory portable audio players. Everybody makes them, and you will, too. By reading the next sections, you'll be better prepared to handle the mistakes, and you'll waste less time getting back to listening to your music.

Starting off on the right foot

Follow your manufacturer's directions for starting and prepping your portable audio player when you first get it. Make sure that you install the recommended software and have the minimum required specifications for your computer to make it work. If you have everything in place in the beginning, your journey will be that much easier.

My controls aren't working!

Most likely, this means that your lock switch is on. Most players have a function that allows you to turn off the controls so that you can put the player in your pocket without worrying about accidentally turning the player off, skipping tracks, or changing the volume. It's a handy feature, but it can sometimes throw you when you first try to change something on your player. Just make sure that the lock control is off (check your owner's manual if you're unsure of where it is), and you should be back to normal.

My player doesn't turn on!

You've spent a lot of money on this player, and now you can't even get it to turn on! Relax. Your problem can probably be solved with one of a couple simple solutions. First, make sure that the lock control I previously mentioned is off. Second, make sure that you're working with a good battery. If you have a rechargeable unit, plug it in and see whether the additional power makes a difference. If you have a replaceable-battery unit, go ahead and put in a fresh battery.

You may run into a different situation, like the one that happened to me one Saturday night. I was using my iPod to provide music for a gathering of people, along with another CD player. I came back to the iPod after playing a track from a CD to find my portable audio player wouldn't turn on. The lock switch was off, but I couldn't get any response from the iPod, no matter which control I used.

Visions of technical support and warranty clauses ran through my head until I was reminded of the iPod's Reset function. The thing to remember in this case is that all operating systems and hard drives may sometimes require a reset. It's the same reason manufacturers build the function into computers and Windows XP, and hard drive players have the same function built into them. Check your user's manual for the correct reset sequence for your hard drive player. When you execute that, the player should be up and running again, with your data intact. If that doesn't work, try it again. If you're still working on it minutes later like an ER doctor working on a patient, you may want to return to those visions of technical support and warranty clauses.

My computer doesn't recognize my player!

So you've plugged your player into your computer, expecting to hear the familiar Windows XP chime of welcome for a new device. After waiting for more than a minute, nothing is there. Don't panic yet; some more simple solutions exist to getting your device working.

If your system doesn't chime to acknowledge the addition of a new external device (and you're sure you have your speakers on), the first step is to check the Safely Remove Hardware icon in the lower-right corner of your screen for the name of your external device. Double-click this icon to bring up the menu that's shown in Figure 9-8.

Figure 9-8:
Showing all connected external devices in Windows XP.

Make sure that the device isn't listed in this menu. If it's not, make sure that the USB or FireWire cable is solidly connected to both the computer and the portable audio device. Second, make sure that the portable audio device is turned on. Most computers don't recognize a device that isn't powered on when it's connected to the computer. Those two troubleshooting tips should correct the vast majority of your problems.

If your device is listed but you can't get the software to recognize your device, make sure that you've installed everything the manufacturer listed in its instructions. Without those installations, the computer can't work properly with your portable audio device.

Looking for Music in All the Weird Places

You don't have to have the latest portable audio player to listen to digital music on the go. Audio playback functions have been built into a number of devices that you may not ordinarily think about. I cover these devices in the following sections.

Personal digital assistants (PDAs)

These palm-size units incorporate most basic functions of a personal computer into a compact unit that can fit into your pocket. These units don't have a great deal of memory to devote to digital music, because much of the memory goes toward running the operating system and keeping programs and documents. Still, units that run the Windows CE operating system carry a version of Windows Media Player on them, and many can also use external memory in the form of the memory cards that I've previously discussed. With the combination of the player and the external memory, you can take a decent-sized music collection with you and enjoy the benefits of a PDA to boot.

Cellular phones

You're probably already carrying one of these devices around with you (at least, everybody I see in restaurants and bank lines is using one). Why not expand your phone's capabilities and put an MP3 player in it? Motorola, Siemens, and other manufacturers sell add-on players for about the price of a flash memory portable audio player. These players use the phone's power and take memory cards to store the music.

Some cell phones can also download music directly to the phone, either as files or as ring tones. Just be judicious in your choices of music. You don't want to hate a song just because it's what you hear every time the boss calls you at home for some unexpected overtime.

Gaming devices

You may have to poach one of these devices from your kids to test this out, but some hand-held gaming devices can also play MP3 and WMA files. If listening to music and playing video games are things you want to combine into one device, look to the Nokia N-Gage or Nintendo Game Boy Advance. The Game Boy requires some additional hardware, but both devices can handle music in addition to the latest games.

Chapter 10

Feed Me, Seymour! Transferring Songs to Your Portable Audio Player

. . . .

In This Chapter

▶ Hooking up your portable media player

▶ Moving songs between the computer and the portable media player

▶ Understanding the legal issues surrounding the transfer of media player files

. . . .

I've spent countless hours ripping music from my CD collection to my home computer for the express reason of putting it on my portable audio player. I love being able to take thousands of songs with me wherever I go and having them available anytime. I've mentioned before that I'm an addict, and I'll seek treatment soon. But I doubt I would have spent that much time ripping music if it weren't so easy and quick. A truly frustrating experience would have just driven me away, because I have very little patience for uppity computer equipment.

While it's easy to get your player connected to the computer and start the transfer of songs, it can seem like a daunting task if you haven't done it before. In this chapter, I take a look at transferring files with the Windows Media Player software that's already built into Windows XP and with some proprietary software. That way, you'll be ready for whatever comes down the road when you buy your portable audio player.

Hooking Up Your Portable Player

One way or the other, you have to get your files from your computer to your player. Both the maker of the portable audio player and third-party manufacturers make various types of connecting devices for the player. Still, it boils down to two types of connections. The player attaches to your computer via either USB or FireWire connections.

Plugging it in

Connecting USB and FireWire devices to your computer is as easy as finding the jack and plugging in the device. Both types of devices are hot-swappable — in other words, you can connect and disconnect these devices without turning your computer off. However, you must stop these devices before you unplug them. Because a small amount of current flows through these cables (both USB and FireWire cables can power devices), you can damage the computer or the device if you disconnect the device without first stopping the computer's connection to the device. The following is a simple process, but it's one you should observe each time you unplug a USB or FireWire device:

1. **Click the Safely Remove Hardware icon in the lower-right corner of your screen.**

   This icon looks like a green arrow over a grey rectangle, as shown in the lower-right corner of Figure 10-1.

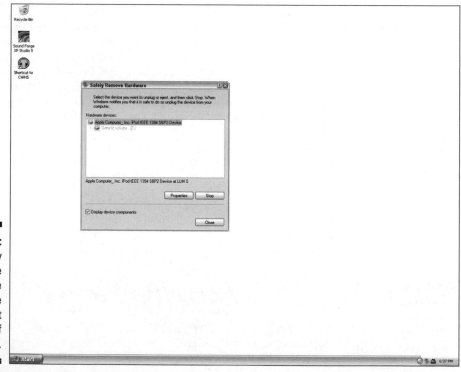

Figure 10-1:
The Safely Remove Hardware icon in the lower-right corner of the screen.

If you don't see the icon in the corner of your screen, click the gray arrow in the same area of the screen, as shown in Figure 10-1. That expands the tray and shows you all the available icons. You should now be able to see the Safely Remove Hardware icon.

2. **Find the device you want to remove from the menu that appears.**

You're choosing from a list of all the external devices connected to your computer.

3. **Select the device you want to remove, and click the Stop button.**

You'll see a message like the one shown in Figure 10-2. You can now safely remove the device from your computer.

Figure 10-2:
Ready to
remove
hardware.

USB

USB connections are common on all current computers, and most units produced within the past three years have at least one of these connections available. The jacks look like small rectangles and can be found either on the front or the back of the computer. A USB cable can only fit into a computer one way, so don't worry about putting it in wrong. If it's in, it's in right. The other end of the cable may be smaller or look differently, like the cable shown in Figure 10-3.

Figure 10-3:
The various
USB con-
nections.

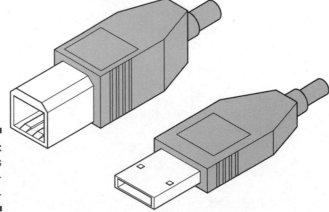

USB connections can support two transfer speeds. USB 1.1 provides the slower speed, but it's also the most common. USB 2.0 is considerably faster than both USB 1.1 and the first version of FireWire, but USB 2.0 is just now becoming standard on home computers.

FireWire

Officially known by the standard name IEEE 1394, this standardized type of connection was popularized by Apple (and renamed by Sony as iLink). Until the advent of USB 2.0, FireWire was the fastest connection available for external peripheral devices. A new and faster version of FireWire connections is now available, but it is not yet standard on home computers. FireWire connections are not usually included on PC motherboards, so you need to purchase an internal FireWire card to take advantage of this connection (shown in Figure 10-4). The standard connection is rectangular with two corners edged off, but smaller connectors and jacks can be used in the FireWire standard.

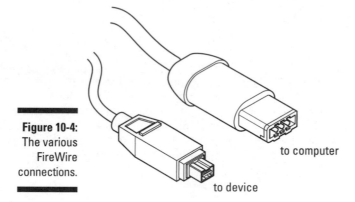

Figure 10-4:
The various
FireWire
connections.

to computer

to device

Transferring Files to Your Portable Audio Player

You can use a variety of software to manage files on your portable audio player. Many players require you to use their proprietary software, and some players interface with Windows Media Player. The first player I demonstrate works with Windows Media Player (after installing some linking software provided by the included CD — and Internet updates).

USB connections

The Rio Chiba player advertises that it's compatible with Windows Media Player, among other players. That means you can use the Copy to CD or Device tab in Windows Media Player to manage the files on your portable audio device. Follow these steps to set up the software and transfer your music files:

1. **Install *all* the software that's recommended by the manufacturer.**

   As you can see in Figure 10-5, the installation CD starts automatically on insertion. To make the Chiba work with Windows Media Player, you must install all the software and drivers on the CD, in addition to the available Internet updates. In this case, the device updated itself automatically. You may have to download software from the company's Web site as well.

Figure 10-5: Installing the new software on your computer.

Always check the manufacturer's Web site periodically to see whether any new information or updates are available for your portable audio player. These updates can help your player run better and can solve any technical problems you may have.

2. **Connect the portable audio player to your computer.**

   Make sure that the device is powered on when it's connected so that the computer can recognize it.

3. **Open Windows Media Player, and click the Copy Music to CD or Device tab.**

   This brings up the view that allows Windows Media Player to transfer files.

4. **Select your device from the drop-down menu in the upper-left corner of the screen.**

   As you can see in Figure 10-6, I've selected Rio Chiba from the menu, and Windows Media Player lists all the available folders.

5. **Select the music that you want to transfer to your player using the drop-down menu in the upper-left corner of Windows Media Player.**

   I've chosen a file that's included with every version of Windows Media Player 9. You can also choose files from your My Music folder or any other location on your computer.

6. **Click the Copy button in the upper-right corner of Windows Media Player.**

   This transfers the files from your computer to the portable audio device.

7. **Check the menu on the right side of the screen to make sure that all the songs made it to the device.**

   As shown in Figure 10-7, you can see the file is now on the Rio Chiba. You may now disconnect the device (making sure to stop it using the Safely Remove Hardware icon if necessary) and take your music on the road.

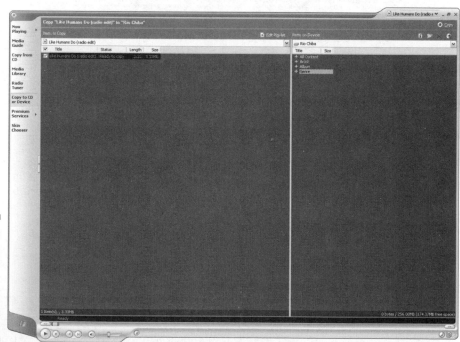

Figure 10-6: Copying music to your portable audio player.

Figure 10-7:
The
completed
transfer
process.

FireWire connections

In this case, I'm going to show you how to use one of the most popular media players (iTunes) with the FireWire cradle that's included with the iPod portable media player. Because of the close connection between iTunes and the iPod, the transfer process is even quicker. It can be a drawback, though, if you don't like to use the software that's associated with the portable media player. Choose your players carefully. Follow these steps to install the software and transfer your music files:

1. **Install *all* the software provided by your manufacturer.**

   Starting to sound repetitious, isn't it? iTunes also automatically updates when you make an Internet connection. When the installation and update are finished, activate iTunes. You then see a screen similar to what's shown in Figure 10-8.

2. **Connect the FireWire cable to your computer.**

   The iPod can also connect to a computer via a USB 2.0 connection, but it's preferable to use FireWire. This not only connects the device, but it also charges the iPod's battery while it's connected. If you have a docking station, you can also connect it to the cable at this time.

Figure 10-8:
iTunes in
Windows
XP.

3. **Connect the iPod to the docking station or cable.**

   The computer should recognize the device, and it will show up on the left menu of iTunes.

4. **Right-click the iPod, and select Update Songs, as shown in Figure 10-9.**

   This automatically syncs the songs in your iTunes library with the iPod. You may also change the options to update the iPod automatically, or you can manually drag the songs that you want to the device.

5. **Right-click the iPod, and select Eject.**

   This allows you to disconnect the device from the computer. Note that the Eject command is followed by the name you gave the device when you first loaded it (the name I gave mine is a long story).

You have to stop or eject any device from your computer before physically disconnecting the device to avoid damaging any components.

Figure 10-9:
Updating
the iPod in
iTunes.

Legal Concerns

So after you've transferred files from your computer to your portable audio device, can you copy files from your portable player to another computer? That depends.

The iPod allows the files to be stored on the player, but it doesn't allow them to be moved to another computer. It also restricts the amount of times you can burn the file or share it among computers. Other devices may allow you to transfer freely, but files that you've purchased from online services may have copy protection that prevent them from being transferred to another system.

As long as the files remain in your possession, it's not going to be a problem. Just remember that you have to retain your original copy of the files — you can't sell that and keep the copies.

Part IV
Quiet in the Studio

The 5th Wave   By Rich Tennant

MIXING THE FIRST
"RUDE AUDIENCE" CD

© RICH TENNANT

"I laid down a general shuffling sound, over dubbed with periodic coughing, some muted talking files, and an awesome ringing cell phone loop."

In this part . . .

*I*f you've got a song to sing (and record), these next few chapters will help you get that song on disc. You'll learn about setting up a digital audio workstation's hardware and software, and you'll also pick up on the basics of how to use these devices and programs.

Once you've got that down, you'll learn what goes in to mixing your music and laying the songs down on CD (or even the Internet). It's never been easier to get your music heard.

Chapter 11

Building Your Studio

*W*hether you're a serious independent musician looking to record a masterpiece or just a hobbyist who likes to jot down the occasional tune, this is an exciting time. Audio-recording technology that used to be available only to pro-level studios has been digitized and placed in the hands of the common artist (well, as "common" as artists can be expected to be). This gives someone who wants to record his or her music both the power and the opportunity to make it happen. Not only is the gear there, but it's also cheaper than renting out a hundred-dollar-an-hour recording studio.

No amount of technology can make you the next Phil Spector if you don't have the musical ideas already in you. However, the technology makes it easier for you to get these ideas recorded and made public. It's like getting a new Porsche after trading in your old Pinto. You get there a lot faster with the sports car, but you still have to know how to drive.

This chapter shows you how to get your computer up and running as a simple recording studio, including taking a look at hardware and connections. For more in-depth information on home recording, I recommend checking out *Home Recording For Musicians For Dummies,* by Jeff Strong (published by Wiley).

Putting Your Studio in the Box

Take a look at the interior of a recording studio. If you've never seen one, use your favorite search engine to look up a picture of the control room of a major studio. It looks a little complicated, doesn't it? All the boxes and lights and wires trailing all over the place can be enough to make the most curious techie go blank. So many tools and toys all over the place can make it hard to know where to start.

The good news is that you don't have to deal with this when you set up your computer. You can get software that virtually takes the place of the equipment you see in the recording studio. With your computer and a couple hardware additions, you'll have a home recording setup in no time. It won't be Abbey Road, but it can work for what you need from it.

Make sure that your computer can meet the needs of home recording. This goes far beyond the minimum operating requirements set forth by Microsoft for Windows XP or the manufacturer of the audio software you choose to install. Remember that recording audio is one of the most demanding applications you can run on a computer, so you need plenty of hardware muscle to back up your recording demands.

The processor

I address the computer's processor in Chapter 2, and what I write there applies here. You want a fast processor, and getting a dual-processor system can be helpful. The more power you have here, the better. However, it's important to take other factors into account. (It just couldn't be simple, could it?)

The Intel processor has lost ground to AMD in most sectors of the computer-manufacturing business, but most PC-based musicians continue to insist that the Pentium processors outperform the Athlons when it comes to audio recording. Some of this may be attributed to the mojo-oriented personalities of some musicians and recording engineers. This isn't in reference to any of the Austin Powers movies, although quite a few musicians and recording engineers may seem stuck in the past. In this case, I'm talking about the tendency for these people to attribute near-mythical qualities to certain pieces of equipment. It's the reason some musicians would rather spend hundreds or thousands of dollars repairing a fading piece of gear instead of buying a new replacement. Think of it as maintaining a classic car as opposed to getting a new automobile.

Still, some evidence suggests that Intel processors perform better with music-recording and -editing software in competitions against AMD processors. At this point, though, remember that how the processor interacts with the rest of the system is as important as how many instructions the processor can address per second. I prefer to use Intel processors in my recording based on past performance, but if you already have an Athlon processor in your system, I wouldn't worry. Most software manufacturers use Intel systems for their testing machines, but AMD processors should be able to carry the load. I recommend using an Intel Pentium 4 processor rated at a minimum of 2.4 GHz (or its AMD equivalent), and I would shy away from the budget-minded Celeron and Duron processors. Remember, you want muscle here.

Memory

This is another part of the system that you should bulk up. The type of RAM you get depends on the motherboard of your computer, but try to get at least 1GB of memory in your system. Not only does this enhance the functioning of your computer, but you also stave off the threat of obsolescence to your system for a bit longer. Memory also comes with different clock speeds. Look for memory rated at 400 MHz or above when buying your machine.

Before adding memory to your system, check with your computer's manufacturer to determine the correct type of RAM to add. You must get this specific type of RAM for your computer to function correctly.

If you can't afford more physical memory, or if your system has reached the limit of RAM it can handle, you can still beef up your system's memory using virtual memory. *Virtual memory* is space on your hard drive that the processor views as additional physical memory. The computer places information on the hard drive section and refreshes it with new information as it would with the normal amount of physical memory, although the rate of data transfer is slower because hard drives transfer information more slowly than physical memory does.

It's a good idea to have your virtual memory set to at least one-and-a-half times the amount of physical memory installed on your system. When you get to 1GB RAM and above, your system may limit the amount of virtual memory that you can set aside. In any case, try to have as much virtual memory as possible in the paging file. Follow these steps to change the amount of memory that's devoted to the paging file:

1. **Click the Start button, and right-click the My Computer icon.**

   This brings up the options menu for your system.

2. **Choose Properties from the menu that appears.**

   You see a tabbed menu of options relating to your system, as shown in Figure 11-1.

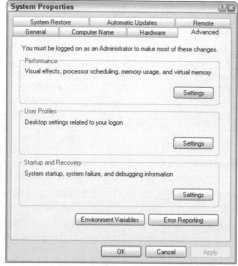

Figure 11-1:
The System
Properties
tabs in
Windows
XP.

3. **Click the Advanced tab, and click the Settings button in the Performance section.**

This shows you the amount of memory that's devoted to your paging file.

4. **Change your Initial Size amount to the total shown in the Maximum Size amount, as shown in Figure 11-2.**

This sets aside the maximum allowed hard drive space for virtual memory. Refer to the example shown in Figure 11-2.

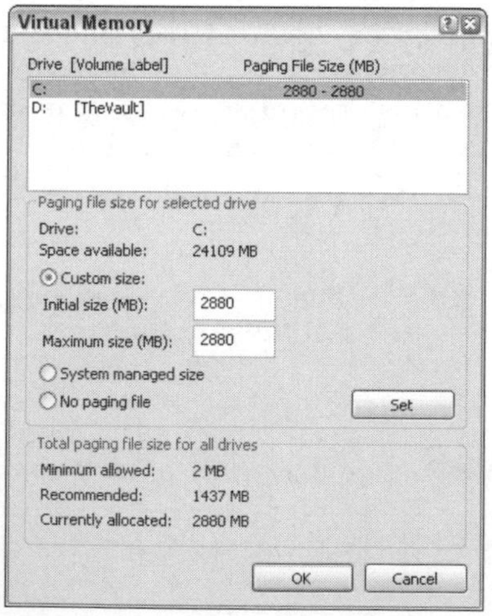

Figure 11-2:
The
maximum
allowed
virtual
memory.

The hard drive

I named a section of my hard drive "The Vault" because that's basically what the storage device is. It's a place to put all the files or songs you're not using, ready to be ordered up at a moment's notice. However, the hard drive plays a big part in the recording process. This is the virtual tape where all the tracks are laid down, so you have to make sure everything runs smoothly. Otherwise, you get the digital equivalent of crumpled or eaten tape, and it sounds as bad as the real thing.

First, make sure that you have enough hard drive space. In Chapter 2, I mention that it's a good idea to have at least a 100GB hard drive. If you're delving deep into recording, you may want to either get a larger drive or even install a second hard drive on your system. In fact, it's a good idea to have your sound recorded on a different drive than the one that contains the program you're using to do the recording. If you can't manage that, you should at least partition your drive so that the computer can address that part of the drive faster. Regardless of the size of your hard drive, make sure that it has a data cache (about 8MB) to ensure that information can flow even during seek times.

The drive can be partitioned before it's formatted and loaded with Windows XP, or you can use a program like Partition Magic to partition the drive after you've loaded Windows XP. This can be a risky and complicated procedure, though, and you'll gain more benefits by using a second hard drive for recording. In the long run, the extra expense will more than pay for itself.

The second concern is the speed of the hard drive. Measured in rotations per minute (or rpm), this relates to how quickly the drive can move to access or record data. You need to have at least a 7,200-rpm drive, and anything faster is helpful. Drives rated at 10,000 rpm are a big benefit. You pay more for faster drives, but it's worth the money if you're serious about recording. The drive should also have a fast (low) seek time (about 7 to 8 milliseconds) so that it can find and record data quickly.

Finally, make sure that you keep your drive in the best possible working condition. Using tools already present in Windows XP, you can clean and defragment your hard drive to keep it running in the best possible condition. Think of it as tuning up a car. Cleanup and defragmenting tools are found in the same place, so the following steps show you how to take care of them both at the same time:

1. **Click the Start button, and select My Computer.**

   This shows you the available drives on your computer.

2. **Right-click the hard drive or partition that you want to clean up, and select Properties from the menu that appears.**

   You see a tabbed menu (like that shown in Figure 11-3) that displays the amount of space left on the selected drive or partition, among other things.

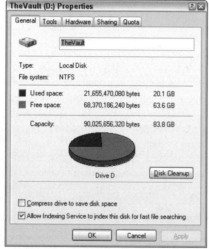

Figure 11-3:
The properties of a hard drive in Windows XP.

3. **On the General tab, click the Disk Cleanup button.**

   After reviewing the hard drive or partition, Windows XP presents a list of items that can be deleted. These items normally include files stored temporarily on the drive, cached Internet data, and other expendable information that can be trashed without consequence.

4. **Select the actions you want to take, and click the OK button.**

   This gets rid of the unnecessary files and frees hard drive space.

5. **Click the Tools tab, and click the Defragment Now button.**

   The Disk Defragmenter window, shown in Figure 11-4, allows you to analyze and defragment the drives or partitions on your computer.

6. **Select the drive you want to examine, and click the Analyze button.**

   The Disk Defragmenter examines the drive and reports whether the drive needs to be defragmented. If you've never done this before, your drive probably needs to be defragmented.

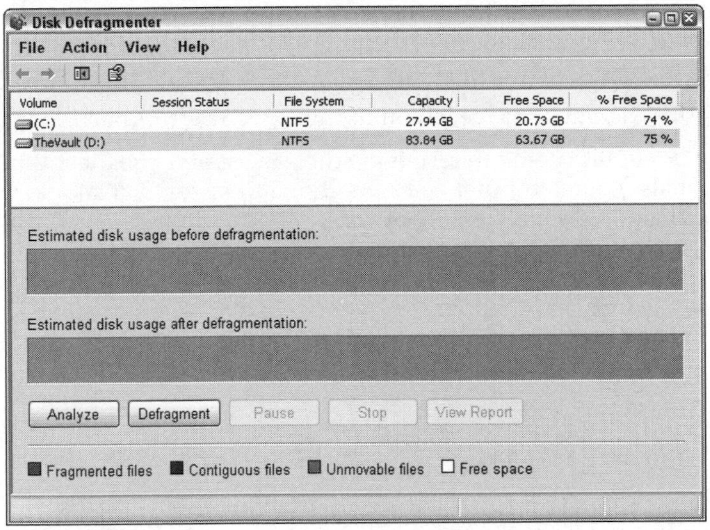

Figure 11-4:
Defrag-
menting the
hard drive.

7. **If the analysis recommends defragmenting the drive, click the Defragment button.**

   This process can take a while, so you may want to go get a soft drink right now. The defragmenting process is shown in Figure 11-5.

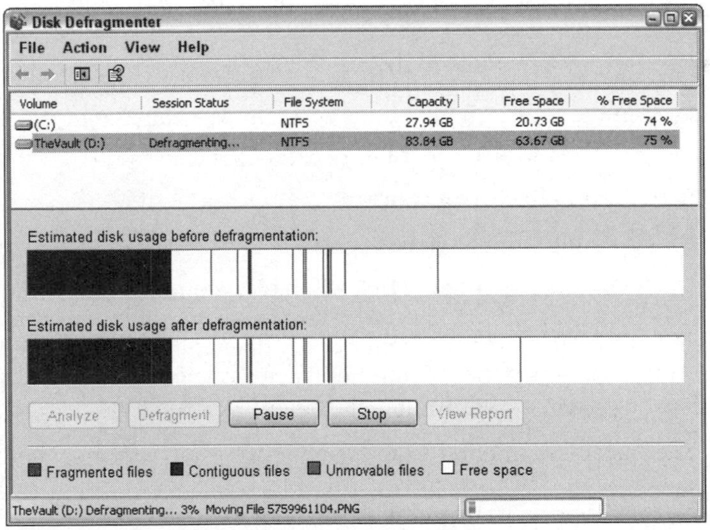

Figure 11-5:
The defrag-
menting
process.

Defragmenting the hard drive consolidates the parts of files that have been scattered around the hard drive and places them closer together. It's like alphabetizing your CD collection or arranging your tax receipts. Everything becomes quicker and easier to find; this places less strain on your system and reduces file access time. Depending on the degree of fragmentation, this process can take some time, but it's the easiest and cheapest thing you can do to make your computer run smoother and faster. You should repeat this process about once a week, depending on how often you use your system.

Audio files, especially those files used temporarily to record sound, are among the most fragmented files found on your computer. Make these cleanup and defragmenting functions your friends, and visit them often.

Dealing the Sound Cards

In Chapter 2, I describe the sound card as the audio interface for the computer. It plays the audio files through however many speakers you had connected to the computer, and it takes in any signal you feed it. Your current sound card can handle anything you want to play, but the territory we're about to head into needs some specialized hardware to adequately handle audio recording.

The main difference between consumer-grade sound cards (like the ones that come with virtually all computers) and specialized audio-recording sound cards is the number of inputs on each card. While "normal" sound cards have only the line-in function I described earlier, audio-recording sound cards can contain from 2 to 24 (or more) inputs. So why do these cards need so many inputs to import sound? It all relates to a concept called *multitracking*.

Multitracking

In the early days of recording (back when dinosaurs used to set up the mics and musicians were often forced to take a break to quest for fire), songs were recorded on one microphone strategically placed in a room. The band would perform the song, and they would hope everyone got it right the first time. If someone made a mistake, or one instrument was too loud or soft, they would have to decide whether to start over or just keep the recording, warts and all. If your studio time and money were running out, the decision was often made for you.

The invention of multitracking changed this. Engineers could now capture each instrument individually, and musicians could go back and re-record their parts without disturbing the overall song. It was still an expensive process most of the time, but it was now easier to get a better-quality recording.

Given that the technology has filtered down into the hands of consumers, it's now inexpensive to put together a home digital multitrack studio. It's also helpful for solo artists to have this technology available, because they can more fully realize songs on their own by layering track upon track to make their own recordings or demos (examples of songs used as a basis for recording the finished product later).

To record multiple tracks, artists can either lay down several tracks at the same time or add the tracks one at a time. To record several at one time, the computer requires a specialized sound card with multiple inputs available. The sound card maps each of the sound sources to a different track in the software-recording program that's being used. The number of tracks that can be recorded at any one time is based on the number of inputs available as well as the power of the computer system being used. Recording multiple tracks cleanly at the same time take a lot of power, and your computer may not be able to handle all the tracks the sound card could potentially record.

Internal versus external sound cards

In Chapter 2, I describe internal sound cards (both with and without a breakout box) and external sound cards. In this case, for any sort of multitracking or quality recording, you need external gear. Even if your motherboard has a built-in sound card, that only suffices for normal media playback. If only because you need the extra space for connecting your sound sources, you need some sort of external box. It also makes it easier to connect sources when you don't have to struggle behind the computer.

The question at this point is whether you want to get an external sound module or a sound card that is internal to the computer. If you have a PCI slot available in your computer, I recommend going with the breakout box variety. You get a faster rate of sound transfer when you go the direct route rather than using USB 2.0 or FireWire. However, if you have no available space or you're working on a laptop or in another portable environment, the external module is the best way to go. One benefit of Windows XP is that it has a driver for just about everything already preloaded in your system. Depending on the external sound module you buy, you may be able to just plug the thing in and be ready to go.

The manufacturer may have other ideas about what driver is the best to use with your system. Always check your instructions and determine the proper installation process. Using a little precaution often pays off.

Remember that you get what you pay for, so size up what you need before you buy the unit. The important factors to consider are the number of inputs you need, whether you need preamps, and the quality of sound the module can produce.

The inputs

The standard input on the regular consumer sound card is a ⅛-inch minijack. While this may be fine for casual home microphone and Webcam use, it's not a good option for recording musical instruments because of the relative lack of sound quality. Instead, sound cards designed for home recording include a couple of different types of standard inputs.

¼-inch connections

If you play electric guitar, bass, or other electric instrument, you're already familiar with this type of connection. You may have also seen this type of connection on higher-end headphones. This type of connection is commonly used in both the instruments and the amplifiers, connected by cords with male plugs on both ends. This type of connection is usually present on an external sound card or on the breakout box of the internal sound card. These types of connections are available in either mono or stereo configuration, as shown in Figure 11-6.

Figure 11-6:
Mono and stereo ¼-inch connections.

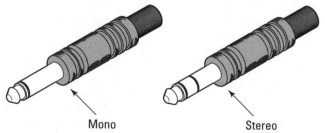

Mono   Stereo

XLR connections

This type of connection is used for microphones or connections from other pieces of recording equipment. The XLR connection looks like a large cylinder with three prongs in a triangular pattern (male) or three holes in the same pattern (female), as shown in Figure 11-7. This type of connection is favored for use with recording consoles or mixing boards because it transmits a balanced signal to the equipment.

Figure 11-7:
Male and female XLR connections.

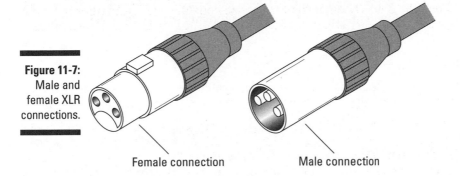

Female connection   Male connection

Before the inputs — the preamp

It's possible to just plug an instrument into the sound card and get a sound out of it. But the sound is nothing you would want to use in a recording (unless you envision a recording featuring thin and tinny sounds due to lack of signal). Between these instruments and the sound card come devices that boost the volume and shape the tone of that signal, making it ready to be recorded and mixed. These *preamps* are inserted in between the instruments and the recording equipment.

Technically speaking, these devices bring the instrument signals up to "line level," that is, ready to be laid to tape (or hard drive, as the case may be). Beyond that, all kinds of other factors can be introduced at the preamp level. From tube to transistor, from analog to digital effects, and even including the elusive "mojo" factor, these devices play a huge part in coloring the sound that gets recorded.

It's not uncommon for professional recording studios to have several different kinds of preamps available for different uses. However, you probably won't be interested or be able to purchase all of those boxes and devices to make your home recordings. External sound cards and input devices usually have a preamp built into them, so check for that when you purchase the device. Otherwise, be prepared to shell out another hundred dollars or so for a budget-minded home recording preamp. Some preamps are tailored to certain types of instruments or microphones, so be sure what you get either does what you want or can be used for recording other types of instruments.

Internal preamps

Some devices, such as the external sound card shown in Figure 2-4 (back in Chapter 2), include internal preamps. In the diagram, only a gain boost knob is shown, although some others may include basic tone-shaping controls. This can be helpful if you don't want to spend extra money on preamps after you've bought the sound interface. Don't expect too much, though. You inevitably get what you pay for.

Mic preamps

These devices are usually tailored for microphones, hence the name. They are placed between the console and the mic, and they usually add "warmth" and fullness to the sound.

Direct boxes

These devices used to interface an instrument (guitar, bass, keyboard, and so on) with the recording console. It can do just that, or it can take a more active role and help shape the tone of the instrument. Because guitarists usually prefer to record using any number of amplifiers (these folks believe in the "mojo" factor like no other instrumentalist I've ever seen), direct boxes are found more in the case of bassists and keyboardists.

If you're a musician and you have a guitar, bass, or keyboard amplifier, you already have a preamp. The question is how to get the signal from your amp to your sound card. You can either place a microphone in front of the amp (a delicate art I can't even begin to explore here) or look for a "preamp out" jack on the amp and plug it directly into the sound card.

Do not plug the speaker-out jack from your amp into the sound card. Way too much power is coming out of that jack for the sound card, and you're liable to harm your equipment. Burning circuits are never a pretty smell.

Bits and Hertz

If you've spent a lot of time around digital recordings (not the process, just the output), you've probably heard this terminology. The standard rate for digital recording is 16-bit, 44.1-kHz. This means the sound that was recorded for the CD was sampled a little over 44,000 times a second, and each sample contains 16 bits of information about that sound. I have a few CDs in my collection that proudly proclaim that they were re-mixed and remastered in 20-bit sound (which means that more information about the sound was included in the recording), but it's still been mastered down to the CD standard for sound. That is, the sound was recorded and mixed at a higher resolution and then translated through a process called *dithering* to the CD standard. The sound will be better than one that wasn't recorded at the high resolution, but it's still going to the same format.

You should know that better sound is possible. Think of moving up from a regular camera you purchased in a drugstore to a higher-end professional camera. You can still take pictures with either, but the pro camera can capture more detail. Professional gear can record sound up to a 32-bit, 192-kHz level, but this level is not necessarily available to the entry-level home recording artist. Still, you should be able to get 24-bit, 96-kHz sound for about $250 at the time of this writing.

So how does this additional information help you? First, it's good to capture as much detail as you can in the beginning. It's easier to start great and work your way down than to start mediocre and then make the sound worse. The "mojo factor" also makes an appearance here. Higher sample and bit rates can capture higher frequencies than lower sample and bit rates. While you may not be able to hear these sounds, some engineers theorize that the inaudible frequencies still have an effect on the audible ones, subtly changing the sound. If that inaudible sound isn't there, the audible sound will be different. Make sense? Yeah, physics was never my strong suit, either. But it's important to remember that computers are now capable of playing audio over and above CD-quality audio. Given the right set of speakers, your computer can sound better than your regular stereo system without much effort. Starting with good quality will net you better results in the long run.

Setting the Wavetable

The basic sound card merely does the job of converting analog signal to digital signal and vice versa. It's the portal between the two different audio worlds. However, some cards also carry their own sounds along with them. These sounds are found in a *wavetable*.

The wavetable is either synthesized (artificially created) or sampled (small recorded sounds) audio that's arranged to be triggered by MIDI signals. When the sound card receives a MIDI signal, it sends the appropriate sound to the speakers, and you hear the sound. This can be triggered either by MIDI files or incoming MIDI triggers from other sources, such as external keyboards or files from the Internet.

The wavetable is placed directly on the sound card, so you don't have to install anything to get it to work. Wavetables are automatically triggered by any MIDI signals coming into your computer. These are often sounds licensed from manufacturers like Yamaha, although the sound card maker may have included its own sounds to keep costs down.

MIDI's bad rap

I discuss how powerful a tool MIDI can be in the section "Stuck in The MIDI with you." But first, I want to address a misconception about this language that makes it seem like a joke.

If you've spent any time surfing the Internet, you've probably been to That Site. It's the site that pops up all kinds of windows when you first access it. It probably also has all kinds of cheap little animated graphics on it, too. The whole thing looks like a seven-year-old scattered his attention span on your screen and then left for ice cream. The worst part is yet to come, however.

That's right — you hear background music. Without warning, your speakers are suddenly blaring the worst bleeps and clangs you've heard since the cat got loose on Grandma's electric organ. You can't reach the volume or close the Web site quickly enough. When blessed silence finally arrives, you're left only with a cold sweat and the memories of hideous sound that leave you forever cursing the day some tech geek invented MIDI.

In this case, MIDI is indeed partly responsible. Someone embedded a horrible MIDI file in the Web site that played automatically, making your browsing experience a living nightmare. Still, some of the fault falls in your lap — or, more specifically, your sound card's virtual lap.

Remember, MIDI is just a set of instructions about what musical notes should be played and what instruments and stylistic variations should be used. It's up to you whether they're played by a symphony orchestra or the elementary school glee club from down the road. It's a bit of an over-simplification, and no amount of gilding is going to make an unimaginative MIDI file sound good. But when a MIDI file is created by an inspired player and sent through a good, quality synthesizer or wavetable, you hear good music. Again, it's better to start out with good equipment and hear what you're supposed to hear the first time.

It's also wise to avoid That Site in the future. If you can't do it for yourself, do it for the sake of the children.

Stuck in the MIDI with You

You've already been introduced to MIDI with the sound card and wavetable functions, so this is the best time to explain exactly what MIDI (short for Musical Instrument Digital Interface) is. Remember, MIDI is a set of instructions for sound modules to interpret and play. However, it can be so much more.

MIDI basics

MIDI information tells a sound device what note to play, when to play it, how loud or soft to play it, and what type of instrument sound (known as a *sound patch* or just a *patch*) to use. This information is transmitted along 16 "channels," and instruments can be set to receive MIDI information from any of these channels (or all of them at the same time). Think of it like a business's telephone system — a receptionist could take messages from any of the lines in the office, or you can direct-dial a specific office.

MIDI channel number 10 is reserved for percussion and drum set sounds. Any messages you send on this channel are interpreted as percussion sounds. Any of the other channels can be used for instrumental sounds.

Three basic types of MIDI ports exist, and each type uses a special five-pin cable, as follows:

- ✔ The IN port receives MIDI data.
- ✔ The OUT port sends MIDI data.
- ✔ The THRU port sends MIDI data through the device without modifying the data.

This is important if you have many different devices hooked up in a line but you only want certain devices to receive data. This keeps the data chain connected without bogging it down with unnecessary commands. Computer-based sequencing programs can also receive MIDI data via a USB or FireWire cable.

When connecting MIDI cables, remember that you have to connect the OUT port of one MIDI device to the IN port of the next device. This is counter to normal logic, and it's one of the most common mistakes beginning MIDI users make.

The international MIDI specification allows 128 patches (numbered 0—127), and each number is attached to a specific type of sound. For example, the traditional acoustic piano sound is always found at 0, while the eminently useful gunshot sound effect is located at 127. Why does the numbering system start at 0? It delves into the specific nature of how computers recognize numbers, and as such is rather boring. Just remember that all the patches start at 0. And don't feel that MIDI is limited to just these 128 sounds. That's just the international specification that all devices that handle general MIDI must subscribe to. Manufacturers can and do tailor their own specialized sounds to different patches. Just don't expect it to sound the same if it's not played on the device that you used to write the song.

The huge benefit of MIDI is that it can act almost like a word processor for musical notes. Editing MIDI instructions is roughly like editing a text document. You can change any of the parameters (such as patches or channels), and you can also do more global edits like quantizing the notes (for the rhythm-impaired, it aligns the notes to fit the tempo of the song). You can even change the key and tempo of the song. MIDI can also add basic sound effects like reverb (a slight echo that makes the sound seem like it was created in a large room or hall) or chorus (a thickening of the sound to make it seem like more than one instrument is playing). Anything can be modified using a sequencing program or device (I talk about these items in the section "Sequencing MIDI," later in this chapter).

After you have the MIDI data recorded as you like it, you can make your sound device play the MIDI instructions and record the sound made by the device. Imagine an actor being videotaped acting out the final version of a script. The audience never sees the script; it only sees the final product. Because MIDI instructions are so easy to change and the file sizes are so small, virtually all electronic musical instruments (for example, keyboards) use some form of MIDI in producing sound.

Sequencing MIDI

You need software to sequence MIDI data, just like you need some type of word processing software to compose documents on the computer. *Sequencing* is the process of creating the MIDI instructions for your synthesizers and other MIDI devices to reproduce. Think of it like the punched paper roll you give to a player piano to make the instrument play the notes. You also need some kind of MIDI input device, but these devices can take many forms (I discuss this in the section "Oh, THAT Kind of Keyboard," later in this chapter). After you have everything connected, you have three ways of recording MIDI data: real-time sequencing, step-time sequencing, and drawing in MIDI data.

Real-time sequencing

Press the red button and play — this method is just like recording regular audio. The software runs a steady time line and sequences the musical input (or events) as the time line runs through. If you're an experienced player, this may be the quickest and most natural way to create a MIDI file. However, if you're not a proficient musician, this is probably not the way to go.

Step-time sequencing

With this type of sequencing, you preset the rhythm of the note you want, such as a quarter- or half-note. You then use your MIDI input device to select the note and loudness you want. If you're sequencing a lot of the same rhythms, this can be an effective way to enter precise data. However, if you're considering complicated musical passages, this could be time consuming.

Drawing in MIDI data

This last method doesn't require any sort of instrumental skills. Sequencing programs or notation programs (programs that create sheet music) provide the manual placement of notes by pointing and clicking your mouse. Again, this can be a slow and time-consuming process, but it allows precise placement of notes. If you can read music, you can use the standard staff and notation to write out your music. The program translates that into a MIDI file, and you're ready to go. If you're not comfortable with that format, the sequencing programs can provide a grid to plot out what notes (with what parameters) happen when. Each sequencing program has a different layout, but they all function about the same way.

Oh, THAT Kind of Keyboard

Up to this point, I've referred to keyboards as the normal typewriter or QWERTY keyboard, but here the keyboard also means a piano-type instrument. Aside from that similarity, though, the type of keyboard can vary wildly.

MIDI controller

This type of keyboard is only capable of transmitting MIDI data. It looks like a standard electronic keyboard, but it has no on-board sounds, like you may find in a normal synthesizer. This keyboard connects to a computer via the standard MIDI jack, the sound card's joystick port, or a FireWire or USB port.

In this case, consider your keyboard needs before you purchase something. If you're not a proficient player, a small keyboard with little key sensitivity is fine and more cost effective. If you're used to playing a normal piano and you need the fine control that kind of instrument offers, you should invest in a high-end controller that makes you feel more at home.

The type of connection also plays a factor. If you're using an older computer, you can use the joystick port of your sound card. Any modern computer can handle a USB or FireWire connection, though, and the Plug and Play convenience makes this kind of connection valuable. This can be especially helpful if you're using a laptop, where portability and conservation of space are at a premium.

Synthesizer

This is the most common kind of keyboard because it also carries its own sounds on-board. This keyboard can both receive and send MIDI data, which makes it another resource you can use. Otherwise, you should consider the same factors that you would with a MIDI controller. You just have to take the sound-outs of the synthesizer and patch them into the sound card to record your sound. Otherwise, you can use the sounds contained on the sound card or in the software you use.

Drum machines

If you've listened to popular music anytime within the last decade, you've heard these machines. These are basically specialized synthesizers that produce percussive sounds, and they come with integrated sequencers that you can use to record MIDI data or sound.

Making the buy

You may remember Truck Stop Sushi from earlier in the book as an example of using the Internet to promote a band. Now that they're back from their national tour, it's time to write more material. The lead singer also writes the songs for the group, and he wants to work his computer into the songwriting process. (He paid a lot of money for this machine, and now he's just using it to find his local weather forecasts and order Precious Moments figurines from eBay.)

The computer is a couple of years old, and he just has a regular stereo sound card in it. The lead singer writes using an acoustic guitar, so he needs a couple of microphones to plug into a sound card that can record multiple inputs at the same time. He also decides to get an inexpensive

MIDI keyboard to create simple drum patterns or to tap out other ideas (he *really* wants to work in ocarina on this album).

The singer buys a small sound card with a breakout box that handles two mic inputs. He also decides to get a mic preamp that can make his vocal mic sound beautiful (he is a lead singer after all — always gotta sound perfect, even on a demo). He already has the mics from the band, and a USB-connection MIDI controller completes the process. For about $900, Truck Stop Sushi now has a quick-and-dirty demo studio. Now, they can finally realize that two-disc concept album based on a mosquito's life. That's heady stuff.

Other input alternatives

As technology advances, you find more ways to record MIDI data. Most instruments, from percussion to wind to strings, are capable of producing MIDI signals with the assistance of additional technology. Either real instruments or wholly new constructs can be used to make MIDI files. You can also find "virtual keyboards," or programs that with a mouse click or the press of a key on your QWERTY keyboard, generate a MIDI note. This last piece of software lacks precision and control, but at least it gets the note out there.

Chapter 12

Laying Down a Few Tracks

In This Chapter

▶ Finding out what most recording software has in common

▶ Evaluating your needs and getting the right software

▶ Hooking up your new home studio and getting it running

At some point, you've probably heard a debate between a PC user and an Apple user. The exchange may start about seemingly meaningless details, but it likely devolves into a raging argument that not only calls into question the meaning of the other's existence but also likely the circumstances through which the person came into existence. The point is that this is a contentious issue, and it's not likely to end soon. As long as both platforms exist, you will find differences.

Because this book focuses only on the tools available to Windows XP, I can at least avoid that debate in these pages. The Apple folks turned away as soon as they saw the title. Now all I have to deal with is the slightly less contentious debate over which recording software is the best. They all do basically the same thing — it's just a matter of which one does what you want better than the rest.

If you've done any sort of reading about digital multitrack recording or talked to someone who knows about the subject, you may have heard the name Pro Tools. It's not a loose description of the software but an actual brand name for an industry-standard pro-recording system. Pro Tools is available for Windows XP, but the home recording user has a great deal of other options. In this chapter, I compare these options and give you an idea of what's best for you.

Common Features and Functions

Quality home recording software can handle a few key functions that are necessary to make a good audio file. However, each of them is known for a certain specialty. For example, Acid made its name for its innovate use of sound loops, while Cakewalk started out as a MIDI sequencer. Because of customer demand and advancing technology, each program has been forced to take on aspects of the others. Still, you'll find that most stay true to their roots.

Multitrack Capability

This is the basic function you need. As I mention in Chapter 11, this can be used to either to record several tracks at once or to layer sound upon sound. The important consideration here is how many tracks you need to record simultaneously. Some software can only handle one track at a time, while others can record multiple tracks at the same time. In Chapter 11, I review the hardware necessary to handle functions like this, and now I take a look at the software restrictions.

Software manufacturers list the parameters of their recording software on their Web site, so you can find out how many tracks the software can handle. For example, one program may be able to handle only 16 or 24 tracks of audio, while another can go to a theoretically unlimited number of tracks.

Nothing in the world of recording technology is unlimited. When a manufacturer indicates that its software can record an unlimited number of tracks, it really means that "you can add as many audio tracks as you like, but eventually your computer will become slow as molasses — at which point you can't be productive." The unlimited part is determined by your computer's hardware and how clean and neat you keep the software on your machine.

Manufacturers also often differ between audio and MIDI tracks in their specifications. For example, you may see one that advertises "up to 24 audio tracks and an unlimited number of MIDI tracks." Because MIDI instructions take much less memory and processor strength to run, you can have a greater number of those kind of tracks. Just realize that MIDI tracks cannot record anything from a mic or a direct line, like from a guitar or a bass.

Audio recording

You may be wondering what is the difference between this section and multitracking. In the previous section, I discuss how many tracks the software can handle. Here, I discuss the overall quality of those tracks and what you can do to manipulate them.

Each piece of software has its own audio-processing engine. This determines the quality of sound that you can get from each track of audio. You need to match this with the hardware you purchase for your home recording studio. For example, Cakewalk Home Studio is capable of handling 24-bit audio at 96 kHz, a respectable setting for home recording purposes. However, if you're just using the sound card that's built into your budget motherboard, you may only be able to record 16-bit, 44.1-kHz sound. Both the hardware and the software ends must be covered to take full advantage of the higher-end recording quality.

Each track also has its own volume control, and you should be able to pan each track somewhere in the stereo field. (At this point, it's highly unlikely you'll find anything at this level that's capable of being recorded in 5.1 or 7.1 surround sound.) At this level, you're looking for how you can modify or enhance each track, through the use of envelopes, or automated functions. *Envelopes* are curves or plots that automatically change or alter the volume, panning, or other effects on each track. While it sounds complicated, it's really not. It's just like telling a word processor where to make words bold or how to make the font size larger or smaller. Figure 12-1 shows an envelope represented in Cakewalk Home Studio.

The line in this figure shows where the volume is increased and decreased. This function is automated — the playback follows the envelope's line whenever the tracks are played back and when the track's audio files are mixed together.

You also need to take into account how many effects each track can handle. Effects include things like audio compression (making softer passages louder and louder passages softer to allow louder volume), equalization (the boosting or lowering of certain frequencies), or distortion — common effects that you may want to put on one track, but not the entire recording. Some programs may only allow a certain number of effects to be placed on each track, or you may once again see the "unlimited" tag applied here. Each effect takes up more processor and memory resources, so the number of effects you can use depends on the hardware strength of your system.

Each software program uses audio drivers to allow a better interface with the sound card than what is normally used with regular audio playback. Look for WDM or ASIO driver compatibility in both sound cards and the software. These compatibilities allow better playback of audio and MIDI data. Using other or earlier audio drivers may introduce *latency* — a lag between when you play a note and when you hear it from your computer's speakers. Windows XP is capable of handling these drivers with ease, and it's the first Windows operating system to do so.

Sound editing

In addition to the ability to record audio, some programs also provide the ability to edit the audio after it has been recorded. This can be as simple as cutting and pasting different parts of the audio, or it can be as deep as drawing in different sections of the waveform. Programs like Adobe Audition started out as waveform recorders and editors, so this kind of function is ingrained in its functionality. Programs like Cakewalk Home Studio started out as MIDI sequencers, so you don't find as much audio-editing capability.

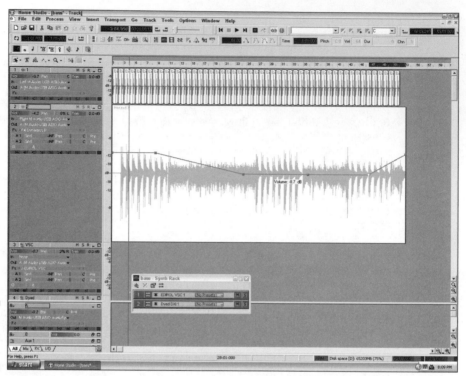

Figure 12-1:
A volume
envelope.

Traditional cut-and-paste (known professionally as non-linear) editing allows clips of audio or MIDI to be removed from their current location and placed elsewhere. The advantage of this is that the editing in nondestructive — this type of editing doesn't lose data, and you can always undo what you've done if you're not happy with the results. This is compared to linear, destructive editing, such as splicing tape. Once you've made a cut, you've made a cut. Once that clip has been thrown away, it's gone. The digital tools allow you to avoid the pitfalls of accidentally destroying music. Some programs also allow "slip" editing, or moving the edges of the clip that's played back. This doesn't alter the clip, but it does affect what's played back during the course of editing. Again, this is a simple process that can be undone if you're not satisfied with the end result.

MIDI recording

I've already mentioned the number of MIDI tracks the software may be able to handle. The important concepts here are how to choose and manipulate the MIDI data after it's been recorded. Each program has different capabilities.

For each MIDI track you set up, you must set up the channel it receives data on, the MIDI channel the data will be recorded on, and the patch used to play back the data. You should also be able to determine which audio device receives the MIDI instructions from each track. For example, you may want your keyboard to play the instructions from one track and the drum machine from another track.

Much like audio, the software should also be able to cut and paste the MIDI data from one track to another. You can also make multiple copies of that data to create a full track of looped MIDI instructions. You can do this with audio as well, but because of the pinpoint accuracy MIDI allows, you can make the track sound a little more precise. Cutting and pasting also allows you to double the melody or rhythm phrase with two or more instruments, raise or lower it an octave, and do other things with the composition. You can't easily replicate these effects with digital audio.

Looping

This concept has long been prevalent in hip-hop and other popular music, but it took on a new dimension when the multitracking program Acid came along. Previously, you were limited to what you could do with a section of audio as far as tempo, length, and pitch were concerned. After the section was recorded, it was pretty much set in proverbial digital audio stone. A new looping process changed all that.

With Acid, users were able to manipulate sound clips like never before. Clips of audio could be moved to new keys, stretched to two or three times their original length, shortened, moved to new tempos, or looped indefinitely. This functionality was so popular that many manufacturers rushed to add this kind of compatibility to their programs. This kind of tool can be very beneficial for new composers, and it's especially useful for laying down repetitive rhythms tracks or just sketching out ideas. You can hear your song at a variety of tempos and keys, which can help you develop new ideas.

User interface

All the functions in the world aren't going to help you record audio if you can't find your way around the program. Each of these recording programs has a different way of presenting controls and data to you, although you will find some common appearances.

The most common way of looking at the recording is to show each track with the controls to the left and the data to the right. Figure 12-2, taken from Cakewalk's Home Studio, shows this view.

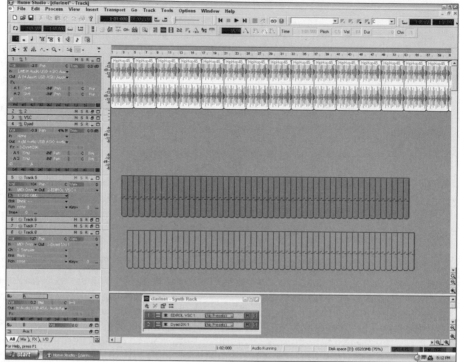

Figure 12-2:
A common view of multitrack audio and MIDI recording.

Another common view is the Mixer view, as shown in Figure 12-3. This looks exactly like the mixing board you may be familiar with, and that's why many software manufacturers include it. It's a sight that many people are familiar with, so it's easier to control than a new interface with a new learning curve. Many home recording artists use both tracks and mixer views in conjunction to record their audio.

Other views help you edit data more precisely, whether it be for audio or MIDI. These views vary from one program to another.

Control surfaces

When a software recording program is created, all the controls are represented virtually on-screen. However, it's sometimes cumbersome to mouse to each control and move it — in any case, it's not as convenient as placing your hands on a real mixer. You can use the QWERTY keyboard to create shortcuts for functions like playback, rewind, and saving data. Still, many people prefer a physical control surface to use in the recording process.

This kind of device has controls that are familiar to those who have recorded audio before. Things like knobs and faders can be connected to controls in the software via MIDI, and then the surface can be used to move these functions around. You still have to use the mouse and keyboard, but it could make the process seem a little bit more natural. Also, because Windows XP has many drivers preloaded, surfaces connected by USB or FireWire (as the vast majority are) can be easily installed and recognized. The only challenge is getting the controls mapped to the right functions in your software.

You have to analyze your needs when buying a control surface as well. Because each track requires a separate control strip (a fader and set of knobs attached in the same general area), you need to consider the average number of tracks that you'll need and make sure that you have enough room on the control surface. Additional functions like MIDI or audio inputs can be handy as well.

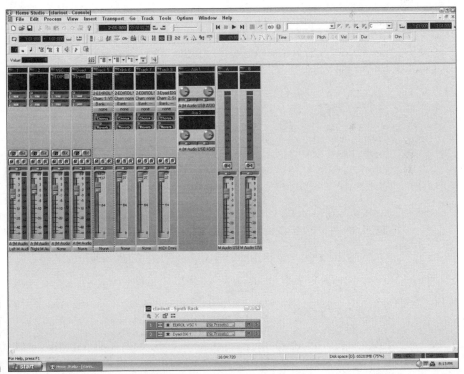

Figure 12-3:
The Mixer
view.

Plug-ins

Any program listed here can record and edit audio and MIDI to some extent. The ability to use effects can make a program stand out among its peers, and this is where plug-ins are effective. Like a new piece of studio equipment, *plug-ins* are software additions that allow the processing of audio and MIDI in a way that wasn't initially programmed in by the software's manufacturer. For example, one plug-in may add new distortion algorithms and another could simulate the sound of various types of guitar amps.

A variety of plug-ins are available, but only certain ones work with certain recording programs. Pro Tools has a unique set of drivers, so you probably won't run into these drivers unless you're using a Pro Tools rig. Cubase and other sequencers use sequencing based on a technology called VST, while Cakewalk and Acid use plug-ins based on DXi technology. You can't use these plug-ins across platforms by themselves, but software has been written to port these plug-ins to other programs.

Remember that these plug-ins require more processor strength and memory — yet another reason to invest in the best-quality hardware you can get initially. They also represent another investment, because some of these plug-ins can cost hundreds of dollars. Be sure that the plug-in can perform the function you want and won't represent a money pit.

Mixing

This is a standard function that every software recording program can perform. Each audio track's volume and place in the stereo field are combined into one stereo or surround-sound track (again, the latter is rare in this type of software), ready for burning or playback by a media player. The difference is in the way that the mixing function is handled. After the levels are set and automated to your specifications (using envelopes), the process is usually handled automatically. This saves time and makes sure that everything is handled according to how you have it set, reducing the possibility of mistakes. When the file is mixed, you have the final product.

Exporting

After the final product is mixed, you're left with a high-quality audio file ready to be burned or played back. However, it's going to be a huge file, and you may want to compress it for quicker and easier transport or to save space on your hard drive. In addition to creating a WAV file, the software recording program should be able to create different types of files, like MP3 or WMA. Otherwise, you may have to invest in another conversion program to put the file in your preferred format.

Mastering

After the track has been created, you may need to perform additional processes on it to make it sound better. This process, called *mastering,* can include compression, overall track volume changes, and equalization of certain frequencies to make it sound better during playback. This can be a tricky process, and to find out more about mastering, check out *Home Recording For Musicians For Dummies,* by Jeff Strong (published by Wiley). What you need to be concerned with right now is whether the program can handle additional plug-ins for mastering, along with the ability to work on audio files in general as opposed to track editing.

Burning

You've seen this function a billion times, but it takes on a special significance when working with audio-recording software. Burned CD-Rs can be played in normal CD players, but commercial CD recordings are burned to what are called Red Book specifications. This won't be of much concern unless you're producing commercial recordings. However, it's something to look for if you're considering making CDs that look and sound exactly like commercially produced recordings. Even if they don't burn to Red Book specifications, certain software programs may be able to burn audio CDs in the same manner as other computer burning programs.

What Do You Want to Do?

Quite a number of programs are available to you, each tailored to a different type of user and even genre of music. Here, I guide you through a few common home recording scenarios and discuss what kind of software best fits that situation. You can evaluate your own needs against these examples and decide what will work best for you.

Just beginning

You're coming in fresh to making music, and you don't have any experience with recording audio. It may seem a little daunting, but some software is made just for you, at little or no cost. Go ahead and jump in — the digital water's fine.

I recommend that you start with a program called Acid Xpress, which is available as a free download from http://acidplanet.com. The price is right, and the program has just enough built-in functionality to give you a good music-making experience. The program is limited to eight tracks of audio, and the ability to use plug-ins or effects on each track is disabled. This is just enough information to find out how to navigate multitracked audio and to understand how to mix tracks. You don't have MIDI functionality here either, but that can wait until you're a little more familiar with recording in the Windows XP environment.

You also get the opportunity to work with loops that have already been created for you and to get a sense of how to put music together. You can either buy loops on CD or download a few for free from the same site. With these loops, you can do simple insertions and deletions in a nondestructive environment. You may not be creating any masterpieces, but it's a great way to start understanding the process. If you play an instrument, you can also plug it in through the sound card and record tracks along with the loops.

Intermediate/project studio

If you have experience in home recording or audio in general, you may be more comfortable using advanced recording software. If you're concerned only with digital audio, a program like Adobe Audition (a program Adobe bought from Syntrillium when it was called Cool Edit Pro) is a valuable tool. Included in this program are both a multitrack recorder and a powerful waveform editor, and it has a looping capability that's similar to Acid. This is a professional-level recording tool, but it remains in the price range of many of those who are interested in home recording.

If you want to work with a MIDI sequencer or combine that with digital audio, a program like Cubase SE or Cakewalk Home Studio Version 2 can handle these needs. The main difference between these two is that Cubase SE natively handles VST plug-ins and Cakewalk uses DXi (although Cakewalk includes a program to port over VST effects to function inside Cakewalk). At this point, you should consider getting the digital audio interfaces and preamps that I discussed in Chapter 11.

Professional

At this point, you're looking at investing several thousand dollars in gear and software. This level is reserved for producing commercial-quality recordings. The studio must be able to handle a variety of instruments and situations, and it's not something an inexperienced hobbyist should consider.

Professional recording is currently dominated by Pro Tools, although PC-based programs like Steinburg's Nuendo and Cubase SX and Cakewalk's Sonar are making inroads into the field. You can run these programs on home PCs, but the initial software investment alone is several hundred dollars. Add that to the necessary plug-in and hardware purchases, and the bill skyrockets.

Loop-based recording

If you want to specialize in loop-based recording, like pop, hip-hop, or dance music, several programs are designed with those needs in mind. Acid Pro is the most prominent name in this field, but Ableton Live has also won converts to its product. You should also look at drum machines and synthesizers, because these are the tools of the trade in such music. Reason products also specialize in looping (specifically ReCycle), but it's a much better example of another valuable type of software for the home recording artist — the soft synthesizer, or *soft synth.*

Soft Synths

No, the term does not represent Nerf's entry into the music world. These programs are specialized sound programs that react to MIDI input and generate sounds based on patches that you've chosen. Soft synths represent a huge savings in both space and money, because you can fit the sounds of several synthesizers inside a computer and call them up at a moment's notice. They also tend to be much less expensive because you don't have to purchase the keys and electronics that come with normal synthesizers.

Like plug-ins, these synthesizers are based on VST or DXi technology. Remember that you must tailor your soft synth collection to the recording software you work with. Programs may even come with built-in soft synths. For example, the Edirol and Dyad soft synths are built into Cakewalk software (see in Figure 12-4).

The big name in soft synths is Propellerhead's Reason software. This package includes several virtual modules that can create or sample sounds, loops, and drum sounds, along with a sequencer that can create basic loops. The software also includes effects modules that can be patched into the signal paths of the created sounds and samples. The soft synths produced by Native Instruments have also earned a great deal of popularity.

The things to look for in a quality soft synth are quality of sound and the ability to customize those sounds. Programs like Reason allow you to move sounds and effects around to create new and different sounds, and it also produces quality stock sounds. As I noted previously, be sure that the soft synth is compatible with your recording software. This is another reason that Reason is so popular — it interfaces with so many different software packages.

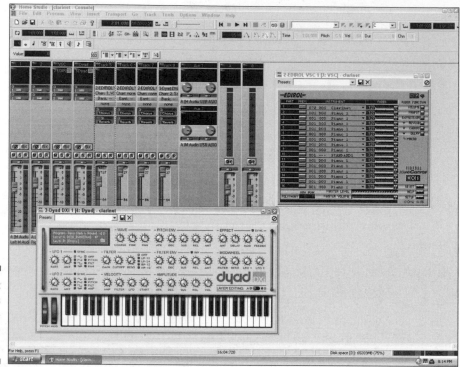

Figure 12-4:
Soft synths
in a record-
ing environ-
ment.

Finally, the effectiveness of the soft synth depends on the use of WDM or ASIO drivers to reduce the amount of lag between the time you strike the keys and the time you hear the sound. Because the computer is using both the recording software and the soft synth software, the sound card is pretty busy. The soft synth requires a direct connection to that sound card to make it work. Even a delay of 20 to 30 milliseconds is noticeable to someone play-ing the keyboard. WDM and ASIO drivers can reduce the latency to less than 10 milliseconds, which is virtually unnoticeable to the player. The goal is to make the recording process as trouble-free as possible. Again, this is where Windows XP shines. WDM drivers are native to Windows XP, and ASIO drivers are compatible with the operating system as well.

Hooking It All Up

So, you have all the tools ready to go, and you've followed the manufacturer's instructions when installing the software. Now, you have to get your computer set up to handle the software properly. This task varies from one system to another (Cubase, for example, requires the addition of a hardware key to operate), but you should look for some common functions. I use Cakewalk Home Studio to illustrate the process, but you should look for these things regardless of the software you use.

Is everybody here?

The first step is to make sure that all your gear is recognized by the program and is usable. The program lists all the gear it can detect, as shown in Figure 12-5.

Typically, the software lists audio and MIDI devices separately. This is also where you set the default devices (that is, those devices the computer and software automatically turn to) for the recording program.

If you don't see all the devices you have listed by the software, it's time to run through some basic troubleshooting steps. The following steps can serve you well in any computer-based activity you undertake:

1. **Make sure that the device is turned on.**

   It's obvious, but people (never you, of course) still manage to forget it. The device should be drawing power either from a wall outlet or from the USB or FireWire connection.

2. **Make sure that the device is properly connected.**

   Again, this may seem obvious. Still, if the USB or FireWire cable is not plugged in properly at both ends, the computer can't recognize the device.

3. **Make sure that the device's drivers are loaded.**

   Windows XP is preloaded with many drivers, but the manufacturer may require additional software to function. Read the instructions, and make sure that all the right software is installed.

Figure 12-5:
A list of available devices in Cakewalk Home Studio.

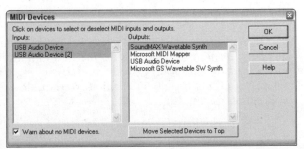

4. **Make sure that the computer is recognizing the device.**

   Right-click the My Computer icon and select Manage. On the Device Manager menu, you'll see a full list of devices that are connected to the computer. If you've followed the previous steps and still don't see the device, it's time to call the manufacturer's technical support line.

Reducing latency

Latency is a problem for both audio and MIDI recording. Rhythm is so important to the recording process that any interference with the music's timing can throw that process off. The goal here is to get the least amount of latency in your system. The amount of latency depends on the amount of memory and your processor speed; it also depends on the drivers you're using. If you use normal MME drivers (pre–Windows XP drivers), latency of 50 to 100 milliseconds is common, even with good hardware. With WDM or ASIO drivers, you can significantly cut these times, as shown in Figure 12-6.

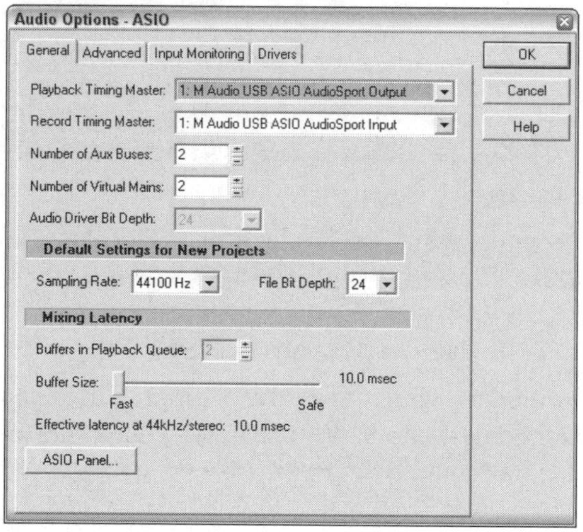

Figure 12-6: Reducing latency.

Each program has some method for managing latency. Check the manual for the software you buy to determine that program's method of handling this problem, and tweak the settings for your system. Keep the latency as low as possible. When you start noticing problems like distorted or slow audio, you've reduced the latency too much.

Where have all the files gone?

You've spent a lot of time so far making sure that your hard drive or drives are partitioned and functioning correctly. To keep those drives functioning properly, you need to know where your files will be saved. Because you want the music files to be saved to the largest partition or hard drive (again, because these files are large and easily fragmented), the software recording program gives you a choice of where you want to save those files.

Each type of file should have a separate folder to assist in keeping everything organized. For example, the temporary recording files (where the audio you record is saved until it's saved and named) can be saved in one folder, the loops you bought or made can be saved elsewhere, and your finished files can be saved in a third folder. Setting up these folders helps you better manage your file structure and makes recording quicker and easier.

Removing what you don't need

Programs like games and instant messenger services may be fun, but their functions can interfere with the audio-recording process. These programs take up system resources, and pop-up windows (like those associated with instant messenger communications) can throw off the recording process. It's best to disable these services when recording — or better yet, don't install them.

Loading down your system with desktop wallpaper and screensavers can also cause problems. Keep photographs off of your desktop, and don't download involved screensavers that could pop up while recording long tracks. The basic rule is that anything that doesn't directly improve audio functioning should be kept off the system.

Several other system modifications you can make to your system will improve its performance as a digital audio workstation, such as turning off Automatic Updates or the System Restore function for your hard drives. However, this can impair many of the safety functions built in to Windows XP. It's like taking your motorcycle helmet off because you want to ride lighter and faster. If you truly want to tweak out your system for making music, check out guides like the one found at www.musicxp.net. A quick search of "Windows XP digital music" on Google will also turn up more advice on this subject. These should be used if your machine will only be handling digital audio. Otherwise, keep your helmet on, Evel.

A Comparison

Table 12-1 allows you to compare the functions of the various software recording packages so that you can decide which one is best for you.

Table 12-1		Software Packages and Features				
Name	*Audio*	*MIDI*	*Loops?*	*Plug-Ins*	*Exporting*	*Burning?*
Cakewalk Home Studio	Unlimited	Unlimited	Yes	DXi, VST	WAV, MP3, WMA, Real	No
Cubase SE	48	Unlimited	Yes	VST	WAV, MP3, WMA	No
Pro Tools LE	32	256	Yes	HDM	WAV	No
Screenblast Acid 4.0	Unlimited	Unlimited	Yes	DXi	MP3, Real, WMA	Yes

Chapter 13

Recording, Looping, and Editing

· ·

In This Chapter

▶ Getting good sound from external instruments

▶ Understanding and using audio clips and loops

▶ Layering audio tracks for a fuller sound

▶ Undoing and fixing your mistakes

· ·

You've already built your computer, and your musical equipment is hooked up and ready to go. Your software is loaded and has recognized all the external hardware. You've managed to retain a sizable portion of your sanity, and you're ready to unleash your works of musical genius upon the world. All that's left now is to record your songs.

You need to follow some basic rules when you're recording audio on your computer, and I take a look at them in this chapter. This information can get you going on the way to recording audio, but it's just a first step. For more in-depth information on the ways of home recording, I recommend picking up a copy of *Home Recording For Musicians For Dummies,* by Jeff Strong (published by Wiley).

Setting Up Your Project

You need to set up a few things before you even connect your instrument to your computer. These settings will affect how you use your equipment to record audio and sequence MIDI events for every project you do. Look for these settings in every piece of recording software you use:

- ✔ **Tempo:** This is the speed of the song. Each project has an overall tempo assigned to it, although you can change that tempo in the middle of the song later.

- ✔ **Bit rate and sampling:** This determines the original resolution of the audio you record. It's a good idea to record at the highest possible bit and sample rate so that you have the best quality possible before you dither it down to the CD standard.

- ✔ **Input definitions:** This involves telling the recording software where the audio or MIDI signals are coming from. The software presents a list of all possible inputs, and you select which ones you want to use in the recording.

- ✔ **Templates:** The recording software may present you with templates for recording set ups, like 16 tracks of audio or a mix of audio and MIDI tracks. You should also be able to customize these templates to adapt to the type of projects you usually record. For example, you can set up a template for all of your MIDI devices and audio inputs and set the program to default to that template.

Where's It Coming From?

All the sound cards I've recommend up to this point have multiple inputs, so you need to tell the computer which audio signal you want to record. Imagine trying to write down everything four people are trying to say at one time. It's an impossible task, and the recording software won't even attempt it. You need to specify which input goes to which track so that the proper audio signal can be routed to that track.

First, make sure that you have enough tracks to handle the inputs you have available. This process can vary from one program to another, but as an example, you insert additional tracks in Cakewalk Home Studio by choosing File⇨Insert from the main menu. Most programs have a similar command. You're now ready to assign inputs to those tracks. Views in each recording program differ, but they'll look similar to what's shown in Figure 13-1.

Notice how you see a menu of available inputs to choose from. Pick the input that's connected to what you want to record, and you're ready to go. That track now only takes a signal from that input.

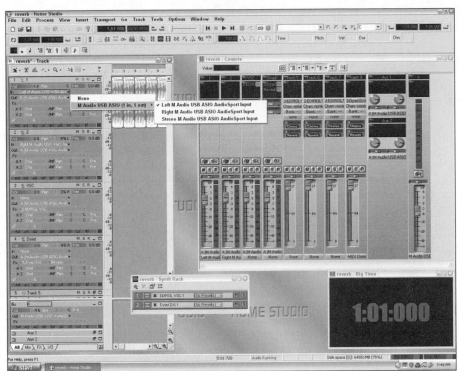

Figure 13-1:
Choosing a
track's
input.

Leveling It Out

If you've seen a lot of music videos, you've run across at least one where the group is in the recording studio, singing or playing their guts out while someone sits at a large mixing board, pushing buttons and knobs and faders (sliding levers that control volume) and capturing the perfect track, or layer of audio. This process may have lost some of its mystique after being used so many times in the video-making process, but it's still a vital part of recording music.

You're doing the same thing on your computer, although the mixing board has been moved inside the machine, and you control it with a mouse or an external control surface, like I describe in Chapter 12. The important part in this process — whether you're manning a huge console or pushing pixels with your mouse — is getting a good recording with a strong signal, or level. The audio you're recording should be as strong and clear as possible without distorting. Distortion can be good if you're trying to get a certain sound (like the true rock spirit inherent in every good distorted power chord on the electric guitar), but it's better to use a different effect to get that sound than just pushing up the fader. This is because, as I've tried to emphasize, digital distortion is virtually always a harsh and nasty experience that's not worth listening to (unless you're performing in Nine Inch Nails, but that's the only pass I'm willing to give at this point).

In Figure 13-2, you see a normal signal coming through the Mixer view in Cakewalk Home Studio. The signal is strong and present, but it's not heading into the dreaded red zone above the 0 level on the meters.

In Figure 13-3, notice how the level is bouncing up and over the 0 level of the fader. This results in a harsh distortion, tainting the sound and making it unusable. It's time to start over.

Stay away from the distortion, and you'll be fine. This is why you see people always checking mics or instruments to make sure that everything sounds okay.

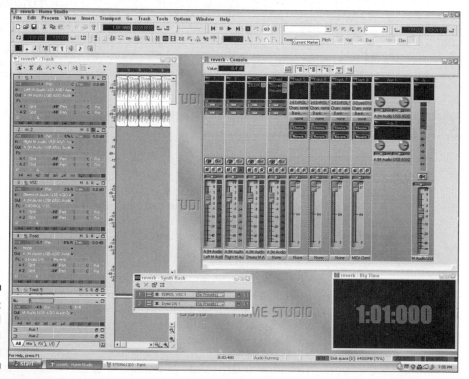

Figure 13-2:
A normal signal being recorded.

Basic Sound Levels

When you're recording audio into a Windows XP–based digital audio machine, the signal is going through at least two possible points of level adjustment inside the computer itself: the Windows XP sound mixer that I discuss in Chapter 3 and the recording program itself. If you're using an outside preamp or an electric instrument, you have other chances to boost or cut the volume level. So how do you adjust the levels to get the proper sound? It can be quite confusing (and I think that's why so many sound engineers seem a little insane at times).

First, always get the strongest signal that you can from the electric instrument you're playing or sampling. That means making sure that the volume knob is turned up all the way on the electric guitar, bass, or keyboard you're playing (or is at the center position if you're using an active instrument, or one that has a preamp built into it). Keeping the signal too low at the source means that you don't get the full potential of the instrument recorded, and you may end up recording some noise with the signal as well. This noise results from electrical sources getting too near the instrument or from other sources inside the computer, like fans or other noise-making parts.

If you have a preamp between the mic or instrument and the computer, make sure that the gain on that device is turned up as far as possible without continually lighting up a clip signal. Virtually all preamps have a light that turns on when too much signal is flowing through them. It's okay to have the occasional flash of light if you're recording through an analog device, but remember to stay away from digital distortion (I sound like a broken record, I know). If that light is on constantly, it's time to turn down the gain knob on your preamp.

Now, your signal has wound its way through your equipment and it's in your computer. You have only two more steps to take before your signal is ready to be laid to virtual tape on your hard drive. Open the System Mixer by double-clicking the speaker icon in the lower-right corner of your screen. Select Options⇨Properties, and change the radio button from Playback to Recording. Now adjust the volume about halfway up. (You may have to adjust it again later.) Leave the Windows XP Audio Mixer window open for now.

Some sound card manufacturers may include separate audio mixing or virtual patchbay software with their product. Your recording software may also ask you to choose what audio inputs you want the software to use. It's impossible to address each and every one of these examples in this book. Just be aware that, though the process may be similar, there could be extra steps involved in setting your levels. Follow your manufacturer's instructions.

The final step is using your recording software. You can adjust the volume in a couple of different views, but I show you how in a mixer view first. The exact position of the volume controls differs from one software package to another, but the views will be similar. The goal here is to set the fader to 0, as shown in Figure 13-4.

When you play now, the signal should fluctuate between the –2 dB and –6 dB level. If it's outside that range, you need to go back to the Windows XP Audio Mixer and move it down. If the signal doesn't reach that range, push the fader in the Windows XP Audio Mixer up. Your signal is now at its optimum level, and you can use the recording software to make fine adjustments from here.

So what does this whole numbering system mean? It's the amount of decibels that are going through the inputs. It's measured in negative numbers because the software isn't adding volume to what's coming in. That's a good thing — when you boost a signal using the mixer, you can introduce noise and distortion. Need I remind you how bad noise and digital distortion can be for your recording? It's okay to go a little bit above the 0 level, but too much can be a problem.

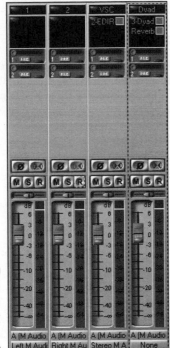

Figure 13-4:
A 0 level in
the Mixer
view.

Basic Sound Effects

From the title, you could assume that I'm going to discuss the sound for a
movie or television show. The effects I talk about in this section won't always
be as obvious as the "Thonk!" you hear when someone gets smacked in the
head with a frying pan, but they are a vital part of the recording process. They
define how you hear so much of the music that's made, and a great deal of
these effects are already present in any recording software package you buy.

This one goes up to 11

Yes, I'll finally let up on distortion and let it join the accepted realm of recorded
audio. You may occasionally hear it referred to as "overdrive," "crunch," "fuzz,"
or another similar adjective, but it refers to the sound a signal makes when it's
pushed to high levels. This is normally used on guitars to get a rock or metal
sound, from slightly distorted to a full-on scream. If you're looking for a more
modern sound, it can also be used on drums, vocals, or other instruments to
get a unique sound.

Let the good times roll

So how do you know what "the right way" is? With so many theories and rules, it's impossible to tell you the one right way to use effects. It involves the effect you're using, the software you use it with, the elusive "mojo" factor, and many other things. My advice is to read as much as possible but also to trust your ears. You're not going to break anything by twisting a few knobs here and there to see what the effect sounds like — within reason. (It's probably not a good idea to boost the volume until you blow out your speakers.) Play with these effects and find out what they do, and don't be afraid to move anything around.

Did you record this in a cave?

Short for *reverberation,* reverb can make the instrument sound like it's in any environment from a small club to the Grand Canyon. The key is creating small delays of the sound (a few milliseconds or so) and using those delays to create the illusion of depth. It simulates the natural echo of a space. If you overuse it, it can smear all the sounds you record into one jumbled mess. Used the right way, though, it can enhance the recordings you make.

There will be a slight delay . . .

Delay takes the reverb effect to new and higher levels. Instead of providing small delay times, this effect can go up to a full second or more, depending on the type of delay you're using. You can also set the amount of delayed sound you hear and the number of times that delay repeats. If you've ever heard the chiming, repetitious guitar sound from U2's The Edge, you've heard delay at work.

Join the chorus . . .

Chorus is another delay-based effect that gives a musical instrument a thicker sound. Chorusing a signal slightly delays a copy of the signal and plays both signals back, giving the illusion of two or more instruments playing at the same time. The rate of delay can be varied to allow for more or less "shimmering" in the sound.

All things being equal . . .

Also known as EQ, equalization allows you to boost or cut certain frequencies within a given audio signal. It sounds more complicated than it is, and I guarantee that you've used EQ before. If you've ever tweaked the treble or bass knob on your stereo, you've used a form of EQ. However, the EQ that you find in these digital recording programs is a bit more precise than just the treble or bass knob. It allows you to change certain parts of the sound to be more prominent or to reduce any offending distortion or dominance.

What are my limits?

If you've heard any popular music within the last ten years, you've heard compression at work. It's not an obvious effect, but it's one that producers and engineers apply to virtually every song that comes out of a recording studio. Compression means smoothly lowering the highs and boosting the lows so that the track sounds louder overall. A song can be played at a higher volume when no overly loud peaks are in the track. Compression can also be used on individual instruments to smooth out a particular sound, like vocals or guitars.

Limiting is a form of compression that simply prevents the signal from going over a certain threshold. This is most valuable when you're trying to prevent a distorted peak in a track.

The rest of the show

A multitude of other audio effects are available, including wah-wah (think of a '70s funk guitar sound similar to "wakka-chikka"), phaser (another delay-based effect), and others. The only way to truly know what these effects can do is to experiment with them and see what you get. Quite a few are available with the recording software, and others can be added as plug-ins. Feel free to experiment, and listen to a lot of music to get ideas of the various possibilities.

Using Effects

You can add effects to the audio you record in two basic ways. You can either process them directly to the audio, or you can run the tracks through the effects using the virtual workings of your recording software. Each method has its advantages and disadvantages, so read carefully and decide which is appropriate for each situation.

When you insert the effect into the track, it's like running the signal through another piece of equipment, like a guitar pedal or an effects unit. This process can vary from one software package to the next, but I demonstrate how to perform this action in Cakewalk Home Studio. Right-click at the top of the track and select Effects⇨Audio. Choose the effect you want from the menu shown in Figure 13-5.

The advantage of this method is that it leaves the original audio unprocessed, so you can turn the effect on and off quickly to hear how it sounds either way. It does draw more processor and memory power though, so stacking multiple effects on each track may cause the program to slow or stall.

Processing the audio directly takes some time on the front end of the process, but it saves some strain on your system. For example, right-clicking the audio clip, selecting Effects⇨Audio, and choosing an effect from the pop-up menu (as shown in Figure 13-6) to get the effect allows you to directly change the audio. The clip now plays with the desired effect, but if you don't like the effect, you can undo it (as I discuss in the section "Uh, I Made a Mistake . . .," later in this chapter).

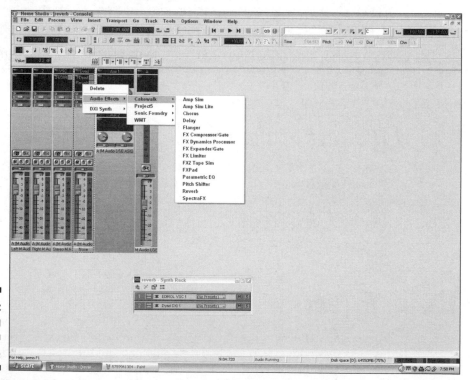

Figure 13-5:
Putting an effect on the track.

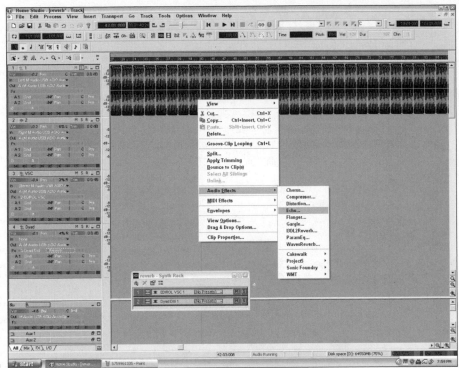

Figure 13-6:
Directly
processing
the track's
audio.

The Click Track

A lot of music is recorded today with a click track. This metronomic pulse is based on the tempo and *meter* (beats per measure) you've selected for the song (as shown in Figure 13-7), and it provides a constant tempo for you to record to. This is extremely helpful if you're layering on audio tracks, because everything is recorded to a common speed reference point. It's also helpful in sequencing MIDI events, because it gives you the ability to quantize events like notes or rhythms. You can also turn the click track on or off, depending on what you need.

Figure 13-7:
The Click
Track
toolbar in
Cakewalk
Home
Studio.

Clicking the Record Button

Before you record any audio, you first have to "arm" the tracks you'll be recording. It's a safety measure to make sure that you don't accidentally erase any data or record something you don't want. It's as simple as clicking a button.

Look at Figure 13-8, and notice that the "R" button on the track has been depressed. This indicates that the audio going into this track will be recorded when you click the Master Record button.

After you've armed all the tracks you're going to record, it's as simple as clicking the Record button and letting it fly. Good luck!

It's a good idea to insert a "lead-in" to any song you record so that you don't have to try to start the song right when you click the Record button. Either let the click track in the song go for a few beats or program in a quick MIDI sequence that leads into the main audio recording.

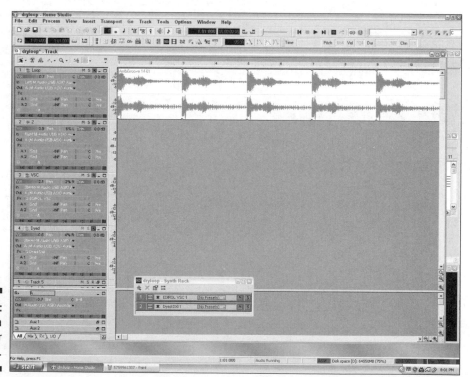

Figure 13-8:
Arming a
track for
recording.

You can record from the beginning, or you can move the cursor to a specific point in the recording and record from there. Most software packages also allow you to "punch in," or start recording, in the middle of an already-recorded track and record over what was there, leaving the previous part unaffected. Punching in also gives you a little lead-in to the point where you want to record (commonly referred to as *"pre-roll"* — a reference to the old analog tape days), allowing you to start playing along for a smoother transition. For example, in Cakewalk Home Studio, select Transport⇨Record Options⇨Auto Punch and set the time you want to punch in, as shown in Figure 13-9. Click the Record button, and you're ready to go.

Figure 13-9:
Punching in.

Layer Upon Layer

Congratulations on recording your first tracks! It just gets easier from here, I promise. I'll assume here that you first recorded the basic tracks for your song, and you now want to listen to what you've recorded and either erase it or build upon what you already have.

The first step is to disarm the tracks you recorded. If you don't, you may accidentally record over some of the audio you've already laid down. You can rewind now and play back what you've recorded. If you want to redo what you recorded, you can either use the program's Undo function (which is usually located in the program's Edit menu) or right-click and select Delete on the clip itself. Repeat the above recording process until you get what you want.

If you have what you want and you're ready to add more audio, simply arm the other tracks and record what you want to add. This leaves the earlier tracks unaffected, and you can change the individual properties as needed. Repeat this process until you have recorded everything you need.

Sampling a typical recording session

The lead singer for Truck Stop Sushi has creative ideas fairly bursting out of him following a relaxing stay in a small Appalachian mountain town (he really likes rustic handicrafts). He sits down in front of his newly built digital audio workstation to lay down some of his ideas.

He's just going to use an acoustic guitar while he sings, but he's planning on doing two passes at each song. It may seem easier to do them both at the same time, but he wants to be able to change the volume of each one later. If he were to sing and play at the same time, even into different mics, they would still pick up both signals and the sounds would be irrevocably mixed.

The lead singer sets up a click track to play guitar and clicks the Record button, going over the lyrics in his head and marveling over his genius the entire time. Sometimes the marveling gets the better of his thought process, and he's forced to re-record and punch in a couple of times during the guitar process. After the guitar portion is finished, the singer goes back and records the vocals. While recording, he decides he wants to put in some guide tracks for the drummer. He inserts a new MIDI track and starts playing his keyboard on MIDI channel 10, sketching out some percussion ideas.

Deciding to give himself some time between recording and the final mix, he decides to save his files (always a good idea) and step away from the computer for a bit. After all, he has some birdhouses to stain.

Repeating Yourself

As I mention in Chapter 12, a program called Acid revolutionized the way loops of audio are used in music. This program (and the similar functions adopted by many other software programs in the wake of Acid's release) allows segments of sound to be extended or changed in ways not possible before. I'll use the free version of Acid (available for free download at http://acidplanet.com) to demonstrate this because the program is easy to get and to use. While they are not in the same format, programs like the soft synthesizer/sequencer Reason and its companion Recycler can handle their version of loops in much the same way. Remember, this is a very easy and useful function that's been built into a great deal of programs.

You can alter three major attributes of Acid-style loops: tempo, key, and repetition. Like the regular audio or MIDI clips you've seen before, you can also cut and paste these loops and put them wherever you want.

When you first install the free version of Acid (called Acid Xpress), a sample song pops up, giving you a multitude of loops to choose from. You can also start new programs and experiment with different loops there. This is a good place to start, though, so I start with this view and go from there.

Keeping a steady beat

This attribute is very easy to change. Simply locate the Tempo slider on the left side of the screen (as shown in Figure 13-10) and change it to the speed you want. The time is measured in beats per minute, or BPM. A tempo of 120 BPM is the standard "dance" music tempo, so you can use that as a reference point as you increase or decrease the tempo.

In addition to changing the tempo for the entire song, you can also insert points at which you want the song to speed up or slow down. Move the cursor to the point in the song where you want to change the tempo, and select Insert➪Tempo/Key Change from the main menu, as shown in Figure 13-11. This allows you to speed up or slow down the song from that point on.

This change remains in effect unless you insert another change to a new tempo, or until the song loops back on itself.

Each loop is recorded at a specific tempo, but extreme changes in tempo may cause loops to sound different. It's also easier to speed up a loop than to slow one down. A drum loop recorded at 92 BPM can be sped up to 110 BPM with no effect, but slowing a loop from 100 BPM to 60 BPM makes it sound jagged and strange.

Figure 13-10:
Changing the overall tempo of the project.

Figure 13-11:
Changing
the tempo in
a specific
place in the
song.

What key was that in?

Much like tempo, you can change the key of a song in many ways. First, I look at changing the overall key of a project. Look for the tuning fork next to the Tempo slider that's shown in Figure 13-10. Click the tuning fork, and you get a list of available keys. Choose one, and all the clips are adjusted to that key. Drums and loops without a specific pitch stay the same.

To change keys at a specific point in the song, follow the directions for changing the tempo at a specific point that I presented in the previous section. Instead of concentrating on the tempo section, change the key to what you want. All the pitched loops change to that key until another change command is inserted or until the song loops back on itself.

Additionally, you can change the key of a particular clip in the song, leaving the rest of the song's loops unchanged. This only applies to loops with a pitch or reference note — drums and other unpitched loops are not affected. Follow these instructions to change the properties of a loop:

1. **Right-click the clip that you want to change and select Properties from the menu that appears.**

   This brings up the attributes for that clip.

2. **Find the Pitch Shift input box.**

   This is the second value down in the window that opens when you select Properties.

3. **Raise or lower the amount of semitones by which you want to shift the clip's pitch.**

4. **Click the OK button to change the clip's properties.**

To only change a part of the clip, split it off from the rest of the clip by placing the cursor where you want to change the pitch; then right-click the clip. Select Split, and you change the clip from one part to two. You can then right-click the part of the clip you want to change and shift the pitch from there. You can do this as many times as you want to change pitches. The overall key of the song remains the same.

Repetition

Acid and other loops contain information that allows the recording software to easily manipulate the data of one sound clip. Instead of copying and pasting a loop multiple times, you can extend a loop to repeat multiple times while it remains one large clip. That way, you can change the properties of this extended clip all at once instead of performing the change multiple times on several small clips. You can also move the edges of a loop inward so that only a portion of the loop is affected.

When you place your cursor over the right edge of the loop, notice how the arrow changes into a small box with an arrow inside. Hold down the left mouse button, and drag the edge to the right. The loop extends as the cursor is moved until it reaches the point where you want to stop it. The extended loop looks like what is shown in Figure 13-12.

If you move the loop edge to the left, the loop only plays the portion of audio that's shown. You can also perform the drag on the left edge of the loop and extend or shorten the loop from there.

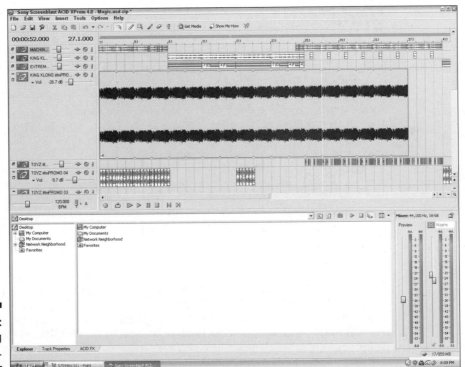

Figure 13-12:
Extending
the loop.

As you can see, loops are an extraordinarily fluid musical tool. They are especially helpful for laying down repetitive rhythm tracks or long, unchanging musical passages. These loops are available for download or purchase at several locations on the Web and in music stores. With the aid of a program like Screenblast Sound Forge or other similar programs, you can also record audio and create your own audio loops.

Uh, I Made a Mistake . . .

Nobody can get it perfect every time, track after track. At some point, you're going to have to make some sort of correction to your tracks. That's okay, because digital audio allows you to move and edit audio without harming it. This is called *nondestructive editing,* and it's part of what makes digital audio editing such a powerful tool. Any change can be moved or undone without harming the audio you've recorded (until you've clicked the Save button), unlike the accidental erasures or loss of audio quality you would deal with in analog recording.

Undo

Drill this into your head early, and be prepared to use it often. This key sequence can save your recordings and your sanity more than once in your recording career. Remember this key sequence: Ctrl+Z. By pressing this sequence (or using the Undo command in your recording program), just about anything you've done can be undone. Your change is gone, and the audio you modified is back the way it was. No harm, no foul. This feature is a godsend when you accidentally record over something or you want to erase a track quickly when you're sure it's not what you want.

In the following paragraphs, I take you through an example of how this beautiful function works. I've recorded a bass track. It sounds okay, but I want to use a chorus effect on it. I add the chorus effect by right-clicking the track and selecting Effects⇨Audio⇨Chorus. I pull down a present from the menu shown in Figure 13-13, and clicking the OK button runs the track through the effect.

The whole process runs smoothly, but when I play back the track, I realize it just doesn't sound good. Because your ears are the final test for any audio you produce, bad-sounding audio has to go. Instead of re-recording the bass track, just press Ctrl+Z, and everything is back to normal. It's a beautiful thing.

Figure 13-13:
The Effects
menu.

Selective undo

You may not have immediately realized you made a mistake. Suppose you get
a few edits or effects into a project when you realize that the cut you made
earlier has some audio you wanted to keep. In that case, it's valuable to be
able to undo that cut without changing what you had done after that point.
Some software packages keep a list of actions you've performed, like cuts and
effects processing. By going through this list, you can choose what you want
to remove and only take care of that action. For example, this list can be
opened in Cakewalk Home Studio by choosing Edit⇨History from the main
menu, as shown in Figure 13-14.

Figure 13-14:
Selective
undo in
Cakewalk
Home
Studio.

Re-recording

If at first you don't succeed, just delete the clip and try again. Click the clip you want to get rid of and press Delete. The track is cleared, and you're ready to go again. Some software packages also allow you to record several "virtual" tracks on one track. You can then record multiple times on the same track and choose which take you prefer.

If you're not sure whether you want to keep the track, but you don't want to delete it, go ahead and record the part on a new track. You can mute the one you're not sure about and come back to it later. Most software packages have an "M" button on the track that you can use to mute the audio.

Some recording programs will hold on to old takes even after you've stopped using them. Follow your manufacturer's instructions on cleaning out these old tracks, and you'll save space on your hard drive for your new masterpieces.

Chapter 14

Mixing the Music

• •

In This Chapter

▶ Dialing in the levels and stereo settings for your songs

▶ Rendering your music to one file

▶ Making the final cuts and putting the songs in order

▶ Burning the final mix of your CD

• •

Getting all the individual instrumental and vocal tracks recorded is a big step in the creative process. But you have to do more before you can put your music out to the adoring masses. All of those tracks have to find their space and be combined into one file for play through portable audio players, computer media players, CD players, or any musical device you want to pump it through.

While movies and television have heartily embraced surround sound, the vast majority of today's music is still produced in stereo. You can record music in a multichannel format, as heard in the DVD-A and SACD formats. This technology is quite expensive and not for the beginner or even intermediate digital audio user. For now, I concentrate on mixing your tracks in stereo and getting them ready for your audience.

Processing . . . Processing . . .

Back when dinosaurs ran the tape machines and the first musicians climbed out from the primordial ooze (a tradition repeated to this day), mixing the song required real-time attention from the engineer and, for larger mixing boards, automated gear that moved the faders. All of this had to be done in real time, and a missed push of a fader or twist of a knob could ruin the whole thing. It could be a long and arduous process, especially if the studio had already run out of coffee and muffins.

Windows XP–based digital audio workstations can't provide coffee and muffins, but they can simplify the mixing process for you. Because the parameters of the track can be easily automated, you can set envelopes for each track and let those envelopes take care of watching the faders and knobs during mixing. Also, you don't have to mix it in real time. Digital audio can be mixed more quickly because the computer isn't lifting audio from tape; instead, it's crunching your audio's numbers and putting them all together. First, though, it's important to get your tracks in order.

Finding your place

The process of mixing can be very complicated — it's a specialty for a great deal of engineers who do just that. However, you should keep some basics in mind to help you put everything together and make a good song.

The stereo mix

As you've no doubt heard many times before, stereo music contains two channels of audio, and the instruments in the song are given different volume levels in each channel. The effect is the illusion that you can hear that instrument or vocal coming from a particular place in space. You may hear a rhythm guitar coming from your right side, while the vocals are front and center and the bass is off to the left. And don't forget the quick succession of drums flying in front of you during that one moment in the song. All of this is accomplished using *panning*.

Each track has a panning control on it that determines where the track lies in the stereo field. The Panning control is usually located just above the fader in the Mixer view, as shown in Figure 14-1. It's a simple control — move it to the left and the sound goes toward the left speaker. Moving it to the right brings the sound in that direction.

If you leave all the panning controls in the center of their range, your sound can come out muddy and unclear. It's like having an entire band set up in the middle of the stage — it's crowded and it's hard to pick out what's happening at any one time. Moving the instruments around can make them stand out. In addition, follow these basic guidelines:

- Any lead vocal or strong melody lines should be placed in the center of the track — this is what you want your listener to focus on.
- If you have individual drum tracks, imagine yourself in front of a drum set and place the sounds accordingly. The bass drum and the snare can go in the middle, while the toms and cymbals can be spread across the field.

✔ If you're using a rhythm loop or don't have the instruments separated into different tracks, consider copying the drum track into another track and panning one hard right and one hard left. This gives the illusion of drums surrounding the track while leaving some space open in the middle for the other instruments.

✔ Put the bass, guitar, keys, and so on in different spots around the field; just make sure to give them some room to breathe.

✔ Panning can also be used for different effects or to get a listener's attention. Try panning a dramatic chord across the stereo field to give it a little extra push. You can also take the guitar from the left side of the field to the center when the big solo comes up (your audience loves it when you do that).

Figure 14-1:
The Panning
control.

It's best not to overuse it — think about trying to follow a band that's running nonstop around stage. It's a nice show, not a musical performance. Use panning to get attention and to make a point, but don't let it run wild.

A good way to control these panning effects is to use a panning envelope. I discuss envelopes in Chapter 12, but I want to give you a specific example here that shows how panning works. Look at Figure 14-2 for a sample guitar track.

Here, the guitar is chugging away on rhythm on the right side until it comes time for the big solo, when the melody is moved to the center for maximum attention. After everything's said and done, the guitar moves back to its previous location and the song eventually fades out, leaving the band ready to rock another day.

Figure 14-2:
A panning
envelope.

Track levels

You already made sure that each track had a good signal and that the overall volume level on each one was good. Now, instead of focusing on the volume of each separate track, listen to the entire song. See what dominates the mix or what needs to be given a little more emphasis. You can manipulate the faders from there and give the song a little more balance. Tracks may require different volume levels throughout the song, too. A chugging rhythm guitar may need to be loud during the intro, but it could fade into the back when the vocal comes in. Or, a solo may need to be louder than the rest of the mix for emphasis (any musician loves it when you bump up his solo). This is another great spot to use envelopes. Figure 14-3 shows a guitar that rides up and down in the mix, depending on what the song needs.

Leave some time between the recording process and the mixing process. You'll be surprised what you can hear after you've taken some time and come back with "fresh ears." If possible, have a friend listen and give you a second opinion. (Just make sure that you can take what he says without coming to blows.)

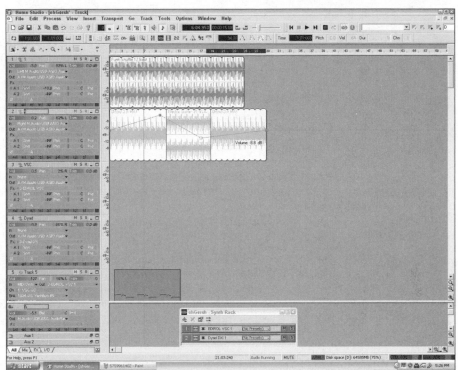

Figure 14-3:
A volume
envelope.

Rendering tracks

After you have the volume levels plotted out and each track has found its place in the stereo space, it's time to mix everything down and make the final track. This is quite the easy process in theory — it's as simple as selecting File⇨Export in most programs. However, it's good to have a deeper understanding of the process of rendering.

Rendering is the process of crunching numbers and bringing all the tracks together into the stereo track that you can play on media players and portable audio devices. The computer takes the digital information from each track and plots out where everything goes, making the final product. This doesn't take place in real time — in other words, the software is just taking the information and putting it together as quickly as possible. This saves time over a normal mix.

Rendering is a processor- and memory-intensive process. Depending on the bit rate and hertz resolution, this could require a lot of power. It also takes a lot more power to combine a large amount of tracks compared to a fairly small number. Time really isn't that much of a factor here, because the process of rendering generally takes less time than the length of the song. Just don't expect to do much else on the computer while the rendering process is taking place. This would be a good time to get more muffins and coffee. You can never have enough.

Any MIDI sequences you route through soft synths will be rendered to audio during this process. However, if you're sending any MIDI sequences to external devices, like a keyboard or drum machine, you'll need to record the audio output of those devices prior to mixing.

You have to set a few parameters when you're rendering your tracks. These parameters affect what gets into the song and how the song ultimately sounds.

Who gets in

Be sure to select the tracks you want to go into the final mix. All the instruments and vocals going into the song should be unmuted and activated. And, as you would probably assume, anything that's not going in should be muted or hidden. It's fine to keep alternate tracks or takes in the saved project just in case you change your mind, but make sure that only what you want gets into the final mix.

File format

At this stage, it's best to export your music into a high-quality, uncompressed format, like a WAV file. A great deal of programs can export to MP3 and WMA files, but those files can lose information. In this case, it's best to keep the highest-quality audio to begin with and then move down from there if necessary. You can always make a compressed file of the master file later.

Never make a compressed file from another compressed file. For example, just because iTunes can convert a file from WMA to AAC doesn't mean it's a good idea to do so. It's like making a photocopy of a photocopy — you lose information between compression formats. Start large and make it smaller as you go.

Resolution

Remember, it's best to start with the highest quality possible and go down from there if necessary. When you export your file, make sure that it's exported at the highest bit and sample rate that your software and hardware can handle. If your sound card and software can handle 24-bit/96-kHz resolution, go ahead and use it. If you're burning to a CD, you can export a 16-bit/44.1-kHz copy as well. That way, you already have a copy ready for burning without running it through an additional conversion process.

Multiple mixes

You're going to repeat this process several times, if only because you may want copies at high- and CD-quality resolution. You may also hear something you don't like in the mix, or you may want to bump up another part. You may just want to try something different. The beauty of this kind of mixing is that you can try several different options in a relatively small amount of time without running through expensive tape or studio time.

You Can't Have Two Masters

Mastering is another engineering specialty that makes the song ready for burning or final distribution. Mastering includes compression, limiters, and equalization to make the music stand out and sound level and equal. This is a highly oversimplified description of the process, and it's not something that can be fully explained here. Again, for more information, I recommend reading *Home Recording For Musicians For Dummies,* by Jeff Strong (published by Wiley). However, in the following sections, I give you a few simple tips that you should look for when you're finishing up your music.

No, not a cold compress . . .

A small amount of compression on the track can make it sound a little louder and punchier. If that's the effect you want, you can add the compression in a sound-editing program after you're done mixing down the track. Most sound-editing programs have a preset available, so look for something like "Final Mix Compression" and apply it to the track. Remember, though, the magic of Undo — you can always take back the compression or re-tweak the song if it doesn't sound good.

Demanding equality

If your track sounds bass-heavy or if you want to add something to the midrange or high frequencies, a little equalization (EQ) may be just the thing you need. Remember that it's better to subtract levels from too much of a frequency than add volume to too little of a frequency. Therefore, consider sliding something out of the mix before you try boosting a level. This can help you level out the frequencies across the spectrum, so don't be afraid to give it a shot.

Making the cuts

Depending on what you used to start the track (such as clicks into the down-beat), or if you just wanted to take a section out, you can use the sound-editing program to delete information you don't want in the song. Just high-light the offending section and take it out. Judicious use of this function can really tighten up a song.

You're fading in and out

This is a fairly standard component of the modern song — when you don't have an ending, just fade it out. When the track is completed, it's easier to set up an envelope that fades out the overall volume. You can also fade a track in for an unusual effect. Feel free to experiment.

Chapter 15

Finishing Up Your Song

Most likely, after you've recorded a song, you'll want to share it with others. If not, that's okay — just put it in the vault and keep writing. If you do want the public to hear what you've been doing, Windows XP's tools can help you to get your music ready. The important consideration at this point is who will be getting the songs.

You now have more options than ever to receive digital music legally, and taking advantage of those routes means that more people can hear your music. You just have to customize your files to make the most of what's available. Making your music easier to get can only help.

In Chapter 14, I note that it's best to export an uncompressed WAV file or similar format when you're making your final mix. That way, you can use a sound-editing program to make compressed audio from the original copy and make sure that you lose a minimal amount of information. In this chapter, I take a look at what formats work best with various avenues of distribution.

Online Distribution of Files

Suppose that you're giving these files away on your own site. You're free to do whatever you want with them, and your only concern is that the maximum number of people can listen to them. In this case, you should use a file format that all the popular media players can handle (such as MP3). You may want to post different versions at different resolutions so that those folks with dialup connections can at least get a sample of the songs, while those with cable or DSL service can hear a higher-fidelity version.

Online distribution services like iTunes, Music Rebellion, and others have specific types of files that they sell. In this case, you have to obtain the appropriate technical specifications and create your file to match their needs. You must also check out their copy-protection schemes and determine what you have to do during the encoding process to make the files secure.

Streaming files give you a way to let people listen to your music without downloading the file to their computer. Formats like Real and Windows Media Player can be enabled for streaming, and you can put links on your site so that the files can be accessed from there (see below). Formats like Real and Windows Media Player can be enabled for streaming, and you can put links on your site so that the files can be accessed from there. If you have some experience in designing Web sites or working with the Internet, you can write a file that allows you to stream MP3 files as well. You use three lines of code to tell your browser the kind of file it's dealing with, information about the song, and where to find the MP3 file. To make this file, open Notepad and type in the following code:

```
#EXTM3U
#EXTINF:60,Artist Name - Song Title
../Audio/SongTitle.mp3
```

The first line tells the browser that it has identified an M3U file. The second line gives the media player the length of the song and other identifying information. Just insert the pertinent information about your song. The last line tells the browser where to find the song. Save the file with a .m3u extension, and put a link on your Web site to this "in-between" file. Remember, this is an option only if you've had some experience in dealing with Web coding. The advantage is that you have a more universal file format for your audience to stream.

WMA files require an .asx metafile. Create an ASCII text file containing the following tags:

```
<asx version = "3.0">
<title>Insert Title Here.</title>
  <entry>
    <ref href = "http://mydomain.com/myfile.wma">
  </entry>
</asx>
```

Save this file with an .asx extension and link to it from your Web page. Windows Media Player (versions 9 and later) also supports progressive downloads, which allow playing while the song is downloaded. The only difference is that the file remains on your machine after playing.

For RA files, create a .ram metafile that contains only one line — the address of the actual RA file. Save it with a .ram extension, and link to it from your Web page in the usual way.

While streaming files don't end up staying on your machine, there are several programs out there that enable the recording of streaming files. If you want to let people listen to your music without actually giving it away, know that this is still possible even if the file is streamed.

Burning Down the Tracks

Making a normal audio CD is more expensive than just producing a file for Internet distribution. After all, you actually have to make the CD for distribution. Still, you can be assured that almost everyone owns a CD player and can play your music. Plus, it's nice to sidle up to someone and hand her a copy of your CD, along with the cheesy pickup line of your choice.

Most burning programs can create standard audio CDs from just about any type of audio file available. The problem is that the program first converts the audio to the 16-bit/44.1-kHz WAV file needed to burn a standard CD. If you already have that WAV file ready, you don't have to worry about how the compression scheme will affect what goes down in the audio. Keep your file in WAV format if you're going to be making CDs.

You need to pay a little more attention to the track sequence here. After all, this is the order in which people will hear your songs, and you want to leave an impression on them. You can do this by dragging the songs in the order you want them into the burning program of your choice, including Windows Media Player, as shown in Figure 15-1.

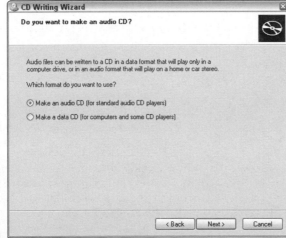

Figure 15-1:
Burning your tracks in Windows Media Player.

You can also use programs like Roxio or Nero to enhance the effects between songs, such as the amount of time between tracks or cross-fading music. This gives your CD a more professional sheen. Figure 15-2 shows examples of how to work with your CD, in this case using Nero.

Figure 15-2:
Enhancing
your CD
with Nero.

When you're ready, go ahead and burn the song. Many third-party burning programs like Roxio and Nero also offer ways to print CD labels. In any case, make sure that you clearly print your name and the song titles on the CD. That way, there's no confusion about what's on the disc.

It's not a bad idea to put a copyright notice on the label as well. Legally, your material is protected by copyright the moment you write or record it. Registering that copyright with the government is where it all gets tricky.

Part V
The Part of Tens

The 5th Wave   By Rich Tennant

"I could tell you more about myself, but I think the playlist on my iPod says more about me than mere words can."

In this part . . .

Digital music is full of fun little facts and features that can sometimes fall through the cracks. The Part of Tens collects those tidbits and puts them together for your enjoyment. Look at these next few chapters as the added bonus to the rest of the book.

You'll find out about digital music toys, sources, and artists that you may not have considered before. Have fun!

Chapter 16

Ten Valuable Ways to Tune-Up Your Digital Music

I wanted to collect some of the more valuable tips from earlier in the book and add some additional hints here to give you a checklist for your computer. These are free and easy ways to keep your system running smoothly and to keep your hair from being pulled out in a fit of frustration. If you follow these words of advice, you'll have an easy time keeping the music going.

Keeping Only What You Need

When you first get a computer, you're faced with a blank slate. You probably have a large hard drive with what looks like a lot of free space, and you may want to load it down with any software that catches your fancy. While having a number of programs on a good-looking machine may seem on the surface to be a good idea, this can lead to problems down the road. Windows XP is an efficient operating system, but it can only handle so much, and the same goes for your processor, RAM, and hard drive. If you find that you're no longer using a program, use the Add or Remove Programs icon in the Control Panel to remove the program from your system.

Never just delete the program from your hard drive without using the Add or Remove Program tool. Doing so may cause problems when your computer looks for files that are no longer there.

Keeping Your Looks Simple

It's also a good idea to stay away from a large number of themes and screen-savers. Not only do these features take up storage space, but they're also often not written efficiently, and they could cause problems with your computer's normal functioning. If you must customize the way your computer looks (I admit to using a Matrix screensaver on my work system), just keep the amount of files on your system to a minimum. Keeping the appearance of your overall system simple makes it run faster and more efficiently.

Defragmenting Your Hard Drive

It's especially important to defragment your hard drive if you're recording audio on your computer (which is why I bring it up in Chapter 11), but it's also a good idea even for regular office or entertainment computers. Files and programs get scattered across your hard drive through normal computer use, and defragmenting the drive makes it easier for Windows XP to find what it's looking for. To defragment your hard drive, follow these steps:

1. **Choose Start⇨My Computer.**

2. **Right-click the drive that you want to defragment.**

3. **Choose Properties, and click the Tools tab.**

4. **In the Defragmentation section, click the Defragment Now button.**

Using the Disc Cleanup Utility

Right-clicking a hard drive in My Computer and selecting Properties also opens the Disc Cleanup Utility. This is a great way to get rid of temporary files, compress old files, and free space on your computer. Giving your computer more free space, in turn, allows it to run smoother. You'll be surprised how much hard drive space you get back after you run this utility.

Using Only the Media Players You Need

You already have Windows Media Player on your system, and you'll probably also end up getting other players (like iTunes, if you plan to use the iTunes store) as you go. For the most part, these programs only duplicate the functions of the others, with a few exceptions (you must have Real Player to play the Real format, for example). At worst, multiple players can interfere when playing various files, because the players can run into conflicts over common resources. When you've decided what player you like, get rid of the rest. It'll simplify your life.

Playing Your Files with One Player

Each time you load a new media player on your machine, you must decide which player will handle each file format by default (that is, which player is called up automatically when a song is selected). This can get confusing when you're working with common file types, like MP3 or WMA. Unless you're careful when you set up a new player, it could take over the playback of all the media files, even if you want to keep certain files associated with your original player. When you're setting up a new player, be careful to specify which player handles which file formats. You can always reset these preferences using your favorite media player. For example, in Windows Media Player, you can reset your options by following these steps:

1. **In Windows Media Player, select Tools⇨Options.**

   This tabbed menu should look familiar by now.

2. **Click the File Types tab.**

   You see the menu shown in Figure 16-1.

3. **Select the file types you want to play with Windows Media Player.**

   You can either make Windows Media Player the default player for everything or pick and choose what you want.

4. **Click the OK button to close the menu.**

   Your choices are finalized, and Windows Media Player handles only what you want it to.

Figure 16-1:
The File Types tab in the Options dialog box.

Keeping Your System Free of Viruses and Spyware

You've heard of them on the news and maybe even experienced an infection or two. Viruses, worms, and to a lesser extent, spyware can cause major problems with your computer's operations. You can get viruses and worms from e-mails or even from just connecting to the Internet, and Web sites can place all kinds of programs on your computer that track your network usage. Fortunately, it's easy to keep your system free of these bugs. *Always* keep a virus-protection program running when you're connected to the Internet, and use programs like Ad-aware or SpyBot to scan your system and delete programs that may have been placed on your computer during your Internet travels.

Keeping Your Files Organized

A hard drive is a large space to have to look through to find one file. If you don't keep your files in a specific place, they can be hard to find. Use folders and clear filenames so that you know what is being stored where. Choose a main folder to store your music, and then use smaller folders inside that main location to categorize your files. Finding that one song or document is a lot easier that way.

Emptying Your Trash

It may seem self-evident, but remember that deleting files only places them in the Windows XP Recycle Bin. This folder, located on your computer's desktop, holds these deleted items until you're sure that you want to get rid of them. If you're holding a lot of items in the Recycle Bin and you're sure you want to let them go, right-click the Recycle Bin and choose Empty Recycle Bin. This permanently deletes the files and frees hard drive space.

Burning Off Your Files

If you want to keep some files around but you're only going to use them occasionally, use the Windows XP burning utility to put them on a CD and get them off your hard drive. You'll have a backup copy, and you have freed some space on your hard drive.

Chapter 17

Ten Legal Download Sites

*I*n Chapter 7, I detail a list of various music download sites, both fee-based and free. If all you're interested in is downloading audio files, I suggest reviewing that chapter. However, a wealth of free and low-cost software is available on the Internet that can be obtained by a simple browser selection. Here, I take a look at some very informative and useful sites that can provide you with some great tools.

iPod Lounge

This site, located at `http://ipodlounge.com`, is obviously directed solely at one brand of portable audio player. However, you can find out just about all you need to know at this location. Not only do you find a support community that exchanges information and tips about the iPod, but you can also download additional software that does everything from backing up the iPod to putting a Bible on the screen. In case you want to play around with the devices and look for some new uses for the iPod, this is the place to go.

Hit Squad

Hit Squad (www.hitsquad.com) serves as a musician's clearinghouse for software and audio downloads. You can look for music production software, MP3 software, or other packages. You can also find links to additional discussion on music and production, and you can track down recordings or sheet music. If you want to dig deeper into software music resources, consider a visit to this site.

Winamp

I mention this brand of media player in Chapter 5, but the home site for Winamp (http://winamp.com) also provides more than the media player software. You can download a staggering amount of songs, videos, plug-ins, skins, and games from this site. Remember, Winamp allows developers all over the world to write code for this player. You can discover something new every time you visit the site.

Source Forge

Source Forge (http://sourceforge.net) may seem daunting if you're not familiar with open source programming. But when you dig in, you'll find a huge amount of potential in the software products these developers have created. The sound editor Audacity came from this project, and other audio tools are available. It's free to both look around and to download, but these projects also accept donations if you choose.

Download.com

From the name, Download.com (http://download.com) has a fairly obvious intent. You can examine and download freeware and shareware from this site, and an entire section is devoted to music-related software packages. You can also visit `http://music.download.com`, which is the audio file download section of this site. Taking its cue from the original MP3.com, this site allows unsigned bands to post their music on the site and get their songs out to the public.

Version Tracker

Gone through everything that's available on Download.com? It's time to head over to Version Tracker (`www.versiontracker.com`) and see what software is available. This site offers commercial software demos, shareware versions, and freeware programs. Look for audio software as well as updates for programs you may already own. This is a great resource for all your software needs.

ZDNet Downloads

Look in the audio section on `http://downloads-zdnet.com.com` (yes, that's two .coms, I know) for more freeware and shareware audio programs. This site is linked to both commercial and independent resources, so you can get a good sampling of what's available.

Analog X

Take a trip over to `www.analogx.com` for information and software related to music production. The highlight of this site is the extensive list of music software that's available as freeware or shareware, along with technical news and the music and rambling of the site's owner. This is an interesting site and resource.

Vorbis

I mention the Ogg Vorbis audio format several times in this book. It's an open source audio format that's designed to be the counterpart of MP3 and WMA. This site (`www.vorbis.com`) is loaded with information about using and creating audio with the open source technology. Dig deeper into digital audio — you can find several interesting audio projects on this site.

Archive.org

It would be impossible to archive the entire Internet. And really, how many dancing hamsters does one really need? Archive.org (www.archive.org) just focuses on the good stuff with its Live Music Archive. Thousands of taping-friendly bands have concerts hosted at this site in .shn format. This freeware compression scheme requires some additional software downloads for listening, but the huge amount of music available should be enough motivation for you to take up some extra space on your hard drive.

Chapter 18

Ten Download-Friendly Artists

*W*hile Metallica has made more news over the downloading debate than they have made music in the past few years, some artists have embraced the growing digital trend and tried to make it work for them. This chapter focuses on those artists who endorse the use of free or purchased downloads as part of their artistic business.

The Roots

Their mix of hip-hop, jazz, and other styles was already a singular sound. They also took the singular step of making themselves available on the Internet. Not only does their official Web site (`http://okayplayer.com`) act as a Web-based community for fans of their music and similarly minded artists, but they've also given permission to the folks that run `http://therootslive.com` to host live recordings of their concerts and make them available for free download. That's especially important because, in my opinion, they're one of the most exciting live bands out there today. Make a visit to one of these sites and be amazed.

Charlie Hunter

It's unusual enough to find a virtuosic musician who plays both guitar and bass on the same instrument. To make recordings of this music and distribute it free on a Web site is even more unusual. Soul jazz genius Charlie Hunter not only provides three albums' worth of MP3 files for free download at `http://charliehunter.com`, but he also provides cover art for fans to print out and place on their burned CDs. Hunter also puts up tracks in FLAC format for fans to download for a small charge.

Smashing Pumpkins

This group was one of the biggest acts in rock during the '90s, selling millions of copies of its records. Yet, toward the end of the group's life, it was difficult for Billy Corgan to get his record company to release the group's last album in the way he wanted. Because of this impasse, fans of the group were treated to some free music when the tracks were posted on several Web sites endorsed by the band. When Corgan formed his next group, Zwan, the first track was also made available for free streaming on the now-defunct original `MP3.com` site.

The Offspring

This group (found at `www.offspring.com`) also wanted to make one of their singles available for free on the Internet before their record company forced them to remove the song from their site. The group was an equal-opportunity offender, though. They sold merchandise featuring the Napster logo before that file-sharing service got them to stop. The group even tried to use the name "Chinese Democracy" for one of their albums after they found out that Guns N' Roses wanted to use it.

Steve Coleman

Steve Coleman is a pioneering musician. This saxophonist constantly researches new theories and evolutions in jazz music. Those who want to partake of these musical treatises can download MP3 versions for free at http://m-base.org. Coleman offers either full or partial downloads of several of his albums. You may not find this music at your local record store, so it's definitely worth a listen.

Chuck D. and Public Enemy

Controversial hip-hop group Public Enemy (www.publicenemy.com) has never been quiet or subtle about anything they believe in. Group leader Chuck D. has been very vocal in his support for downloading, and he's also taken shots at the RIAA for taking overzealous actions against those who download music.

Country Joe

He performed at Woodstock, and now you can recapture the magic. Visitors to http://countryjoe.com can browse the site and listen to over 50 tracks. The page acts like a virtual jukebox. The files stream in Real format, but everything is free and you can get a great overview of his work.

The Grateful Dead

These legendary musicians (http://gratefuldead.com) were already famous for the huge quantity of bootlegs of the band's live shows that were circulated by fans. They were notoriously taping-friendly, as long as the recordings were not sold — just traded or given. It seems natural, then, that this band would feel free to endorse similar measures in the virtual world. Especially notable is Dead guitarist Bob Weir's endorsement of iTunes.

Phish

This Vermont-based band followed the same hard-touring schedule as the Grateful Dead, and the band earned a similar rabid following by allowing comparable taping and trading measures. In addition, http://livephish.com sells MP3 or FLAC downloads of live shows of both the band's and members' side projects. Lest you think that the band profits from these sales, the home page of the site proclaims that the net profits are donated to charity.

Wilco

When the group found themselves without a record label for one of their releases, they streamed the album from their Web site (www.wilcoworld. net). The resulting bidding war got the group a new contract and earned them much critical acclaim and respectable sales. To reward the fans that supported them, the group made several alternate takes and other tracks available for download to those who purchased the group's previous effort.

Chapter 19

Ten Songs You'll Never Want to Download

● ●

In This Chapter

▶ Achy Breaky Heart

▶ Winchester Cathedral

▶ How Much for That Doggy in the Window?

▶ I'm Too Sexy

▶ Muskrat Love

▶ Girl You Know It's True

▶ My Heart Will Go On

▶ She Bangs

▶ Ice Ice Baby

▶ Too Shy

● ●

*T*his list of songs is just a sampling I took from close friends and family —
I just asked about some artists and went with whomever inspired the
most fear and dread. Your opinions may differ slightly, but I'll continue with
this list for scientific research's sake. In addition to providing information
about the songs, I searched iTunes to see whether the songs are for sale.

Achy Breaky Heart

The punch line to many a late-night comedian's joke, this Billy Ray Cyrus
song seemed to inspire either undying loyalty or wretched feelings of woe.
More than a decade later, it seems the latter have stood the test of time.
Nothing about this musical experience has aged well.

This song is available on iTunes.

Winchester Cathedral

Not only did this song inexplicably win a Grammy in the contemporary music category in 1966 for The New Vaudeville Band, but I was also forced to listen to it repeatedly while digitizing electronic music as part of the work on my master's degree. Needless to say, it has earned a special enmity in my heart.

Several versions of this song are available on iTunes.

How Much for That Doggy in the Window?

Patti Page probably had no idea how painful this song would become to future generations. She was just an entertainer trying to make a buck in this workaday world. Still, this is as much a crime against humanity as it is a pop recording, so it makes the list.

Page's recording of this abomination is available on iTunes.

I'm Too Sexy

The video proved otherwise for Right Said Fred. They enjoyed one summer of success on this freak of nature and then thankfully faded away to obscurity.

Their song seemingly did as well, because you can't purchase it on iTunes.

Muskrat Love

I had managed to purge this song from my memory before it was brought up to me as part of my research. Neither the person who mentioned it nor Captain and Tennille will be getting a Christmas card from me this year.

This song is available on iTunes.

Girl You Know It's True

Yes, it's an easy one. But aside from '80s freaks, who would want this Mili Vanilli song in his or her collection? It doesn't strike me as a particularly high-demand item.

It's a good thing, too. This song is not available on iTunes.

My Heart Will Go On

Having been drilled into the public's head for many months on the radio and in the theaters during the reign of *Titanic*, this song actually caused some people physical pain. This proved to be a common sentiment among everyone I polled.

Several different versions of the song are available on iTunes. If you're forced to buy this one, do yourself a favor and get the surf-punk version recorded by Los Straightjackets.

She Bangs

I'm sure it seemed like a good idea at the time, but it's looking like a sad mistake now. The original inspired ill feelings, and the subsequent versions haven't redeemed the song at all.

Still, both versions have been made available on iTunes.

Ice Ice Baby

Oh, come on. You didn't expect me to let this one go by, did you? It may be too easy, but it's still a viable point. Again, this one is only for those who absolutely must have every hit from the '90s.

Lucky for those people, this Vanilla Ice track is available on iTunes. Have at it.

Too Shy

Visitors from the Land of Too Many Nonsense Syllables, Kajagoogoo and lead singer Limahl put together a song that continues to haunt my nightmares. It may be a personal problem, but I just can't let this one go.

This song is available on iTunes. You can have my copy.

Chapter 20

Ten Digital Music Toys for the Truly Geeky

*P*art of the fun of having new portable audio toys is adding accessories to make them do exactly what you want in exactly the way you want. This list takes a look at some of the more unique and unusual items I've run across in researching this book. You won't find simple cases or headphone options in this list. These are toys specifically for those hard-core enthusiasts who want something different and special. Note that, given the high rate of turnover in technology, some of these devices may no longer be available by the time you read this. This list is just an overview of interesting devices that are made to work with digital audio.

The BMW

Okay, so compatibility with digital audio probably isn't going to be the deciding factor in the purchase of a luxury car. But it's something that BMW hopes will influence people who love both computing and driving technology to take a test drive. BMW and Apple recently teamed up to offer cars with integral connections for the iPod. Not only can the link offer direct digital audio to the car's sound system, but drivers can also control the iPod from the steering wheel. You never know — this could be just the thing you need to justify the purchase.

SliMP3

This tiny device appeals to both geek function and fashion. The player attaches to an Ethernet connection and connects to the user's PC, which acts as a server. It can play either MP3 files from the computer or streaming radio from Shoutcast or Live365. The device is a transparent combination of plastic and circuit boards, with a readout for artist and song information.

LT Laser Turntable

If you've ever wanted to spend as much on an audio component as your first car, this is a great place to start. Not only does the LT Laser Turntable produce audiophile-quality sound, but the laser used in the reading process also does not cause the wear and tear a needle can produce when dragged across vinyl. This device is only recommended for those who want to keep their old records in *really* good shape.

Philips MCi250 Wireless Broadband Internet Micro HiFi System

Quite a name, eh? This player needs a long name to describe everything it does. Not only can this stereo system play normal CDs and receive local AM/FM stations, but it can also receive Internet radio stations over your home wireless network. You can also use the system to find out more information about the songs you hear on the radio. Finally, you can get MP3 files from your computer and listen to those as well. This device frees your audio from your computer and puts it anywhere in your house.

Belkin iPod Backup Battery

You're on a long journey, and you can't make it to a wall outlet or FireWire cord to recharge your iPod. The music can keep on going if you have this external battery backup available to you. This device claims to add 15 to 20 additional hours to the life of your iPod and may allay your fears over nasty reports about the iPod's battery life.

Laks Memory Music Watch

Check the time and hear the rhymes on this combination timepiece/flash memory portable audio player (it's a good thing I don't write catalog descriptions for a living, eh?). This watch carries 256MB of memory, along with an integral MP3 player and USB connection. You can even use it as a portable storage device for other files.

C. Crane FM Transmitter

This device is one of the many transmitters made to broadcast portable digital audio files to an FM radio anywhere, anytime. This one stands out for its ability to transmit anywhere within the listenable FM spectrum up to a distance of 70 feet. You could conceivably force everyone in the house to listen to whatever you want, and isn't that what you've always wanted to do anyway?

Groove Bag Tote Speaker Purse for iPod

The looks of the iPod are praised almost as much as its functionality, so it's only natural that fashion accessories would follow the technological lead. Felicidade made this bag with both style and usability in mind. The purse contains both a carrying pouch for your iPod and two small speakers that make the purse act like a portable stereo. Finally, fashion sounds as good as it looks (still not winning points for that catalog job, am I?).

Sonic Boom Bag

I love portable audio players, but I'm just not the purse-carrying type. For those who fall into a different bag, this backpack features a flat-panel speaker system built into the fabric. You can place any CD player or portable audio device into the case, and a volume control is located in a carrying strap. This should be enough to keep you mobile and entertained for a long time.

PlusDeck 2

I loved getting a cassette deck in my first car — finally, no more AM radio. I'm not feeling the same desire for my computer, but the PlusDeck 2 is still a cool idea. This cassette player fits into the same kind of slot used for CD or DVD drives in your computer, and it can both record and play back audio through Windows XP. It even comes with its own recording software. Now you can make modern MP3 mix tapes the old-fashioned way.

Chapter 21

Ten non–Windows XP Sources for Digital Music

*Y*ou can purchase downloads or order CDs online all you want, but some other sources don't directly involve Windows XP. You can tie these sources into the computer eventually, but the first step is to move away from the computer and see what else is out there.

Concerts

Get out and see a live show! Not only will you likely have a good time, but you can also bring home a CD with you. Sometimes you don't even have to purchase them — up-and-coming bands may pass out samplers to promote their music, and even Prince included a free CD with every ticket on his Musicology tour.

Conferences

It's especially popular to give out CDs at conferences related to music for promotional purposes, but other industries (such as travel, wedding arranging, and so on) likely have sampler CDs or other musical items available from those looking for work. Again, it can be a good source of what's coming up musically. Pay attention!

DVDs

One of my favorite movies of the last ten years was "Standing in the Shadows of Motown." Not only did it spotlight a group of fantastic yet unknown musicians, but it also included a second disc that carried digital sound files of the Funk Brothers playing music from the movie. You can listen to these files, and you can use the included Acid Xpress software to remix these songs — talk about great building blocks! Other DVDs are packaged with extras like audio CDs or other musical goodies. Shop around!

Video Games

If you want to hear some unreleased tracks from certain artists, head to your latest video game console. From Journey to the Wu-Tang Clan, artists have coupled their music with the video games. You may not be able to play these songs on your computer or CD player, but it's worth it to a completist to pick up these games.

Giveaways

The marriage of Pepsi and iTunes was just the first of corporations giving away songs to attract attention to their offerings. Sony has also given away music to sell its products. As more online music stores jump into the fray, look for some free offers to expand your collection.

Used CD Stores

One man's trash is another man's treasure. If you look hard enough, you can find some obscure gems in the cutout bins. Just because the CD didn't sell well doesn't mean it doesn't have good music. And more-popular CDs make their way into used CD stacks for a variety of reasons. Check it out, save a buck, and add to your digital music collection.

Promotional Offers

I've received more than one CD in the mail as an incentive to buy an upcoming release. This may become a more rare occurrence as online distribution of music becomes more popular, but CD sales still ring the cash register. Therefore, companies still want you to buy their product and they promote it to get those sales. Look for fan clubs and other artist organizations and sign up. You may get more promotional messages from the artist as a result, but that's the price you pay.

Satellite Radio

This digital broadcast can be taken from car to home to office, depending on the receiver you buy. Both Sirius and XM Radio offer many channels dedicated to different genres and interests. It's like having Internet radio stations wherever you go. You can hear emerging artists and get more information on music than you normally would with regular radio. It's a premium service, but it's well worth the investment if you want more than normal radio broadcasts can offer.

Digital Cable

Digital cable provides a lot of options, including my beloved high-speed Internet connection and music channels. These channels provide commercial-free music through your TV (and any entertainment center options you have hooked up to that TV). The channels offered depend on your cable provider, but you should be able to find something palatable.

"Bonus" Tracks

Whether it takes the form of "hidden" tracks on CDs (unlisted tracks placed at the end of recordings) or promotional EPs attached to magazines like *Rolling Stone,* the incentive is still the same. You get something more with the same purchase price. Especially notable is the *CMJ New Music Journal,* which includes a full sampler with the purchase of each month's issue. That's a great deal of music for the regular price.

Chapter 22

Ten Other Ways You Can Use Windows XP for Music

*Y*ou can find more music than what's available on download services. With Windows XP (and its bundled Web browser, Internet Explorer) and an Internet connection, you can bring music to almost every facet of your world.

Using Google

If you need to find out anything about just about anything, Google is not a bad place to start. Browse over to www.google.com. Type in your favorite artist or genre of music, and see what is available on the World Wide Web. You'll discover articles, reviews, and other tidbits you may never have seen before. It's a wealth of knowledge, and it's all at your fingertips with Google.

Organizing Your Catalog

It's a good idea to keep track of the recordings in your collection. Whether it's because people keep borrowing CDs from you or you need a record for insurance purposes, keeping a record of what you own can be valuable. Use a word processing or spreadsheet program to record what you have, and you can use the program to keep track of your recordings later.

Supporting Independent Artists

I have a soft spot in my heart for artists who are doing anything they can to get their music out to the public. When you buy recordings or other merchandise from an artist's Web site, you're supporting a small business and giving more money to the artists than you would if they were signed to a major label. Don't be afraid to give a new musician a shot — you'll be surprised at how much great music is out there.

Ordering Music

Obviously, I think downloading music (legally) is a great idea. But I want to buy a physical recording from quite a few artists as well. I'm interested in the liner notes and packaging they've included with the CD, and I can always rip the music to my computer to listen to it on my portable audio device. I've used Amazon (www.amazon.com) and CDBaby (www.cdbaby.com) to buy CDs over the Internet with great results.

Researching Artists

Most artists have Web sites available on the Internet, and fans have also created sites dedicated to their favorite musicians. You can find out the latest news from the artists' Web sites, often before music journalists can get the news to you. Look for the official site to get more information.

Ordering Concert Tickets

Although you can get tickets for most major concerts from Ticketmaster (www.ticketmaster.com), some artists allow you to preorder concert tickets from their Web sites. You can also bid on hard-to-get tickets on eBay (www.ebay.com). The Internet is a great source for finding tickets to see your favorite artist live.

Customizing Your Sounds

You know that Windows XP has system sounds associated with certain functions, like starting up or getting your attention for a pop-up message. You can change these sounds to any WAV files you want. Choose Start⇨Control Panel⇨Sounds, Speech, and Audio Devices⇨Change The Sound Scheme. Here you can select a sound function and change it to your desired WAV clip, as shown in Figure 22-1.

Be sure that the clips you select aren't too long, or you'll end up listening to the same, long clip multiple times. It gets annoying quickly. Trust me.

Figure 22-1:
Changing
your system
sounds.

Creating Sheet Music

If you're a trained musician and you want to create sheet music, you can buy programs that produce exactly what you need. Check out Finale Music NotePad (www.finalemusic.com) for a free trial program to see what you can do. If you want more features and power, you can upgrade to different versions.

Talking to Artists

Services from AOL to smaller Web sites provide chats with artists. Here the fans can ask questions of the artists (and sometimes make fools of themselves). Look for information on news services or the artist's official Web site to see when these events are happening, and browse over to the correct chat site to join in.

Discussing Music with Fans

Many sites have message boards where you can have running conversations on musical topics. After you've registered, you can post messages and join in conversations to discuss any music topic you desire. It's usually a good idea to read over the boards to note basic etiquette for the boards and to see what kind of topics are usually discussed. From there, anything is possible.

Appendix A

Glossary

· ·

*T*hroughout this book, terms may pop up that you'll need to come back to for reference. You likely already read the chapter and just need a little refresher. I've gathered the more important definitions here for your reference so you don't need to go digging back through the chapters.

AAC: This audio compression format is based on the audio layer of the MPEG-4 format. AAC is the format used by Apple's iTunes music store.

AIFF: An older and lesser-seen audio file. AIFF is to Apple what WAV is to Windows. It's an uncompressed audio format still found in the Apple environment.

Analog Sound: Produced from formats like vinyl records or cassettes, this sound is produced mechanically and replayed through direct contact with a needle or a recording head.

Auto-Playlist: A specific type of playlist built on database rules instead of specific songs.

Bit: A unit of data. The more bits you have in an audio file, the better it represents the original recording. For example, CD-quality audio is encoded with 16 bits of information per sample.

Bit Rate: This rate measures the speed at which information is sent over a computer network. It also measures the amount of data played per second by a compressed media file, like MP3 or AAC.

Breakout Box: The breakout box is an external interface for a piece of hardware mounted inside the computer. For example, a sound card could have a breakout box for audio, MIDI, headphone, and FireWire connections.

Burning: The process of placing files on a CD or DVD.

Chorus: An audio effect that uses a slight delay to make it seem as if two or more of the same signals are being played at the same time.

Click Track: A metronomic pulse that allows all tracks in a recording to be captured at the same tempo.

Codec: Short for compression/decompression, this is the digital scheme used to encode and decode digital audio, which allows for decent sound at a lower file size (as opposed to the good sound but huge files sizes of uncompressed audio).

Compression: For digital audio files, this is the process of reducing the amount of data in the file to create a smaller and more easily stored version of the song. For recording purposes, compression is the effect used to lower the peaks and raise the softer parts of digital audio, giving the song a louder and punchier sound.

Defragmenting: The process of rearranging data on a hard drive to allow for quicker access times and easier use.

Delay: The playback of an audio signal milliseconds or seconds after it's played, much like an echo.

Digital Sound: This type of sound is encoded into computer files or optical media and replayed by software media players or CD and DVD players.

Distortion: The sound quality produced by overdriving or processing an audio signal. While it's often a desired effect for guitar tracks, digital distortion is harsh and usually unwanted in recordings.

Dithering: Reducing a recording from a higher bit and sample rate to a lower one.

DVD-A: Short for DVD Audio, the DVD-A format handles multi-channel audio recordings. The full benefits of this audio can only be heard in a DVD-A player (not a standard DVD player).

Envelope: A control that alters the volume or panning of a track using edit points.

Equalization: The process of adding or subtracting sound frequencies from audio playback to tailor the sound to a user's preference, such as adding more bass.

Fader: A control that's moved up and down to control the volume level of an audio device. Mixers will contain several faders to control the volume levels of several audio devices playing at one time.

File Sharing: This controversial practice uses peer-to-peer networks like KaZaa to send copies of digital audio files between users around the world.

FireWire: FireWire is a brand name given by Apple to the IEEE 1394 connection, which allows high-speed data transfers between external devices, like an external hard drive. FireWire connections can also power external devices. Sony calls this kind of connection an i.Link.

FLAC: Short for Free Lossless Audio Compression, this is an open source file format that doesn't lose data while compressing the audio to a more manageable size.

Flash Memory: A small, portable type of memory used in portable audio players and smart cards (used in cameras, PDAs, and other digital devices).

GB: GB is the common abbreviation of gigabyte, a unit of storage representing a thousand megabytes of information. For reference, hard drives and DVDs are usually measured in terms of gigabytes.

Hard Drive: Whether mounted internally or externally, this device stores the majority of data contained in computer systems on a spinning magnetic disc. Smaller hard drives can be found on some portable audio players, such as the iPod.

Hertz: A measure of frequency, or how often something happens. In this book, it refers to both the sound frequencies and the rate at which an audio signal is sampled in digital recording.

Hot Swapping: Changing devices connected to a computer without shutting down or rebooting the system.

Hyperthreading: Hyperthreading is a feature of Intel chips that makes the computer view one processor as a dual-processor system, allowing for faster processing of information.

ID3 Tag: This digital information is attached to MP3 files and contains information about the song, such as artist name, song title, genre, and other categories of data.

Limiting: An audio effect that sets a top level on the volume of an audio signal past which it can get no higher.

Line (or Mic) In: A connecting port for an incoming audio signal.

Looping: Taking a small section of audio and playing it several times in a row. Some audio programs allow you to change the key and tempo of a loop as well.

Lossless Compression: Audio compression that doesn't lose any data from the original file during encoding.

Lossy Compression: Audio compression that does lose data from the original file during encoding.

Mastering: The final stage of the recording process, involving mainly equalization and compression.

MB: MB is the common abbreviation of megabyte, a unit of storage representing a million bytes of information. For reference, flash memory and CDs are usually measured in terms of megabytes.

Media Center Edition: A specialized edition of Windows XP with additional media features, such as radio and television controls.

Media Player: This piece of software plays back digital audio and video files. Examples include Windows Media Player, Winamp, and iTunes.

Memory: Memory is the medium a computer uses to hold information, including programs and audio files, while it is being used by the CPU. *See also* RAM.

MIDI: Short for Musical Instrument Digital Interface, this digital language sends instructions to sound devices (from sound cards to keyboards), which are translated into musical passages.

Minijack: A small (⅛") audio connection mainly used for headphone connections, although it's also used for other basic audio connections.

Mixer: A control that contains several faders, a mixer is used to blend these audio signals for recording purposes.

MP3: An audio compression file format found as one of the layers in the larger MPEG digital file format.

Multitracking: The process of recording several sources of audio onto their own section of tape so that they can be altered without affecting other sections of the recording.

Non-destructive Editing: The ability to alter or change audio without damaging the original source audio.

Non-linear Editing: The ability to move sections of audio around without respect to their original position in the recording.

OGG Vorbis: An open source method of audio compression.

Open Source: Software that is made available (including both functionality and the code used to create the program) to the public for little or no cost.

Optical Storage: Most commonly seen in CDs and DVDs, optical storage burns digital information onto discs and reads them using lasers.

Patch: A sound setting on a keyboard or MIDI device.

PCI: The standard format for mounting internal hardware, such as sound cards, in the computer.

Playlist: A method of organizing music files inside a media player to play certain songs in a certain order.

Plug-ins: Additional pieces of software used to add functions to an existing program.

Portable Audio Players: A portable audio player stores digital audio files for playback away from a computer. These can be based on hard drive, flash, or optical memory.

Preamp: A device that boosts and tailors an audio signal before it's recorded or played back.

Processor: The processor executes millions of instructions per second, telling the computer how to use its software and hardware resources.

Punching In: Recording over a section of a track without re-recording the entire track.

QuickTime: A type of audio or video file specifically tailored for the Apple QuickTime media player.

RAM: Short for Random Access Memory, RAM is the storage medium a computer uses to actively process or play programs or files. The more and faster RAM a computer has, the more programs and files that computer can handle.

Ripping: Taking songs from a CD and converting them to digital audio files.

Real: This audio compression format is a proprietary file type associated with the Real media player, noted for its ability to stream audio and video over the Internet.

Rendering: The process of creating a standard audio track from several previously recorded digital audio tracks.

Reverb: Short for reverberation, this effect produces a slight delay in the sound to simulate playback in a certain space, from a small room to a canyon.

RPM: Short for Rotations Per Minute, RPM is the rate at which the platter of a hard drive spins. Faster spinning hard drives allow information to be found and processed quicker.

SACD: Short for Super Audio Compact Disc, this Sony media format produces multi-channel audio recordings. Although most of these discs will play in normal stereo systems, the full benefits are only realized in an SACD player.

Sample: A slice of information taken by a digital recording mechanism. The more samples taken per second, the more faithful the digital recording will be to the original source. For example, CD-quality audio is sampled at the rate of 44.1 thousand times a second.

Sequencing: The process of recording MIDI events for eventual translation into digital audio.

Skin: A skin is a file that changes the shape and appearance of the media player.

Sound Card: Sound card is the generic term used to describe the hardware used by a computer to produce audio. This hardware can either be mounted inside the computer or connected externally.

Streaming: Playing audio as it's downloaded onto a computer, as opposed to waiting for the entire file to download before beginning playback.

USB: Short for Universal Serial Bus, USB connections allow high-speed data transfer between computers and external devices.

Video Card: An internal piece of computer hardware that creates and sends the visual output of a computer to a monitor.

Virtual Memory: A computer can be instructed to use portions of a hard drive as a type of RAM, allowing the computer to process more programs and files. This is especially important for programs like digital audio recording software, which uses virtual memory to record audio signals.

WAV: This is an uncompressed audio format known for good sound but large and unwieldy file sizes.

Wavetable: Sounds embedded on a sound card and triggered by MIDI events.

WMA: An audio compression format developed by Microsoft to be used with Windows Media Player.

XLR: A three-pin connection used for line-level audio connections, such as those used in preamps or microphones.

Appendix B

Cutting the Wires to Your Music

• •

*H*aving all of your music centralized on your home computer gives you a lot of advantages, but the main disadvantage is that it's all centrally located. Once you step away from that central location (say you leave your home office to relax on the sofa for awhile), you no longer have access to that music. Loading music onto a portable audio player can help, but your computer's hard drive holds a lot more than most portable audio players do. And you're out of luck if you don't want to listen to your music on headphones or smaller speakers.

Wireless networking gives you the ability to access and control your music from any location in your home, provided that there's a strong enough signal. You may already have a wireless network in your home, and they're relatively easy to set up if you don't have one. It will require an initial investment, though. You'll need the following equipment to get a wireless network up and running:

- ✔ A high-speed Internet connection
- ✔ A wireless router (a device that manages incoming and outgoing network traffic)
- ✔ A wireless receiver for each computer on your network (many wireless routers also provide ports for "wired" connection, so a desktop computer may be able to connect through a standard cable, provided it's close enough to the router)
- ✔ A specialized music wireless receiver for your stereo system

Once you have all of these pieces together, it's time to get your network up and running.

Putting Up Your Antenna

The first step in setting up your wireless network is hooking up your wireless router to your high-speed Internet connection (a dial-up connection isn't fast enough to support such a network). Simply connect the router to your cable or DSL modem, and it's active. You won't be able to use it immediately, though. First, you need to configure it.

Every manufacturer will have different ways of configuring their routers, but most of them revolve around a browser-based configuration. It's here that you can handle some important attributes of your wireless router.

Network name

Also known as the SSID, this is the identification for your home wireless network. Most default to a common name, but you'll want to change it when you set up your router for security reasons. It's this name you'll use to connect any wireless devices to the network.

It's important to follow the security procedures specified by your router's manufacturer to prevent outside access to your home network. Unless you do, it's fairly easy to get on that network from any location close to your router. This can allow something as simple as surfing the Internet on someone else's dime, or as malicious as getting access to your home machine and the files on it.

Configuration password

To change the settings on your router, you'll need the configuration password. Again, most manufacturers have this set to a default password like "admin," so you'll want to change it as soon as you can to prevent unauthorized access.

802.11b or g?

Wireless routers will be based on one of two standards, 802.11b or 802.11g. These are a lot of numbers and letters that basically translate to one thing — g is faster than b. However, these routers will only work with compatible receivers. Some 802.11g routers can be configured to handle receivers of both types, but the speed of the network will suffer. It's important to make sure that all of your hardware is compatible.

Getting It All Working

Once your router is broadcasting and you've set up your security protections, it's time to hook up your peripheral devices. Again, the manufacturer will have specific instructions on setting this system up, but you'll have to load some software and drivers to get the wireless receiver up and running on your system. Once that's done, you'll enter the name you assigned to your network and connect to your wireless network.

You'll need to equip every computer with a wireless adapter in order to take advantage of this network (see above bullets). Otherwise, you won't be able to connect to this wireless network. On the positive side, quite a few laptops produced today include integral wireless adapters.

Once this network is set up, you'll be able to hook up your specialized music wireless receiver. This unit sits near your stereo and connects to an available input. You'll need to install software on your computer to configure this device as well. Once this process is completed, the receiver will be able to find the music on your computer and stream it to your stereo.

Several types of these devices are available, and each has their own special features. You might want a remote control to go along with your music (like those offered by Creative and other manufacturers), or you might want the tight integration with iTunes that Apple's Airtunes Express offers. Check out what's offered and choose what fits best with your lifestyle. Some of the more common features include the following:

- ✔ Compatibility with MP3, WMA, and other common audio files
- ✔ Transfer of other files, such as video or pictures
- ✔ Remote controls
- ✔ Display screens
- ✔ Network features, like access to a CD database for information

There's only one problem with the security warnings I gave you — they might cause the wireless music receiver to not function on the network. Make sure everything is compatible before setting up your wireless network.

Index

BUSINESS, CAREERS & PERSONAL FINANCE

Grant Writing FOR DUMMIES
A Reference for the Rest of Us!
0-7645-5307-0

Home Buying FOR DUMMIES 2nd Edition
A Reference for the Rest of Us!
0-7645-5331-3 *†

Also available:
- Accounting For Dummies †
  0-7645-5314-3
- Business Plans Kit For Dummies †
  0-7645-5365-8
- Cover Letters For Dummies
  0-7645-5224-4
- Frugal Living For Dummies
  0-7645-5403-4
- Leadership For Dummies
  0-7645-5176-0
- Managing For Dummies
  0-7645-1771-6

- Marketing For Dummies
  0-7645-5600-2
- Personal Finance For Dummies *
  0-7645-2590-5
- Project Management For Dummies
  0-7645-5283-X
- Resumes For Dummies †
  0-7645-5471-9
- Selling For Dummies
  0-7645-5363-1
- Small Business Kit For Dummies *†
  0-7645-5093-4

HOME & BUSINESS COMPUTER BASICS

Windows XP FOR DUMMIES
A Reference for the Rest of Us!
0-7645-4074-2

Excel 2003 ALL-IN-ONE DESK REFERENCE FOR DUMMIES
0-7645-3758-X

Also available:
- ACT! 6 For Dummies
  0-7645-2645-6
- iLife '04 All-in-One Desk Reference For Dummies
  0-7645-7347-0
- iPAQ For Dummies
  0-7645-6769-1
- Mac OS X Panther Timesaving Techniques For Dummies
  0-7645-5812-9
- Macs For Dummies
  0-7645-5656-8

- Microsoft Money 2004 For Dummies
  0-7645-4195-1
- Office 2003 All-in-One Desk Reference For Dummies
  0-7645-3883-7
- Outlook 2003 For Dummies
  0-7645-3759-8
- PCs For Dummies
  0-7645-4074-2
- TiVo For Dummies
  0-7645-6923-6
- Upgrading and Fixing PCs For Dummies
  0-7645-1665-5
- Windows XP Timesaving Techniques For Dummies
  0-7645-3748-2

FOOD, HOME, GARDEN, HOBBIES, MUSIC & PETS

Feng Shui FOR DUMMIES
A Reference for the Rest of Us!
0-7645-5295-3

Poker FOR DUMMIES
A Reference for the Rest of Us!
0-7645-5232-5

Also available:
- Bass Guitar For Dummies
  0-7645-2487-9
- Diabetes Cookbook For Dummies
  0-7645-5230-9
- Gardening For Dummies *
  0-7645-5130-2
- Guitar For Dummies
  0-7645-5106-X
- Holiday Decorating For Dummies
  0-7645-2570-0
- Home Improvement All-in-One For Dummies
  0-7645-5680-0

- Knitting For Dummies
  0-7645-5395-X
- Piano For Dummies
  0-7645-5105-1
- Puppies For Dummies
  0-7645-5255-4
- Scrapbooking For Dummies
  0-7645-7208-3
- Senior Dogs For Dummies
  0-7645-5818-8
- Singing For Dummies
  0-7645-2475-5
- 30-Minute Meals For Dummies
  0-7645-2589-1

INTERNET & DIGITAL MEDIA

Digital Photography FOR DUMMIES
A Reference for the Rest of Us!
0-7645-1664-7

Starting an eBay Business FOR DUMMIES
A Reference for the Rest of Us!
0-7645-6924-4

Also available:
- 2005 Online Shopping Directory For Dummies
  0-7645-7495-7
- CD & DVD Recording For Dummies
  0-7645-5956-7
- eBay For Dummies
  0-7645-5654-1
- Fighting Spam For Dummies
  0-7645-5965-6
- Genealogy Online For Dummies
  0-7645-5964-8
- Google For Dummies
  0-7645-4420-9

- Home Recording For Musicians For Dummies
  0-7645-1634-5
- The Internet For Dummies
  0-7645-4173-0
- iPod & iTunes For Dummies
  0-7645-7772-7
- Preventing Identity Theft For Dummies
  0-7645-7336-5
- Pro Tools All-in-One Desk Reference For Dummies
  0-7645-5714-9
- Roxio Easy Media Creator For Dummies
  0-7645-7131-1

* Separate Canadian edition also available

† Separate U.K. edition also available

WILEY

SPORTS, FITNESS, PARENTING, RELIGION & SPIRITUALITY

0-7645-5146-9

0-7645-5418-2

Also available:
- Adoption For Dummies
  0-7645-5488-3
- Basketball For Dummies
  0-7645-5248-1
- The Bible For Dummies
  0-7645-5296-1
- Buddhism For Dummies
  0-7645-5359-3
- Catholicism For Dummies
  0-7645-5391-7
- Hockey For Dummies
  0-7645-5228-7

- Judaism For Dummies
  0-7645-5299-6
- Martial Arts For Dummies
  0-7645-5358-5
- Pilates For Dummies
  0-7645-5397-6
- Religion For Dummies
  0-7645-5264-3
- Teaching Kids to Read For Dummies
  0-7645-4043-2
- Weight Training For Dummies
  0-7645-5168-X
- Yoga For Dummies
  0-7645-5117-5

TRAVEL

0-7645-5438-7

0-7645-5453-0

Also available:
- Alaska For Dummies
  0-7645-1761-9
- Arizona For Dummies
  0-7645-6938-4
- Cancún and the Yucatán For Dummies
  0-7645-2437-2
- Cruise Vacations For Dummies
  0-7645-6941-4
- Europe For Dummies
  0-7645-5456-5
- Ireland For Dummies
  0-7645-5455-7

- Las Vegas For Dummies
  0-7645-5448-4
- London For Dummies
  0-7645-4277-X
- New York City For Dummies
  0-7645-6945-7
- Paris For Dummies
  0-7645-5494-8
- RV Vacations For Dummies
  0-7645-5443-3
- Walt Disney World & Orlando For Dummies
  0-7645-6943-0

GRAPHICS, DESIGN & WEB DEVELOPMENT

0-7645-4345-8

0-7645-5589-8

Also available:
- Adobe Acrobat 6 PDF For Dummies
  0-7645-3760-1
- Building a Web Site For Dummies
  0-7645-7144-3
- Dreamweaver MX 2004 For Dummies
  0-7645-4342-3
- FrontPage 2003 For Dummies
  0-7645-3882-9
- HTML 4 For Dummies
  0-7645-1995-6
- Illustrator CS For Dummies
  0-7645-4084-X

- Macromedia Flash MX 2004 For Dummies
  0-7645-4358-X
- Photoshop 7 All-in-One Desk
  Reference For Dummies
  0-7645-1667-1
- Photoshop CS Timesaving Techniques
  For Dummies
  0-7645-6782-9
- PHP 5 For Dummies
  0-7645-4166-8
- PowerPoint 2003 For Dummies
  0-7645-3908-6
- QuarkXPress 6 For Dummies
  0-7645-2593-X

NETWORKING, SECURITY, PROGRAMMING & DATABASES

0-7645-6852-3

0-7645-5784-X

Also available:
- A+ Certification For Dummies
  0-7645-4187-0
- Access 2003 All-in-One Desk
  Reference For Dummies
  0-7645-3988-4
- Beginning Programming For Dummies
  0-7645-4997-9
- C For Dummies
  0-7645-7068-4
- Firewalls For Dummies
  0-7645-4048-3
- Home Networking For Dummies
  0-7645-42796

- Network Security For Dummies
  0-7645-1679-5
- Networking For Dummies
  0-7645-1677-9
- TCP/IP For Dummies
  0-7645-1760-0
- VBA For Dummies
  0-7645-3989-2
- Wireless All In-One Desk Reference
  For Dummies
  0-7645-7496-5
- Wireless Home Networking For Dummies
  0-7645-3910-8

HEALTH & SELF-HELP

0-7645-6820-5 *†

0-7645-2566-2

Also available:
- Alzheimer's For Dummies
  0-7645-3899-3
- Asthma For Dummies
  0-7645-4233-8
- Controlling Cholesterol For Dummies
  0-7645-5440-9
- Depression For Dummies
  0-7645-3900-0
- Dieting For Dummies
  0-7645-4149-8
- Fertility For Dummies
  0-7645-2549-2

- Fibromyalgia For Dummies
  0-7645-5441-7
- Improving Your Memory For Dummies
  0-7645-5435-2
- Pregnancy For Dummies †
  0-7645-4483-7
- Quitting Smoking For Dummies
  0-7645-2629-4
- Relationships For Dummies
  0-7645-5384-4
- Thyroid For Dummies
  0-7645-5385-2

EDUCATION, HISTORY, REFERENCE & TEST PREPARATION

0-7645-5194-9

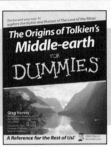

0-7645-4186-2

Also available:
- Algebra For Dummies
  0-7645-5325-9
- British History For Dummies
  0-7645-7021-8
- Calculus For Dummies
  0-7645-2498-4
- English Grammar For Dummies
  0-7645-5322-4
- Forensics For Dummies
  0-7645-5580-4
- The GMAT for Dummies
  0-7645-5251-1
- Inglés Para Dummies
  0-7645-5427-1

- Italian For Dummies
  0-7645-5196-5
- Latin For Dummies
  0-7645-5431-X
- Lewis & Clark For Dummies
  0-7645-2545-X
- Research Papers For Dummies
  0-7645-5426-3
- The SAT I For Dummies
  0-7645-7193-1
- Science Fair Projects For Dummies
  0-7645-5460-3
- U.S. History For Dummies
  0-7645-5249-X

Get smart @ dummies.com®

- **Find a full list of Dummies titles**
- **Look into loads of FREE on-site articles**
- **Sign up for FREE eTips e-mailed to you weekly**
- **See what other products carry the Dummies name**
- **Shop directly from the Dummies bookstore**
- **Enter to win new prizes every month!**

* Separate Canadian edition also available
† Separate U.K. edition also available

Available wherever books are sold. For more information or to order direct: U.S. customers visit www.dummies.com or call 1-877-762-2974.
U.K. customers visit www.wileyeurope.com or call 0800 243407. Canadian customers visit www.wiley.ca or call 1-800-567-4797.